The End of Emp   Gulf

The End of Empire in the Gulf

From Trucial States to United Arab Emirates

Tancred Bradshaw

I.B. TAURIS

LONDON • NEW YORK • OXFORD • NEW DELHI • SYDNEY

I.B. TAURIS
Bloomsbury Publishing Plc
50 Bedford Square, London, WC1B 3DP, UK
1385 Broadway, New York, NY 10018, USA

BLOOMSBURY, I.B. TAURIS and the Diana logo are trademarks of
Bloomsbury Publishing Plc

First published in Great Britain 2020

Cover image: Camels inspected by Sheik Shakhbut, ruler of oil-rich kingdom
Abu Dhabi. (© Ralph Crane/The LIFE Picture Collection/Getty Images)

Cover design: Adriana Brioso

A catalogue record for this book is available from the British Library.

A catalog record for this book is available from the Library of Congress.

ISBN: HB: 978-1-7845-3888-0
        eISBN: 978-1-8386-0079-2
        ePDF: 978-1-8386-0087-7

Series: Library of Modern Middle East Studies

Typeset by RefineCatch Limited, Bungay, Suffolk
Printed and bound in Great Britain

To find out more about our authors and books visit www.bloomsbury.com
and sign up for our newsletters.

This book is dedicated to the makers of the UAE:
the Foreign Office Arabists and the officers
of the Trucial Oman Scouts.

Contents

Illustrations

Maps

Figures

Acknowledgements

I am extremely grateful to the former members of the Foreign Office in the UK and the Trucial Oman Scouts who agreed to speak to me about their experiences in the Trucial States. They provided me with crucial 'colour' about their service in the sheikhdoms during the final years of British imperialism in the Gulf.

This book relies on numerous archives in the UK and the USA. I am especially grateful to the staff in the reading room at the National Archives at Kew, Richmond, who provide researchers with excellent service. Debbie Usher, the archivist at the Middle East Centre Archive, St Antony's College, Oxford University, has assisted me for many years. I am extremely grateful for all her help. The staffs at the presidential libraries in the USA were also very helpful in advising me about their collections.

Rosemary Hollis, Eugene Rogan and Charles Tripp were generous with their time and expertise. Ahmed Al-Shahi kindly gave me permission to consult Peter Lienhardt's doctoral thesis in the Bodleian Library, Oxford University. Shelley Deane, Amelie Jousseaume and Christopher Segar provided me with detailed feedback about draft chapters. I am very grateful to two blind reviewers who commented on my manuscript and made very useful suggestions. Nasser bin Ahmed Alserkal, a very knowledgeable Emirati historian, showed me around Dubai and the Emirates.

I would like to thank my friends and family for their encouragement over the years. Finally, I am grateful for Dr Sophie Rudland's assistance in shepherding this book to publication.

Map 1 The Arabian Peninsula and vicinity.

Source: https://www.lib.utexas.edu/maps/middle_east.html

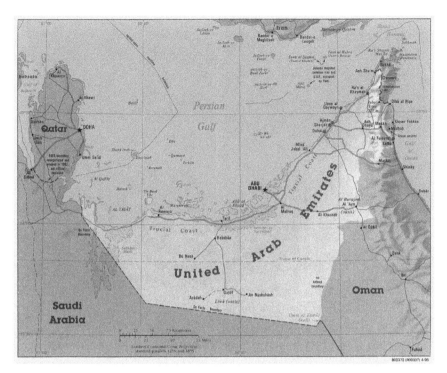

Map 2 The United Arab Emirates (UAE).

Source: https://www.lib.utexas.edu/maps/middle_east.html

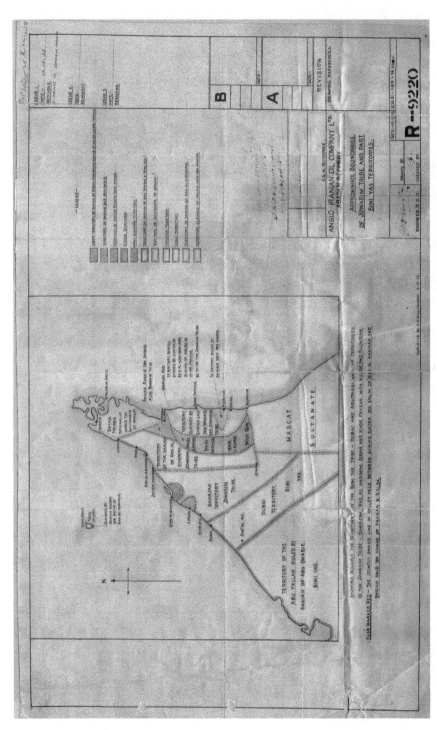

Map 3 Approximate boundaries of Jowasim tribe and part Bini Yas territories, dated December 1935 © BP Archive.

Figure 1 Das Island 1957: the ruler of Abu Dhabi seated in one of the helicopters used for communication between Das Island base and ADMA Enterprise © BP Archive.

Figure 2 The Sheikh of Abu Dhabi (bearded and with bowed head and sword in the back row), undated © BP Archive.

Figure 3 A scene in Dubai harbour, Trucial Coast, 1962 © BP Archive.

Figure 4 Dubai from the air © BP Archive.

Figure 5 Abu Dhabi town Barasti, 1962 © BP Archive.

Figure 6 Aerial view of Abu Dhabi town, 1962 © BP Archive.

Introduction

This book examines Britain's role in the Trucial States from 1948, when the Foreign Office replaced the Government of India as the department responsible for the Persian Gulf, until 1971 and the establishment of the United Arab Emirates (UAE), as the States came to be called on their independence in December 1971.[1] This transfer of authority to the Foreign Office occurred in April 1948, at the end of the British Indian Empire. The Foreign Office managed relations with the Trucial States for over twenty years until the treaty relationship was ended in 1971 and the States gained full independence. The Foreign Office was committed to defend the Trucial States, but it had no power to promote their political, economic and social development. The Foreign Office acknowledged that it did not control events. In stark contrast with other dependent territories, the documents attest that in Bahrain, Qatar, Oman and the Trucial States, the rulers and their subjects did not want the British to withdraw prior to 1971. This book examines the origins of the UAE's historic exceptionalism and considers Britain's soft diplomacy in the Emirates.

The book makes a significant contribution to the existing literature on the Trucial States, and to the origins of the UAE. Historians of the Empire have largely ignored British imperialism in the Persian Gulf. There are various explanations for this omission that include divided control among various government departments, including the India Office, the Admiralty, the Foreign Office and the Treasury. Britain's imperial presence in the Gulf lasted much longer than elsewhere in the Middle East, such as in Egypt or the mandates in Iraq and Palestine. As Peter Sluglett notes, the imperial history of the Middle East has been 'distinctly patchy', with the Eastern Question, Egypt and Palestine dominating the literature.[2]

The book draws on a range of documents, some of which have never been accessed by other historians of the Gulf. In contrast to the existing published studies on the subject, this analysis addresses the complexity of British policy, including attempts to instigate a development policy in the Trucial States, initiating the establishment of regional armed forces and creating the structure of domestic security services. The book examines the impact of the singularly relevant oil industry, as perceived by the Foreign Office, and the processes and procedures followed in attempts to establish new systems of government and governance processes. Finally, the book examines the positive legacy of Britain's role in the Gulf, and assesses the Foreign Office's effectiveness in introducing an efficient system of government in the Trucial States. It shows that, although the British ended the treaty relationship with the Trucial States in 1971, British officers continued to play an important role in the armed forces of the UAE. This indicates how, although the British formally departed from the Gulf at the end of 1971, ties were not severed, and the British remained involved in maintaining the stability of the Emirates. The British had considerable economic interests in the UAE, and strong commercial relations with the UAE were established. These included defence sales, construction and the role of oil companies.

The maintenance of regional stability and access to oil were major criteria for the British following the withdrawal in December 1971. Themes that have not been addressed in the literature on the UAE are discussed here. Very little has been written about how the transition from the social, political, economic and governance pillars of the Trucial States to the UAE was achieved, the establishment of armed forces and the impact of the oil industry in the UAE. The Emirates were transformed from states with no external sovereignty into members of the United Nations. The rulers faced considerable challenges forming a new state, but they were free from British interference in their internal affairs.

Terminology

The terminology used to describe the Trucial States can be confusing. Prior to the signing of the first, annual, Maritime Truce in 1820, the sheikhdoms were commonly known to the British and their representative in India as the 'Pirate Coast'. Subsequently, the sheikhdoms were gradually referred to as 'Trucial Oman', which is distinct from the Sultanate of Oman, which had long-standing relations with the Government of India. Likewise, the rulers became known as the 'Trucial Sheikhs'.[3] The Trucial Sheikhdoms (the name of the ruling family is listed in parentheses) included: Abu Dhabi (Al Nahyan), Dubai (Al Maktoum), Ras Al Khaimah (Al Qasimi), Sharjah (Al Qasimi), Umm Al Quwain (Al Mualla), Ajman (Al Nuami), with today's emirate (sheikhdom) of Fujairah (Al Sharqi) only having been recognised as an independent entity in the early 1950s. Abu Dhabi and Dubai are the two sheikhdoms afforded the most interest, courtesy of their oil wealth and role as a regional entrepôt, respectively. As a result of agreements these sheikhdoms signed with the Government of India, Bahrain (Al Khalifi) and Qatar (Al Thani) were also part of the Trucial system. The sheikhs of Bahrain signed several agreements with the Government of India between 1820 and 1914, and the ruler of Qatar signed a treaty in November 1916 that was very similar to the obligations of the Trucial States. The treaties recognised the independence of the rulers but they forbade piracy, and obliged the rulers to follow British advice regarding their external relations.[4]

In 1928, the Government of India characterised the Trucial States as 'independently administered tribal principalities governed by independent Arab sheikhs'.[5] In May 1936, George Rendel, the influential head of the Foreign Office's Eastern Department, minuted that: 'the Gulf States are a special preserve of His Majesty's Government whose policy towards them rested on a kind of Monroe Doctrine'.[6] By the 1960s, the Foreign Office described the Trucial States as 'independent sheikhdoms in special treaty relations with the United Kingdom',[7] or 'British Protected States'.[8] This terminology is notable because it describes the inherent limitations imposed on Britain's long-standing role in the Trucial States. In a protectorate, such as in Aden, the British reserved the right to make laws for peace and good government, whereas in protected states, the sovereignty of rulers was recognised, and the rights exercised by the Crown had to be acquired by treaties. Britain's relations with the Trucial States were determined by a series of treaties and agreements that led the states to surrender their foreign policy to the Government of India and the Foreign Office. However, the states remained internally sovereign. This meant that British officials could persuade and cajole the rulers to adopt policies such as administrative reform and development, but they could not enforce them. The British were not as powerful as is often assumed, and the personal influence of Foreign Office officials in the Gulf was extremely important. The memoirs written by the officials who served in the Gulf attest to the close relationships that were cultivated with the rulers.

Organisation of the book

Chapter 1 discusses the origins and the significance of British policy in the Trucial States. Shaped by economic and strategic interests, the historical context of Britain's long-standing role in the Persian Gulf is an essential precursor to any study of the Gulf, and of the Trucial States in particular. The interest of the East India Company (EIC) and its successor, the Government of India (established after 1858), in the Gulf, originated in the early nineteenth century. In 1820, the EIC signed the first of a series of treaties and agreements with the rulers of the Trucial States. The EIC represented British interests in India, and had the power to sign treaties and contracts with foreign rulers. These formative agreements created the basis of the Government of India's policy in the Gulf and determined British policy in the region until 1971. The Government of India's policy in the Gulf was shaped by economic and strategic interests, which included trade, and the defence of India's north-western frontier.

Chapter 1 also addresses the structure of British influence in the Trucial States that was founded on the Political Resident in the Persian Gulf (PRPG) and a handful of Political Agents. Until the 1950s, on account of the region's harsh climate, the British presence on the Arabian shore of the Gulf was very limited. Over time, the Foreign Office appointed diplomats who played a central role in cultivating relations with the rulers of the sheikhdoms. The chapter also discusses the characteristics of sheikhly rule that prevailed in the sheikhdoms. This is a significant theme because the Foreign Office had to work within the confines of how the sheikhdoms were run at the time. The system of government in the Trucial States, as far as it existed, was paternalistic and dominated by hereditary ruling families who benefited from the absence of close British control. Finally, Chapter 1 analyses the internal economic structure of the Trucial States. The economic base of the sheikhdoms was very limited, and the largest tax revenue was derived from pearling, but the expenditure of the rulers was confined to their families and the cost of their guards.

Chapter 2 analyses the expansion of Britain's role in the Trucial States during the 1950s. A shift in focus occurred in the 1950s because the Foreign Office was concerned with the maintenance of regional stability, unhindered access to oil, limited administrative reform and development in the region rather than political change. Room for manoeuvre for Foreign Office diplomats was tight because the Foreign Office was forced to rely on the ruling families of the Trucial States. The chapter addresses policy issues, including relations with Saudi Arabia, and the maintenance of British prestige in the region.

There is a significant gap in the historical literature during this period because there is little discussion of Foreign Office attempts to advocate for a development policy in the Trucial States during the 1950s and 1960s. The existing level of development varied between the sheikhdoms. Dubai, for example, was relatively developed because of its long-standing role as the regional entrepôt, whereas Abu Dhabi and the smaller sheikhdoms were characterised by a lower level of development. Chapter 2 analyses the challenges that limited the impact of the Foreign Office's development policy during the 1950s. These included the British Treasury's characteristic parsimony in allocating funds and the very low level of development in the Trucial States. Education was non-existent, and the rulers were very reluctant to adopt British ideas about development in areas such as education because they were perceived at that time to be a significant threat to their long-standing autonomy. The Government of India's previous policy of non-interference had hitherto entrenched the power and authority of the ruling families of the Trucial States. The British became increasingly concerned about the unwillingness of the rulers to reform their regimes and the impact of foreign influence in the Trucial States. Police forces emerged during the 1950s to counter this threat.

A further notable development of the 1950s involves the establishment of security forces in the Trucial States. The British Government routinely raised locally recruited conscripted forces across the Empire that were known as 'levies'.[9] In 1949, the Foreign Office decided to establish a small mercenary force in the Trucial States called the 'Trucial Oman Levies'. The Foreign Office initially established the Levies in order to prevent the slave trade and tribal raiding in the Trucial States, but the Saudi invasion of the long-contested Buraimi Oasis, which lies on the Abu Dhabi–Oman frontier, in the summer of 1952, posed a significant threat to the internal security and territorial integrity of the Trucial States. The Buraimi Oasis was located on a strategic crossroads, and the Saudis had made intermittent attempts to secure the area since the early nineteenth century.[10] The Saudi incursion in the summer of 1952 led to the Levies' expansion, and to a long-running diplomatic dispute between the Foreign Office, which was responsible for the Trucial States' foreign relations, and the Saudi Government. The Levies were renamed the 'Trucial Oman Scouts' in 1956 in order to encourage the recruitment of British Army officers, and that afforded them a high degree of professionalism. The Foreign Office and War Office funded the Trucial Oman Scouts, and British officers and other ranks commanded it until the British withdrew from the Trucial States in 1971. The establishment of the Trucial Oman Scouts was particularly significant because it played an important role in maintaining the peace in the desert hinterland of the Trucial States for the first time. The creation of the Scouts and police forces had long-term implications since they formed the basis of the UAE's armed forces.

Collectively, these developments were significant because they marked a reversal of the heretofore long-standing policy of non-interference in the internal affairs of the Trucial States. The Foreign Office was in an anomalous position. Whitehall officials realised that not only were political and economic reforms necessary but new adaptive policy approaches were an urgent necessity since the British role in the Gulf was subjected to increasing scrutiny internationally and threatened accusations as an imperial anachronism. Change, however, could not be imposed. The Trucial States were a <u>somnolent</u> imperial backwater, but changing strategic, political and economic factors threatened their isolation. The largely self-sufficient sheikhdoms became increasingly vulnerable to outside forces, including the threat of Arab nationalist sentiment that was prevalent at the time. Egyptian Nasserist radio propaganda from Cairo was highly influential. The Foreign Office attempted to cajole and persuade the Trucial State rulers to modernise, with limited success. The Foreign Office was wary of encouraging political reform in the Trucial States because it did not want to weaken the power and authority of the rulers.

Chapters 3 and 4 analyse the period from 1960 to 1967. The sixties were characterised by far-reaching developments in the Trucial States, and in the British government's policy toward them. The Foreign Office was well aware of the anachronistic and anomalous nature of its position in the Gulf. The role of British officials was augmented to guide the rulers of the Trucial States and to prevent the penetration of foreign influence. A notable example was the Foreign Office's determination to preclude the rulers from accepting Arab League assistance in 1965. The role of the Arab League was to encourage economic and political cooperation between its member states. In 1967, the Foreign Office acknowledged that Britain's role in the Trucial States was unlikely to continue beyond the mid-1970s. The fundamental question was how best to manage the process of withdrawal. Chapter 4 addresses this question.

The most important internal development in the Trucial States was the discovery of oil in Abu Dhabi in 1958, and the establishment of its oil industry. The Trucial States faced substantial development challenges and the creation of government institutions. These developments have been scarcely addressed in the existing literature and this book will examine these challenges from a British perspective in detail. One of the major impediments to British initiatives was the personality of Sheikh Shakhbut bin Sultan Al Nahyan, the ruler of Abu Dhabi (1928–66). Sheikh Shakhbut resisted change and British officials (and foreign consultants) found it very difficult to persuade the Sheikh to spend money on much needed development schemes. In 1965, the British Treasury rejected an increase in development expenditure because of Abu Dhabi's increased wealth. The British Government regarded the ruler of Abu Dhabi as an obstacle, and in 1966 the Foreign Office played a central role in his replacement by his brother Sheikh Zayed. In 1967, the Foreign Office observed that Abu Dhabi, the wealthiest Trucial State, faced a variety of problems, including the future unregulated growth of the economy in the sheikhdom as a result of unprecedented oil income, urban and rural development, population growth and the establishment of an effective administrative structure. The transformation and transition of the Trucial States from an impoverished imperial convenience to an oil-rich state makes for compelling lessons for subsequent transitions. Chapters 3 and 4 address this fundamental point.

Chapter 5 analyses the period of 1968 to 1971. In January 1968, the British Labour Government created consternation among the rulers of the Trucial States, when it stated that Britain planned to withdraw from the Gulf by the end of 1971. The decision to withdraw was perceived by the rulers of the Trucial States as a betrayal of a long-standing ally. Helene von Bismarck,[11] Simon Smith,[12] Shohei Sato[13] and Tore T. Petersen[14] have all addressed the policy of the Labour Government from London. However, the process of withdrawal, how Britain systematically separated itself from the Trucial States, has yet to be addressed. Chapter 5 seeks to address this gap. By 1970, the capacity for Britain to hold the reins of control had weakened and the limitations of British power were evident to all. The future of the Trucial States looked bleak. There were multiple unresolved internal and regional issues, not least of which was Abu Dhabi's fraught relations with Saudi Arabia over the demarcation of their shared frontier. Iran's growing regional influence greatly concerned the Foreign Office and the rulers.

Chapter 5 also analyses the future of the Trucial Oman Scouts because they had played a key role in maintaining internal stability. The Foreign Office had consistently failed to persuade the rulers to cooperate in establishing a consultative council. Nonetheless, the sheikhs relied on British advice about the nascent United Arab Emirates's constitutional structure. An important issue arising out of the British withdrawal was the relationship between the sheikhdoms and the kind of political arrangement that would be best suited and most likely to replace the Trucial system. Before and after the British withdrawal in 1971, there was widespread British concern that the newly formed UAE might not endure the persistent competition and marked differences between the respective rulers of the seven emirates, Bahrain and Qatar. Abu Dhabi, on account of its vast wealth, remained the dominant sheikhdom, and the British established a long-standing commercial and defence relationship with the UAE. The rulers of Bahrain and Qatar decided that membership of a federal system was unviable for political reasons, and instead opted for independence. The final denouement was also complicated by Ras al-Khaimah's refusal to join the UAE until 1972. The rulers of the Trucial States were wary of Bahrain joining a union because they believed that the island would have a disproportionate degree of influence in a union of nine states. Bahrain's population was much larger and better educated than the other sheikhdoms, and there had been intermittent outbreaks of violence in Bahrain that were directed against the British and the ruling family. The British belatedly played a central role in the negotiations that led to the formation of the UAE, and the Iranians heavily influenced the diplomatic manoeuvres that culminated in the formation of the new state.

The final chapter addresses the British legacy in the Trucial States. The British legacy in the Gulf was extensive. Formally, the British withdrew in December 1971, but British commercial, military and political interests were significant. The British role in the Trucial States can be best defined as benign. The British government did not contend with internal disorder in the Trucial States that directly challenged Britain's role in the Gulf. The system of low-cost imperialism adopted by the British in the Gulf, and the Trucial States in particular, which relied on ruling families, was relatively successful. The system of imperial control in the Trucial States was beneficial because the Foreign Office made little attempt to interfere in the Trucial States. The British government legacy in Jordan was broadly similar: minimal direct British interference resulted in a positive legacy. After the withdrawal, the role of British officials in the Gulf reverted to traditional diplomatic practices. They were no longer responsible for directing the affairs of the sheikhdoms, and this is reflected in the significant decline in the scope of the Foreign Office records that cover the UAE. Although formal British responsibilities declined after 1971, corporate interests significantly increased. Oil and defence companies played a big role but a wide range of banking, legal and civil engineering firms were present. In addition, in the years after independence, British advisors still ran the police, port and water supply in Dubai. A notable legacy of the British role in the Trucial States was the establishment of armed forces that remained apolitical. The Union Defence Force, the successor to the Trucial Oman Scouts, has to this day not attempted to interfere in politics. In stark contrast with the neighbouring states, the Trucial States were politically stable, and the foundations of a relatively strong, stable UAE assisted by effective and adaptive British policies applied across thirty years.

Sources

This book is based on documentary sources held at a number of archives in the UK and USA. These sources are crucial because of the absence of accessible archives in the UAE.[15] Nonetheless, the researcher needs to be cautious when using the official records. This is because the documents describe events in detail but solely from an official perspective. The first chapter is based on the records of the East India Company and Government of India (after 1858), which are held in the British Library.[16] Since 2012, many of the British Library records on the Gulf have been digitised and can be downloaded for free. This is a remarkable resource for historians of the Gulf region.[17] The Government of India records are the most important source on the Gulf until the demise of the British Indian Empire in 1947. This is because the region was within the Government of India's sphere of influence and the small number of officials who served in the region appointed from the Indian Political Service. The India Office records in the British Library are extensive and under-utilised.[18] Moreover, the documents can be hard to comprehend because they are handwritten and poorly organised; and the absence of permanent British officials on the Arabian shore of the Gulf meant that the East India Company and the Government of India relied on local agents for the bulk of their information. The India Office records provide considerable insight into developments in the Gulf during the nineteenth and early twentieth centuries.

The Government of India also published a variety of publications on the Gulf. The most relevant of these is John Lorimer's monumental *Gazetteer of the Persian Gulf, Oman and Central Arabia*, which is by far the most detailed account of the nineteenth-century Gulf.[19] Other important published sources include the *Bombay Selections*[20] and Jerome A. Saldanha's multi-volume *Persian Gulf Précis*, which provide detailed accounts of events on the ground and the development of government policy.[21] The Government of India also published a series of memoranda during the early twentieth century that provide useful accounts on developments in the Gulf region.[22]

The records at the National Archives (TNA), Kew, are very well organised, and in most cases are easy to comprehend. There is a wide range of sources on the early twentieth-century Gulf at the TNA, because the Government of India/India Office routinely sent documents on the Gulf to the Foreign Office. The latter was concerned with the Gulf, insofar as the developments in the region affected relations with the Ottoman Empire, Iran and Saudi Arabia. TNA records on the nineteenth and early twentieth centuries can be found in a wide range of sources such as the Admiralty, the Cabinet Office and the Foreign Office. In 2017, the Foreign and Commonwealth Office (FCO) – which replaced the Foreign Office in 1967 – released approximately 100 files in two series: FCO 164 and FO 464. These documents are a central addition to the records held at Kew. The FCO is currently processing 600,000 'non-standard files', and a spreadsheet shows that there are numerous documents under review that relate to the Persian Gulf, the Trucial States and the UAE.[23]

In April 1948, the Foreign Office became responsible for the Gulf and the Trucial States. The volume of records on the Gulf States greatly increased during the last two decades of Britain's role in the Trucial States. This book relies on at least 40,000 pages of documents at Kew. It is important to note that this is a sample of the main British documents at Kew, but it provides telling insight into the unprecedented expansion of the Foreign Office's role in the Trucial States in the post-Second World War era. The Foreign Office and, after 1967, the FCO records are by far the most numerous and are well organised. The records of the Treasury are essential since British policy on the Trucial States was heavily influenced by the Treasury's determination to cut overseas expenditure. The Treasury's short-sighted and parsimonious policy had a major impact on the Foreign Office's attempts to fund an effective development programme in the Trucial States. The Ministry of Defence records are also of note because they contain considerable information about the UK's defence interests in the Trucial States.

In conducting research for this volume over a period of five years, a wide variety of documents that have rarely, if ever, been cited are scrutinised and integrated into the British policy story. The large Cabinet Office series contains the records of the Joint Intelligence Committee (JIC). The JIC documents are significant since they contain intelligence assessments on the Gulf, and details on the Trucial States' internal security organisation that are mainly absent in the Foreign Office sources. Other major, but scarcely utilised, sources at the TNA include the records of the British Council and Ministry of Overseas Development (now the Department for International Development, DFID). These sources are valuable because they provide details on development policy and education in the Trucial States.

This book also relies on several smaller archives that hold important records on the Gulf region. These sources are rarely exploited by historians of the Gulf region. They include the BP Archive at Warwick University, and the Middle East Centre Archive (MECA), St Antony's College, Oxford University, which holds a variety of private papers. Furthermore, the Palace Green Library at Durham

University (DUL) possesses the extensive papers of Sir Donald Hawley, who served in the Gulf, and the National Army Museum (NAM), Chelsea, London, includes interesting papers concerning the Trucial Oman Scouts. Researchers can also access financial records at the HSBC Group Archives (the British Bank of the Middle East), London.

This book also utilises records in several archives in the United States. The US National Archives and Records Administration (NARA), College Park, MD, holds the records of the Department of State (DOS). The records of the DOS are voluminous and poorly organised, but they are valuable because they provide a critique of British policy in the Trucial States and the Gulf. American officials regarded the Persian Gulf as a British lake, but by the 1950s the State Department was increasingly concerned about US oil interests. The State Department was extremely critical of the Foreign Office's handling of border disputes between the Trucial States and Saudi Arabia. It was also displeased with the sudden announcement by the Wilson Government in January 1968 that it planned to withdraw from East of Suez. Nonetheless, the British and Americans shared similar interests, most notably regional stability in the Gulf, following the British withdrawal in December 1971. The records in the presidential libraries complement the State Department records because they contain intelligence reports and details of high-level meetings between successive presidents and prime ministers. This book also utilises the Central Intelligence Agency's (CIA) Freedom of Information Act Electronic Reading Room.[24] This is a scarcely known resource that includes a vast number of declassified documents that provide a prescient analysis of British policy in the Gulf.

Altogether, the archival sources on the Gulf and Trucial States in the post-war era are vast, and only limited attempts have been made to fully exploit the archives in the UK and USA.

1

Benign neglect

The Government of India's legacy in the Gulf

This chapter discusses the context of Britain's long role in the Gulf – the Trucial States as well as Bahrain, Kuwait, Qatar and Oman. Britain's position in the Trucial States originated in the early nineteenth century. The East India Company (EIC) and the Government of India (after 1858) dominated the Gulf region for over a century. The policies adopted by the Indian government had a major impact on the evolution of British policy in the Gulf until the demise of the British role in 1971. The Government of India's policy in the Gulf was determined by commercial and strategic considerations. Several agreements and treaties heavily influenced relations with the rulers of the Trucial States, Bahrain, Kuwait and Qatar. The *Pax Britannica* in the Gulf was characterised by the maintenance of peace at sea, and the prevention of what the British regarded as piracy.

The Government of India and the Foreign Office relied on a small number of officials and locally recruited agents in the Gulf. The Political Resident in the Persian Gulf was the key British official in the Gulf. During the post-Second World War era, the number of British officials serving in the Gulf gradually increased. This was a consequence of the Foreign Office's growing intervention in the region. The Political Resident and the British Political Agents enjoyed extensive formal and informal powers. Their most important role was the maintenance of cordial relations with the rulers of the Trucial States.

Sheikhly rule was the dominant form of political organisation in the Trucial States. The Government of India rarely intervened in the internal politics of the sheikhdoms, and the British acted as the sheikhs' guarantor. The Government of India's non-intervention in the Gulf resulted in the hereditary ruling families dominating the politics of the Trucial States, Bahrain and Qatar. The British were determined to secure their interests in the Gulf, but they neglected to introduce any economic, political and social reforms. The Arabian littoral of the Persian Gulf was an imperial convenience, and by the demise of the British Indian

Empire in 1947, the population of the Trucial States had very little to show for the British presence, apart from not being incorporated by Saudi Arabia. The Foreign Office continued to support the rulers in the post-Second World War era because there was no viable alternative to sheikhly rule.

India and the Gulf States

The East India Company's commercial and strategic interests evolved over time.[1] The EIC had perennial strategic interests in the Gulf, which included preventing rival European powers, such as the French, from exerting their influence in the region.[2] The EIC's political and strategic interests on the Arabian shore of the Gulf originated at the beginning of the nineteenth century. During the early nineteenth century, the Company initiated a series of operations in the Persian Gulf in order to counter what it regarded as piracy. Attacks on shipping in the Gulf continued unabated and, in December 1819, British and Omani forces attacked the Qawasim at Ras Al Khaimah, leading to the destruction of the town and of villages nearby.[3] Forts were demolished and the Qawasim fleets were destroyed.[4] The most significant long-term impact of this operation was that the tribal chiefs along the coast signed a General Treaty of Peace in 1820 with the EIC.[5] Under the Treaty, the rulers and their subjects were bound to abstain from 'plunder and piracy', and the Indian authorities tried to ensure that acts of piracy would not go unnoticed and unpunished. The General Treaty was important because it established the basis of subsequent treaties and marked the onset of Britain's primacy in the Gulf that lasted until 1971.

As the head of a naval confederacy, the British regarded themselves as the guarantor of maritime truces and the suppression of piracy. The British believed that their superior strength made them the arbiter of regional power. The British Resident was instructed to abstain from interfering in land wars, and instructed that every opportunity should be taken to persuade the rulers to remain at peace and that acts of piracy would be punished.[6] There were exceptions to this policy of non-interference on land when British interests were threatened. Subsequently, the rulers signed a series of agreements with the Company in 1835 and 1842, and in 1853 they agreed to a Perpetual Treaty of Maritime Truce.[7] As a result of these agreements, the sheikhdoms of the Lower Gulf became known as the 'Trucial States'.

In 1858, the Government of India assumed responsibility for the Trucial States. The British position in the Gulf rested on custom rather than law because there had been no need to define it since no international power challenged British supremacy. In 1892, the rulers of the Trucial States signed an Exclusive Agreement that stipulated: (1) 'that I will on no account enter into any agreement or correspondence with any Power other than the British Government'; (2) 'that without the assent of the British Government I will not consent to the residence within my territory of the agent of any other Government'; and (3) 'That I will on no account cede, sell, mortgage or otherwise give for occupation any part of my territory, save to the British Government.'[8] This agreement remained the basis of Britain's relations with the Trucial States until 1971. The rulers of the Trucial States also signed during the twentieth century agreements concerning the Prohibition of the Traffic in Arms,[9] and the exploitation of natural resources. In 1922, the rulers agreed not to grant oil concessions 'to anyone except to the person appointed by the High British Government.'[10] During the 1930s, the rulers signed agreements for landing rights for the RAF (at Abu Dhabi and Dubai) and Imperial Airways (at Dubai and Sharjah). In return, the rulers received an annual subsidy and a landing fee, but their external sovereignty was significantly constrained.[11] These agreements symbolised greater Indian interference in the internal affairs of the sheikhdoms, which the rulers resented.

The Government of India also signed agreements and treaties with the other Gulf States. Bahrain signed treaties that closely resembled the agreements with the Trucial States. The ruler of Bahrain signed the General Treaty of 1820, but was not included in the 1853 Maritime Truce. However, in 1861, the ruler of Bahrain signed a 'Friendly Convention' with the Government of India, whereby he agreed to 'abstain from all maritime aggressions of every description', as long as he received 'the support of the British Government in the maintenance of the security of' his 'possessions against similar aggressions directed against them by the Chiefs and tribes of this Gulf'.[12] As Rosemary Hollis notes, Bahrain was therefore accorded an explicit guarantee of its independence by the British, which was not the case in the Trucial States.[13] In 1880, Bahrain signed the first Exclusive Agreement with the British, and signed the same agreement as the rulers of the Trucial States in 1892.[14] The rulers of Bahrain also signed agreements in 1898 to suppress the arms trade and in 1912 to establish a wireless station, and in 1914 Bahrain agreed not to sign an oil concession without consulting the Political Agent at Bahrain.[15]

The British also signed agreements with the rulers of Qatar. In 1868, the ruler of Qatar signed an agreement not to breach the maritime peace. However, Qatar only joined the Trucial system in 1916, when Sheikh Abdullah bin Jassim signed a treaty that was similar to the treaties with the Trucial States. In return, the British guaranteed protection 'from aggression by sea' and offered its 'good offices' in the event of aggression by land or sea, as long as such aggression was not provoked.[16]

The Government of India's treaty relations with Kuwait and Oman were different. The Kuwaitis had a more independent relationship with the British on account of Kuwait's historic orientation with the Arab world and its relations with the Ottoman Empire. In January 1899, Sheikh Mubarak bin Salah Al Sabah, the ruler of Kuwait, signed an Exclusive Agreement with a view to forestalling Russian action in the Gulf. Sheikh Mubarak agreed not to receive the agent or representative of a foreign government or power without the previous agreement of the British government. He also agreed not to cede, sell, lease, mortgage or give for occupation any portion of his territory without the prior consent of the British. The agreement implied British support for Sheikh Mubarak's rule and Kuwait's independence, but it remained secret. In 1901, Sheikh Mubarak requested British protection in the face of a Turkish invasion, which was declined. However, Colonel Kemball, the Political Resident, gave the ruler a 'qualified assurance of support, conditional on his continuing to observe the Agreement of 1899'.[17] The Kuwaitis made similar undertakings as Bahrain and the Trucial States on pearls in 1911 and, in 1912, the ruler agreed to establish a telegraph station. In 1913, Kuwait signed an agreement on oil, in which a concession was not to be granted 'to anyone except a person appointed from the British government'. In November 1914, Colonel Cox, the Political Resident, sent Sheikh Mubarak a letter that confirmed Kuwait was 'an independent Government under British protection'.[18] This agreement remained in place until 1961, when Sheikh Abdullah requested that the 1899 Agreement be terminated because it was regarded as dated. The British granted full independence to Kuwait and guaranteed military support, given the possibility of an Iraqi invasion.[19]

In comparison with the Gulf sheikhdoms, Muscat was nominally more independent and sovereign because it signed treaties of friendship and commerce with other states.[20] Oman was different from the sheikhdoms on account of its larger population, territorial space and orientation towards the Indian Ocean. Britain's relations with Oman predated the treaties with the sheikhdoms. The first Anglo-Omani Treaty was signed in 1798 in order to exclude the French from the region during the Napoleonic Wars (1803–15). However, Francis Owtram notes that by the late nineteenth century, Muscat had become a 'de facto British protectorate'.[21] This was the result of the Government of India's 'forward policy' in the Gulf that was expressed in various agreements with the Sultan of Oman.[22]

These agreements were significant because they established the basis of the British imperial system in the Gulf until 1971. The Gulf was open to all maritime flag nations, however, in practice, the *Pax Britannica* was maintained by British naval power, which led to the expansion British and Indian trading interests.[23] The Gulf was a notable example of an imperial backwater that only started to receive significant attention in Whitehall when it became clear that the region possessed vast quantities of oil. Hitherto, the Government of India had scant regard for the Gulf, as long as its economic and strategic interests were not impinged.

The Foreign Office had limited direct contact with the sheikhdoms. Sir Basil Newton, the Ambassador at Baghdad, made an unprecedented tour of the Arabian coast of the Persian Gulf in March 1940.[24] Newton's report is significant because it reveals how little the Foreign Office knew about the Gulf, and the extent to which Whitehall relied on the Government of India and the Political Resident for information about the region. Furthermore, Newton's appreciation of Gulf affairs reveals the extent to which the Government of India's perception of the Gulf dominated British policy.

Political control in the Gulf

The Gulf was a notable example of 'informal empire' because the British avoided formal imperialism – direct overrule of a territory – due to cost and climate. Instead, the British preferred to retain an indigenous political system that they could influence. British control in the Gulf and the Trucial States was based on the Indian model of indirect rule. Michael Fisher defines indirect rule as: 'the exercise of determinative and exclusive political control by one corporate body over a nominally sovereign state, and control recognised by both sides'.[25] This involved delegating authority to local 'bigwigs' responsible for administration, insofar as it existed. In reality, 'independence' was a facade because the British exerted considerable economic, military and political influence. Indirect or informal imperialism relied on an unequal treaty or alliance that defined the extent of intervention in internal affairs and, most significantly, curtailed the rulers' ability to conduct an independent foreign policy. This mechanism of control was appealing because it was cheap and it allowed the British to extract themselves from confrontations with local nationalist feeling.

This pattern of indirect rule originated in the princely states of India in the form of a residency system. The Government of India routinely relied on the

Indian residency system as a means of extending de facto imperial control at the lowest possible cost across the Empire.[26] The mechanism of informal imperialism relied on what Ronald Robinson referred to as 'collaboration'.[27] Without the voluntary or enforced cooperation of indigenous elites, Britain's strategic interests could not be assured.[28] The British could exert overwhelming force over a territory but they could not succeed without mediators within the indigenous society. Robinson contends that the success of a collaborative system was proportionate to the amount of power and wealth invested in it.[29] However, the system established by the British in the Trucial States contradicts this contention because limited financial and military resources were expended but significant strategic and political returns were achieved.

The most important British official who served in the Gulf was the Political Resident in the Persian Gulf (PRPG). The Political Residents played a central role in maintaining British influence in the Gulf. Lord Curzon, the Viceroy of India (1899–1905), described the Resident as 'the uncrowned king of the Persian Gulf'.[30] Until 1953, all the Political Residents were appointed from the Indian Political Service, which consisted of officers seconded from the Indian Army and the Indian Civil Service. The Indian Political Service originated in 1783, when the Company established a Foreign and Political Department and, by 1947, there were no more than 150 members of the service.[31] The duties of the Political Resident evolved over time, but the Gulf represented a limited form of residency control because successive British Residents exercised a very limited degree of internal interference in the sheikhdoms.[32]

The East India Company appointed the first Native Agent at Sharjah in 1823.[33] Several factors account for the East India Company's and the Government of India's reliance on native agents.[34] The Company and the Government of India were constrained by financial limitations while the harsh climate and living conditions made postings to the Gulf unappealing. The Government of India was unwilling to spend resources on its representative in the Gulf, and it was cheaper to employ locals with extensive economic and political contacts.[35] The Foreign Office appointed the first permanent British political officer located at Sharjah in 1948, and their duties were remarkably similar to their Arab predecessors', which highlights how the Indian regime persisted in the Gulf.[36]

The duties of the Political Resident were multifarious and unlike those of an ambassador.[37] His role was a 'criss-cross between those of an ambassador and those of a colonial governor',[38] and included responsibility for protecting Britain's interests in the Gulf, relations with the rulers, the administration of justice, negotiating air agreements, the safeguarding of the sterling area and encouraging the expansion of education.[39] The Residents were very powerful and influential in the Gulf and on decision-makers in India and London. This was because they were the sole channel of communications with the government and rulers. The Political Resident was the most senior British official in the Gulf, and was responsible for Political Agencies that were established from Kuwait to Muscat. The Political Resident had to operate within the confines of the regional and local political system, and serve the interests of the Government of India, the Foreign Office and the rulers of the sheikhdoms; hence James Onley's conclusion that this was the main explanation for the longevity of the *Pax Britannica* in the Persian Gulf.[40] This book shows that the situation was more complex than this explanation.

The Political Resident was based at Bushire on the Iranian coast until 1946, and subsequently Bahrain became the centre of British influence in the Gulf. The system of political influence remained unchanged until 1939. The award of oil concessions and the establishment of an air route through the Gulf led the Government of India to reluctantly appoint a British Political Officer to Sharjah on the Trucial Coast. The Government of India was wary of posting a political officer to the Trucial Coast on account of the region's harsh climate. In 1948, the Political Agent came under the authority of the Political Resident, rather than the Political Agent at Bahrain, and in 1953 the Political Agency was moved from Sharjah to Dubai.[41]

By the 1950s, there were four political agencies – in Bahrain, Kuwait, Dubai and Doha – and a consulate general at Muscat. The Foreign Office gradually increased the number of officials posted to the Gulf. In 1952, there were twenty-nine personnel serving in the region from Kuwait to Muscat, and by October 1960 the number had increased to forty-one.[42] In 1961, in anticipation of Abu Dhabi's windfall income from oil, the Foreign Office established an additional political agency in the sheikhdom.[43] The main role of Colonel Sir Hugh Boustead, who served as Political Agent at Abu Dhabi (1961–5), was to get as close as possible to Sheikh Shakhbut bin Sultan Al Nahyan, the ruler of the sheikhdom, and to try to influence his expenditure on development and the creation of government institutions.[44] The political agents were responsible for day-to-day relations with the rulers, which meant that their first duty was to cultivate friendly, personal relations with the rulers and their subjects.[45] They were also the mouthpiece of British policy, and the interpreter of the sentiments of the ruler.[46] The political agents were required to understand the ruler's point of view, without interfering in relations between them and their subjects.[47] James Craig, who served as the Political Agent at Dubai (1961–4), wrote a colourful description of his role:

The Agent sits in court below the Royal Coat of Arms and sees the old procession of clerks and petition writers. His servants wear turbans and puggarees and long *shirwani* coats. He inspects gaols and pursues smugglers, runs hospitals and builds roads. He takes the salute from the Trucial Oman Scouts, on a sandy barrack square, amid ornamental cannon, pennants on lances, bugles and pipes and drums. He makes State tours with reception tents and dining tents and sleeping tents, trestle tables, carpets and military escorts. He is very much a *bara sahib*.

But he is also a sheikh. All year round he sits and receives his callers; rulers with business of State, tribesmen with pastoral complaints, conspirators with offers of partnership; wealthy merchants seeking agencies; gold smugglers seeking passports; schoolboys seeking scholarships to England. To each he offers, through his coffee-maker girt about with the great silver dagger, the tiny handless cups of black spiced coffee. Twice or thrice a year he sits in full *majlis* while the visitors pour in with congratulations, sweetmeats, Christmas cakes and fat goats. His letters are addressed to 'His Honour, the Most Glorious, the Magnificence of Her Majesty's Trusted One in the Trucial States, the Revered'. He decides fishing disputes, negotiates blood-money, examines boundaries, manumits slaves. He presides over the Shaikhs' Council. He exempts, pardons, appeases; exacts, condemns, ordains. Over a large but undefined field he in effect rules. It is all a far cry from the third room and the Foreign Office canteen.

The Political Agent has, forbye, more orthodox functions. He must persuade rulers and influence public opinion. He must justify (stern task) the workings of the Union Nations and intercept the policies of the Arab League. He must help negotiate oil concessions. He must expound the need for a law on workmen's compensation and even, in settling sea frontiers, explain to an illiterate sheikh the principle of constant equidistance involved in the trigonometry of the median line. He must be severe and masterful when he feels insignificant and ill-assured. He must at times be diplomatic as any conventional diplomatist.[48]

The powers of the Political Resident and the political agents were not entirely informal, as Craig's description shows. The political agents had significant legal responsibilities over expatriates, and they were responsible for the manumission of slaves for years after Indian independence.[49] Nonetheless, one of the crucial roles performed by Foreign Office officials was advising the rulers and, according to Glen Balfour-Paul, 'the boundary between offering advice and enforcing it may have been as narrow as a vocal inflection'.[50] Sir Trenchard Fowle, who acted as Political Resident during the 1930s, summed up Britain's relations with the rulers:

The main factor is that on the whole we possess the goodwill of the Arab rulers and their peoples. One reason for their attitude is that as far [as] possible we let them alone to manage their own affairs in their own way. Briefly we can try to carry out a policy based on the modern methods of 'indirect' rather than older ones of 'direct' rule.

A second reason for the goodwill in question is that in our negotiations with the rulers, over oil, air facilities, ... we give them a square deal. We carry a moneybag instead of a thick stick and are prepared to talk instead of to threaten. This does not imply that our policy is a weak one. In any really serious difference of opinion between the states and ourselves, for example with regard to breaches of their treaties with us, we are of course prepared to take a firm line. The threat, however, of this drastic action has hitherto been sufficient to achieve our purpose, and for the last ten years or so we have been able to obtain our objects on the Arab side, and to enforce the implementing of our treaties without firing a gun or dropping a bomb.

The third and most important reason for the good will of the Arab states is that they regard HMG as their natural protector. This in my opinion is the outstanding and permanent factor, which in all-important issues is at the back of the minds of rulers and their people, and its local importance cannot be over-estimated. It is this consideration, more than any other single factor, which enables us to 'run' the day to day administration of the Arab side with a handful of officials, without payment of a single rupee of subsidy, or the upkeep (on our part) of a single soldier, policeman, or levy, which has a distinct and salutary effect on the minds of any particular shaikh and his people.[51]

Fowle's description remained an accurate portrayal of relations well into the 1950s, and it shows how nuanced the British role in the Gulf was. The system of British influence in the Gulf was based on the Indian model, and little changed after the transfer of authority to the Foreign Office in 1948.[52] Until the late 1940s, the Political Resident relied heavily on 'native agents', namely locally recruited officers, who reported on events on the Trucial Coast. The native agents were valuable because the Political Resident, based on the Persian coast, visited the Arabian shore only intermittently.

The strategic and commercial value of the Gulf meant that the maintenance of maritime security was a crucial interest to the Government of India. The Royal Navy's Persian Gulf Squadron played a 'watch-and-cruise' role in keeping the peace in the Gulf. This meant that the Royal Navy had an important role in assuring peace at sea, and gunboat diplomacy was an important technique that was used to compel recalcitrant rulers.[53]

Nowhere else in the Empire did the British achieve so much with such comparatively little effort. The Government of India dominated Eastern Arabia and the Persian Gulf via the Political Resident. The Gulf States were very different from other examples of British imperialism because there was no civilising mission in the Gulf, and no religious missionary movement such as in colonial Africa. The British presence in the Gulf was minimal; there was no colonial administration in the region and no attempt was made to develop the states. The British were undoubtedly the hegemonic power, but the Gulf was different from British protectorates and protected states elsewhere in the Empire.[54] In a protectorate, the British reserved the right to make laws for peace and good government, whereas in protected states, the sovereignty of rulers was recognised and the rights exercised by the Crown were acquired by treaties. The Exclusive Agreements the rulers of the Trucial States signed with the British forbade them from dealing with the outside world, and imposed on the British the obligation to defend them. Balfour-Paul notes that the indeterminate status of the Gulf sheikhdoms 'wears in retrospect all the marks of that scrupulous impression characteristic of so many of Britain's imperial contrivances'. The British made up the rules of the game as they went along and the result was that no one 'knew what they were'. The Trucial States' status was 'uniquely curious even by imperial Britain's standards of curiosity', but the system worked because it was never seriously challenged.[55] Moreover, the rulers had no one else to turn to, and there was a mutual interest in maintaining sheikhly rule, especially after the discovery of oil. Without British protection, the Trucial States might have been absorbed by their powerful neighbours, such as the Saudis, or merged. Uzi Rabi notes that: 'the Gulf looked out on the world through the small lens of its relations with the British'.[56] British protection had stultifying political implications, and a senior British diplomat described the Gulf political scene as 'paralytic' and referred to the 'bottomless hangover which a state of dependence induces in those who shelter most faithfully under our protection'.[57] But in Sheikh Zayed, the ruler of Abu Dhabi, and Sheikh Rashid of Dubai, the British were fortunate to find two competent leaders in power when they departed in December 1971.

British imperialism in the Gulf had four functions. The *Pax Britannica* in the Gulf protected the sheikhdoms from the larger states in the region. The British also shielded the sheikhdoms from coming to terms with the Ottoman Empire, Saudi Arabia and Iran, and during the 1960s with Egypt and Iraq. The British also succeeded in establishing a territorial status quo but this became increasingly controversial, following the discovery of oil. The British became the protectors of sheikhly rule, and they played an important role in shielding the rulers from the ideological currents that swept the region in the post-Second World War era. The

British protected the traditional political structure in the sheikhdoms because they countered the threat of insurgency and subversion by supporting the status quo from Kuwait to Oman. The final role the British played was that they were the peacemakers amongst the sheikhs. The British succeeded in enforcing an artificial stability and peace between the sheikhs and the tribes who had been accustomed to sporadic conflicts and raiding.

Sheikhly rule and tribes in the Trucial States before oil

It is hard to comprehend the harshness of the environment that prevailed in the Trucial States prior to the discovery of oil. Today, visitors to the UAE observe, especially in Dubai, a remarkable urban landscape. Explorers of the Trucial States and their neighbours provide vivid accounts of the desolation of the region. The British explorer Sir Wilfred Thesiger was one of the most renowned travellers in the Arabian Peninsula. Thesiger wrote a colourful portrayal of the desert interior of the Trucial States:

> The next day we crossed the Sabkhat Mutti. We decided we must make a detour and cross these salt-flats near their head, otherwise the camels might become inextricably bogged, especially after the recent heavy rain. They would only have to sink in as far as their knees to be lost. Camels are always bad on greasy surfaces, so we fastened knotted cords under their feet to stop them from slipping. Here the salt-flats were divided into three arms by crescent-patterned drifts of sterile white sand. The flats themselves were covered with a crust of dirty salt which threw up a glare into our faces and, even through half-closed eyes, stabbed deep in to my skull. The camels broke through this crust and floundered forward through liquid black mud. It took us five unpleasant, anxious hours to get across.[58]

J. B. Kelly, who spent time in the Trucial States in the 1960s, also wrote an evocative account of the area:

> That part of Arabia which lies to the east of Qatar, between the southern shore of the Persian Gulf and the northern rim of the Rub al-Khali, the Empty Quarter, is largely a depressing waste of sand dune, salt flat and gravel plain. It consists, broadly speaking, of a coastal tract with an off-shore chain of islands, and a desert hinterland. The islands begin off the coast of Qatar and end to the north-east of Abu Dhabi town, which itself stands on an island. The coastal tract, a succession of sand and gravel plains interspersed with *sabkhah*, or salt flat, runs from the foot of Qatar eastwards to Abu Dhabi, and then turn north-eastwards,

extending to beyond Ras al-Khaima, the northernmost of the Trucial Shaikhdoms, where it is forced into the sea by the massive cliffs of the Musandam peninsula, which jut into the entrance to the Persian Gulf. The desert hinterland behind the coast is dominated by sand dunes, which grow more formidable in size as they approach the Rub al-Khali. There are two fairly larges oases in the region, Liwa, in the middle of the desert hinterland, Buraimi, at its eastern edge, by the foothills of the western Hajar.[59]

The population of the Trucial States were drawn from three tribes, the Bani Yas, the Manasir and the Awamir, while the population of the Buraimi Oasis belong to two tribes, the Dhawahir and the Na'im. The tribes were loosely organised into sections and subsections, and there was no clearly defined tribal structure as exists elsewhere in Arabia. In many desert areas, each tribe had an exclusive *dar* or homeland, in which it could be found, and where the wells are the property of a certain tribe. This was not the situation in the Trucial States because the tribes freely mingled and the wells were free to all. The tribes did not own settlements, but they did not wander far afield like other Bedouins, preferring to remain on the fringes of the desert.[60]

The tribal structure of the Trucial States was complex because of the lack of defined boundaries between the sheikhdoms and their neighbours. British officials made concerted efforts to demarcate these boundaries, and, in 1955, Martin Buckmaster and Julian Walker, British diplomats serving in the Gulf, conducted a detailed survey of the boundaries of the Trucial States.[61] For British diplomats and officers serving in the Trucial Oman Scouts (TOS), knowledge of the tribes was essential because of the long-standing tendency of tribes to fight one another.[62] The tribes of the Trucial Coast were divided into two categories of nomad and sedentary tribes. By the late 1950s, there was a tendency of some of the nomads to become assimilated with sedentary tribes. There was also an inclination for the nomad tribes to split into smaller groups, who continued living separate lives. The tribes of the Trucial States are divided into two factions, the Hinawiyah and Ghafiriyah, who derived from a civil war in Oman in the eighteenth century.[63]

The ruling sheikhs of the Trucial States were the most important intermediaries with the British. One of the significant long-term implications of the *Pax Britannica* in the Gulf was the system of sheikhly rule that continues to characterise the Emirates today. Abu Dhabi and Dubai were the most important sheikhdoms, whereas the five smaller states were perennially economically and politically inconsequential. The Government of India showed very little interest in the internal affairs of the sheikhdoms. In 1928, it produced a lengthy historical memorandum that detailed the British position in the Gulf since 1907. The authors of this report argued that the 'internal history of the Trucial States in the last 20 years is of no general interest or importance'.[64] Nonetheless, the political complex in the Gulf States underwent a fundamental transformation that was caused by the development of the oil industry.

In the pre-oil era, the sheikhdoms were organised on segmentary lines, rather than being unitary political entities.[65] The sheikhdoms were characterised by one town on the coast that dominated a number of villages, most of which were on the coast, and the desert hinterland. This was the extent of the state, 'the unit over which the authority of one government extends, the maker of peace and war'.[66] The growth of these towns was usually associated with their ruling families, and the rulers were responsible for administering only the central areas of their sheikhdoms through limited powers. Most of the population lived in towns and villages because the land was too barren to allow a livelihood for the majority of the settled population. Rulers presided over a scant administration, and the small size of the state before oil made it difficult for sheikhs to share power.[67] Rulers involved their relatives, for instance in the appointment of *walis*, who were tasked with representing the ruler on the periphery of the state and ensuring that these areas remained under dynastic control. Technological limitations made the administration of the larger sheikhdoms hard to achieve.[68] Rulers also appointed relatives to these peripheral positions in order to prevent undesirable succession, and there were other manifestations of sheikhly rule, including the role of the *muzakki* who collected taxes and customs duties, and *qadis* (judges) who administered law. However, prior to independence in 1971, the sheikhs started to employ 'northern Arabs' from Egypt, Palestine and Iraq in a variety of positions. The rulers were also protected by a small number of salaried but untrained armed retainers, known as *askars*.[69] In Abu Dhabi, Shaikh Shakhbut (ruler 1928–66) retained a small force of about 120 armed tribesmen, who were employed as guides, guards and messengers. The more senior *askars* were deputed to various jobs such as representing the ruler, who always travelled with a large retinue of armed followers.[70]

Amongst the tribes, the sociopolitical role of the sheikh or ruler was crucial. The sheikhs were responsible for defending their followers and, in return, they pledged their loyalty to the sheikh. The system of rule was tribal, patriarchal and oligarchic. Tribal politics was focused on authority over people, rather than territory.[71] The ruler had to earn the allegiance of the people and his performance was critically assessed. A period of bad luck or disputes might reduce the number of followers and through them the territory of the sheikhdom.[72] The right to impose tax was symbolic of the ruler's power, and the extent of the sheikh's authority in wartime was measurable by the number of fighting men he could raise.[73]

Government was based on a selected individual whose decision was final, but the custom of holding a regular *majlis* or council allowed subjects to approach the ruler with grievances or personal problems.[74] The choice of ruler was usually restricted to the family, and the administration was rudimentary if not anarchic. Uzi Rabi notes that the 'most important political factor was that allegiance and loyalty were offered on a personal basis', which meant that the European concepts of the nation state and territorial sovereignty were neither applicable nor comprehensible in the sheikhdoms.[75] The *majlis* worked well in the Trucial States because it allowed public access to the ruler, but there was no desire for representative government. The Foreign Office recognised that the most efficacious form of government was direct personal rule by the sheikh, assisted by a small number of administrators, but even this limited form of rule was very difficult to implement.[76]

The sheikh's government was personal and absolute, but he consulted an informal advisory council that consisted of members of his family, leading merchants and notables. The ruler had to take into consideration the sanction of his forcible removal by members of his family if his conduct was contrary to the interests of his subjects. The ruler exercised an autocratic and personal absolutism, but there was some element of popular participation that influenced his authority.[77] The Government of India recognised the ruling sheikhly families because they enforced agreements, and they became the main channel of influence in the Trucial States.[78] Allen Fromherz notes that in Qatar, the British cooperated with the hereditary Al Thani rulers. This led to institutional development which favoured entrenched tribal interests that placed the ruling family in a dominant position in the sheikhdom.[79]

The Trucial States can be characterised as a chieftaincy or chiefdom. These were power-sharing partnerships that involved pastoral nomads, semi-sedentarised tribesmen, townspeople and a ruler who lived in the countryside or town. Chiefdoms had other notable characteristics, including the role of the ruler who had 'moral authority' over his fellow tribesmen, and was required to provide a 'continuous flow' of goods and services to his followers. These ties were not formally institutionalised because they were focused on the personality of the ruler, and they were based on the segmentary division of society, in which the tribe was bound together by a shared identity based on kinship.[80] Tribal confederacies, such as those in the Trucial States, were characterised by loose alliances between several tribes who controlled a territory. One of the fundamental problems chiefs faced was maintaining their leadership role and the integrity of the chieftaincy. This was caused by the absence of institutionalised authority in a tribal system.[81] Peter Lienhardt argues that the main check on the rulers was the withdrawal of a substantial part of the population if the sheikhs abused their authority. A second limitation on the power of the rulers was the possibility of being overthrown, driven out or murdered. In the Trucial States, there were numerous coups d'état, which suggests that there was not a strong belief in the legitimacy of the rulers. The ruling families persisted, but the rulers did not, which meant that legitimacy lay with the family rather than with a certain person.[82]

The sheikhs were personally responsible for running their states despite the almost complete absence of an administrative system. The Trucial States, with the exception of Dubai, were characterised by a very great administrative weakness because there was no governmental structure that was capable of dealing with development. Dubai, by the 1950s, had a customs administration and a town council, and, in the other sheikhdoms, half-hearted attempts had been made to form town councils.[83] There was no civil service, army or police force, apart from guards (*askars*) employed by the sheikhs. However, there were significant variations between the states concerning the transfer of power between rulers because there was no common system of primogeniture in the Trucial States. In Abu Dhabi and Sharjah, rulers were either deposed or murdered, whereas in Dubai none of the rulers were overthrown.[84] The Government of India was disinterested in these internal power struggles, as un—! long as they did not impinge on British interests.[85] Gradually, the rulers of the Trucial States became less remote as a result of greater British involvement, the development of the oil industry and the consequent improvement in the economy of the states. Enhanced communications, including the widespread use of the radio, and the expansion of education all affected the pattern of rule.

The rulers of the Trucial States acquired power and prestige as a result of being recognised by the British.[86] However, in the pre-oil era, the rulers were constrained by a variety of internal and external forces.[87] Sir Harold Dixon observed that the rulers were expected to be wise, able and courageous, and that their paternalist role meant that they were required to be 'the father of the people'.[88] The absence of a clear line of succession in some of the sheikhdoms, such as in Abu Dhabi, meant that the rulers did not automatically appoint their eldest son as their successor.[89] Sheikhs became rulers as a result of the strength of their supporters compared with their rivals. The ruling family was responsible for the 'election' of a new ruler, but the heads of tribal sections and merchants had an important role.[90]

The rulers and the ruling families had state revenues in their hands. Income was collected from customs duties and pearling taxes, and it was used to support the ruling families.[91] The population was not dependent on the rulers for their livelihood, and, in the pre-oil era, politics in the sheikhdoms was dominated by a coalition between the ruler and merchants. Jill Crystal notes that the merchants connected the ruler with financial resources, and merchants were influential through their presence in the *majlis* and in intermarriage with the ruling family. However, the political influence of merchants varied, and, in Kuwait, where the merchants were well organised, their impact was significant, but less so in Qatar.[92] Merchants were influential because the rulers depended on them for financial support and they were able to tax and extract customs duties. The relationship between merchants and rulers has been characterised as a 'protection racket' because of the way in which merchants subsidised rulers, and, in return, the rulers protected the merchants' trade.[93]

A notable example of the relationship between rulers and merchants occurred in Dubai, which was the main port along the Trucial Coast.[94] Sheikh Saeed bin Maktoum, the ruler of Dubai (1912–58), encouraged local business and attracted migrants from India and Iran. However, the decline of the pearling industry during the 1930s inflicted a severe blow on the merchant community, and the ruler of Dubai exploited new economic opportunities such as the establishment of a British air base in 1934 and the granting of oil concessions. These economic changes upset the balance between the merchants and the ruler, who was no longer reliant on their financial support.[95]

Before oil, the power of the merchants lay in the mobility of their business interests, which meant that they could leave a sheikhdom if the ruler exacted too much tax. Merchants could also take sides in succession disputes, but they did not translate their economic power into institutionalised political influence. Merchants were the only group in the early years of oil capable of opposition to the rulers, but the rulers recognised this. The rulers offered merchants an 'oil pact' that promised wealth in return for renouncing their role in political decision-making, which meant that their formal access to power declined.[96] The growth in oil income resulted in making some of the rulers more powerful and secure than they were in the past.

In the Trucial States, there was a very close relationship between the tribes and the small town-population. As Lienhardt commented, 'the desert made the tribes of the Trucial Coast, but the sea made the Trucial States'.[97] In 1908, the population was thought to be 80,000.[98] In 1939, the Indian General Staff[99] estimated the population had remained static on account of the Trucial States' non-existent health care and the dearth of education, both of which contributed to a high infant mortality rate and short life expectancy.[100] The sheikhdoms were poor countries before oil, whose people, whether they were tribesmen or seafarers, were able to move away from a coercive ruler. In contrast with agricultural peasants, they had relatively little to lose from moving from one place to another because they could take their source of income with them. This freedom of movement preserved their freedom from foreign rule and weakened the grip of their rulers over them. The rulers were only capable of maintaining order in their sheikhdoms, and they never established a complex administration.

The lives of the tribes and settled population were not mutually exclusive, and until the development of the oil industry in the 1960s, the economy of the Trucial States was dominated by a tribal subsistence economy, whereas the littoral population relied on the sea and trade with India and Iran.[101] Pearling and fishing were the dominant maritime activities. The *Pax Britannica* in the Gulf provided maritime security, and the introduction of steamships in the nineteenth century increased demand in India for Gulf pearls.[102] However, the decline of the pearling industry during the 1930s, caused by the development of Japanese cultured pearls, had dramatic economic consequences. The worsening economic situation in the Trucial States was enhanced by the impact of the Second World War. Dubai was adversely affected because it was the most important trading centre on the Trucial Coast.[103]

The rulers of the Trucial States were also influenced by a variety of external forces. One of the significant questions in the historiography of the Gulf is to what extent the treaties the British signed with the rulers were imposed or willingly accepted.[104] J. E. Peterson argues that British protection 'bestowed a legal status on the concept of "shaykhdom".'[105] Lienhardt contends that the British afforded the rulers 'a status higher than the traditional way of life had allowed them.'[106] The Government of India, in the early nineteenth century, was wary of becoming protector on account of its concern that it might be drawn into the unstable and unpredictable affairs of the hinterland. The Government of India's ability to influence events inland was minimal because it lacked the will and resources to become involved in tribal disputes, as long as they did not threaten British interests. The ability to control events was hindered by the range of naval guns, which limited the scope of military operations. The Government of India was also determined to avoid dispatching ground forces for financial reasons and because of the severe climate that characterises the region. The

Indian Government was also concerned that permanent British protection would encourage despotism, and that it would lead the Political Resident to become the arbiter of numerous vexatious disputes and endless claims.[107]

The annual truces were very successful, and the strength of the British position in the nineteenth century was that it alone could stop the endless cycle of violence amongst the rulers of the Trucial Coast.[108] The Political Resident used protection as a method of keeping in power the rulers who were willing to cooperate with the British and keep out of power those who did not. The *Pax Britannica* was mutually advantageous because it benefited the British as much as the rulers of the sheikhdoms. This explains why the system of limited British interference was so successful: it was self-enforcing.[109] The British succeeded in using the tradition of protection in the Gulf, which was based on personal honour,[110] and the treaties were initiated as much by the rulers as by the British. The British froze the existing tribal political map of the Gulf States, and by recognising and protecting certain families as rulers in a territory, they interrupted the historical rise and decline of ruling families.[111]

British protection was not imposed but was sought after by the rulers of the Trucial Coast.[112] Sheikhly authority was 'frail, vulnerable and precarious', and the British Resident was able to hold the rulers accountable for any action of which they disapproved.[113] Only the British, as a result of their maritime supremacy, had the power to stop the pattern of raiding and invasion that characterised relations between the sheikhdoms.[114] The British curtailed tribal raiding in the post-Second World War era, when they established the Trucial Oman Levies in 1951 (the Trucial Oman Scouts from 1956).[115] The Scouts played a very important role in policing the Trucial States and, until their creation, the most important impediment to state formation was the threat of armed tribal opposition to the rulers. The British relied on considerable experience in the Middle East of pacifying tribal populations;[116] however, the gradual establishment of state authority meant that the tribes were 'tamed',[117] which was reinforced by the process of urbanisation that made the tribes easier to control.

Protection had other implications, which included the drawing of boundaries that lessened the power of the rulers. According to Gregory F. Gause III, 'the British sliced up jurisdiction like salami' in the Trucial States.[118] Britain's long-standing role as the protecting power meant that the Foreign Office had a central role to play in any potential unification of the Trucial States. One of the significant criticisms of the British role in the sheikhdoms was that the Government of India failed to take the initiative to enforce the amalgamation of the sheikhdoms.[119] Balfour-Paul challenges this argument and observes that the Government of

India had no interest in uniting the states and the treaties preserved them. Subsequently, the British believed that it was in their interests to leave the situation 'loosely defined'.[120]

The Resident coerced recalcitrant rulers who failed to follow British 'advice', by deposing them or relying on bombardment, fines or banishment. The British intervened three times in Bahrain between 1868 and 1923, and they routinely threatened the rulers of the Trucial States in the interwar years. In 1930, the Government of India seized the pearling dhows of Ras Al Khaimah because the ruler refused to allow a petrol barge for the use of the RAF to be moored in his territory.[121] In 1935 and 1938, the Government of India threatened to seize the Abu Dhabi pearling fleet because the ruler, Sheikh Shakhbut, refused to cooperate in the suppression of the slave trade.[122] Shakhbut repeatedly challenged the British since he was determined to protect his independence. In contrast with the other rulers, Shakhbut refused to sign an oil concession with Petroleum Concessions (Trucial Coast), which was a subsidiary of the Iraq Petroleum Company, until he was coerced by the British to comply with its wishes in 1939.[123]

The British attitude towards recalcitrant rulers was modified following the establishment of the oil industry. Hitherto, the British had relied on threats and, exceptionally, deposed rulers. The economic and strategic importance of the Trucial States meant that the Foreign Office was no longer willing to tolerate rulers who failed to conform to British interests, and, in 1965 and 1966, their families, with British support, deposed the rulers of Sharjah and Abu Dhabi.

Sheikhly rule was transformed as a result of oil income. The rentier state paradigm has been the dominant theory that seeks to explain the longevity of some Middle Eastern monarchies.[124] Its core argument can be summarised as 'No representation without taxation,' but this assumption has been challenged. Michael Herb argues that in Kuwait the rulers are well connected with their population: 'a situation that runs frontally against the chief theoretic claim' of the rentier state.[125] Likewise, Mary Ann Tetreault regards the rentier state paradigm as a 'myth'.[126] Herb contends that 'dynastic monarchy' is a more accurate explanation for the Gulf monarchies' long duration. Reports by British diplomats support this argument. Sam Falle, who was serving in the British Embassy in the late 1960s, commented on how the Al Sabah family controlled the sheikhdom by allocating key government posts to members of the family. Falle observed that:

> The mainspring of the authority of the Sabah family is tradition. The Sabah's were the leaders of the tribal group which settled here in the 18th century and

have always been the ruling sheikhs. The ruling family inherited a tradition of autocratic rule from Sheikh Ahmed al Jabr who ruled between 1921–1950. The present Sabah have therefore inherited an autocratic tradition, while the elaborate apparatus of government of a modern state, which requires licenses and permits of every kind, had increased their power; then the accession of wealth derived from oil, much of which has entered the family coffers directly, has increased it further. Memories are long enough, nevertheless, for the prominent merchant families to have continually in mind the unsuccessful struggles of the past forty years to diminish this power. The Sabah hold all the chief offices of the state.[127]

Following the development of the oil industry, ruling families have monopolised the highest state offices, including the ministries of defence and foreign affairs, known as the 'ministries of sovereignty'.[128] The rulers also distributed family members throughout lower positions of the state apparatus, which has allowed them to establish a robust system for distributing power that has led to an 'unshakeable hegemony' over their states. The monopoly of government posts by the ruling family ensures the continuation of dynastic monarchy because the regime controls the state and ensures that only the family selects the monarch.[129] Fromherz argues that 'clanocracy' or the solidarity of the ruling family is the ultimate guarantee of power, and this is what prevents their deposition.[130] Rulers who failed to rely on their family and did not establish support for dynastic succession were overthrown. Sheikh Shakhbut, the ruler of Abu Dhabi (1928–66), was a notable example of a ruler who failed to rely on his family, and he was obstructive of political and economic changes brought on by a windfall oil income. His family overthrew him with full British support in August 1966.

Crystal argues that, in Kuwait, oil income broke down the ruling coalition between the rulers and merchants, and instead the Al Sabahs were able to deal directly with their population by distributing income.[131] The Al Sabahs centralised power because they were reliable allies and they were a ready-made proto-institution. Oil wealth therefore transformed political life, freeing rulers from their traditional dependency on merchants and established a stable political system. The British tried to expand their role in Kuwait through the appointment of advisors, but their influence was limited by the internal cohesion of the ruling family.

The first dynastic monarchy was established in Kuwait in 1938. The British wanted the ruler of Qatar to follow the Kuwait model by involving family members in the government.[132] Herb argues that pressure from outside the ruling family in Qatar, rather than a succession dispute within, led to the emergence of a dynastic monarchy.[133] The application of this approach to the Trucial States is debatable. Herb argues that a dynastic monarchy emerged in Abu Dhabi in 1966, when Sheikh Zayed became ruler and he appointed his relatives to government positions that existed only on paper.[134] The ruling families of the Trucial States were only able to fully take control of their states when they became independent in 1971 and were no longer subject to British pressure.[135] However, after 1971, all the Emirates, apart from Dubai, were subsidised by Abu Dhabi.

Conclusion

The mechanism of influence the Government of India established in the Gulf during the early nineteenth century was a successful example of low-cost imperialism that succeeded in meeting Britain's commercial and strategic interests. The Government of India had very little interest in the internal affairs of the sheikhdoms, as long as the rulers and their subjects did not challenge British interests. The Government of India allowed the hereditary rulers of the Trucial States a free hand that had significant long-term consequences. By default, the Government of India was responsible for entrenching the authority of the ruling families of the Trucial States. Although the Foreign Office had little direct knowledge of the Trucial States, it adapted Indian methods of indirect rule during the final era of the *Pax Britannica* in the Gulf.

The system of rule in the Trucial States was based on the tenuous authority of the ruling sheikhs. The rulers had to maintain a complex balance between the interests of their families, guards, merchants and tribal affiliations in the interior. There was no recognisable system of government in the Trucial States, and the rulers could not afford standing armies. Nonetheless, sheikhly rule in the Trucial States varied because of the absence of a system of primogeniture. In Dubai, succession was overwhelmingly orderly, whereas in Abu Dhabi, rulers were deposed or murdered. Although the Government of India ignored these internal schisms, gradually it intervened in the internal politics of the Trucial States. However, the system of sheikhly rule underwent a significant transformation, caused by oil income.

Up until the late 1940s, the impoverished population of the Trucial States might have felt that they had very little to show for the Government of India's predominance in the Gulf region. By the late 1940s, the Gulf States, especially

Kuwait and Qatar, were becoming economically significant due to the huge increase in oil income. The Trucial States lagged behind their neighbours because oil was only discovered in Abu Dhabi in 1958. Nonetheless, in the post-Second World War era, the Trucial States became less obscure, and the Foreign Office became far more engaged in their economic and social development. In contrast with the demise of British imperialism elsewhere in the Middle East, the British role in the Gulf significantly expanded.

2

The neo-Raj

British policy in the Trucial States during the 1950s

In the 1950s, British policy in the Trucial States underwent a fundamental transformation. During the late 1940s, the Government of India's policy of non-interference in the internal affairs of the Trucial States was still favoured by the Foreign Office. Sheikhly rule in the Trucial States meant that administration, justice and economic prosperity were unknown in the protected states, and the windfall income from oil was unforeseeable. Bahrain, however, presented the facade of a well-ordered state because it was the most advanced sheikhdom. Changing economic, political and strategic circumstances threatened the isolation of the Trucial States because the Gulf was no longer a remote imperial outpost. The gradual expansion of Gulf oil, sterling balances and the growing strategic importance of the Gulf changed the situation.

The Iran oil crisis in 1951 and the development of the oil industry in Kuwait were decisive factors that led the British to take a more active role in the Gulf. The Iranian oil crisis strengthened the Foreign Office's determination to protect the Trucial States from external threats. A notable example of this occurred in the summer of 1952, with the Saudi occupation of the Buraimi Oasis, which lies on the frontier of Abu Dhabi and the Sultanate of Oman.[1] The Buraimi Crisis was very important because, without British protection, the complicated structure of the sheikhdoms would have been ruptured and there might have been a free-for-all. The Foreign Office was determined to remove the Saudis from Buraimi for reasons of prestige and regional stability. The Buraimi situation showed that there was no effective alternative to the British presence in the Gulf. There was no meaningful grouping of Arab states that could have provided a viable confederation, capable of resisting strong centrifugal tendencies.

There was no reason for the British to withdraw from the Gulf at the time. However, the British position was increasingly regarded as an anachronism and there were competing views about what the Foreign Office's policy should have been. During the Eden (1955–7) and Macmillan governments (1957–63), the Foreign Office failed to establish sound administrative and political reforms of any substance in the Trucial States. The pattern of rule in the Trucial States was unchanged, and the rulers seemed unaware of, and indifferent to, the impact of growing Nasserist propaganda and were unable to do much about this. Similarly, they had little interest in or control over the nascent educational system. The Foreign Office encouraged reform but could only succeed with the agreement of the rulers. The British faced a fundamental dilemma in the Trucial States because they wanted the rulers to reform their administrations, which might have threatened British interests and stability. The rulers seemed to offer the best and only hope, but expected the Foreign Office to secure them against their opponents. This occurred in 1954–6 in Bahrain, where the first post-war manifestation of political discontent and opposition to sheikhly rule occurred.[2] Likewise, in 1957, the Sultan of Oman also sought British assistance against an insurgent movement.[3]

The Foreign Office could do little more than cajole, persuade and exhort the rulers to modernise themselves, their families and their administrations, usually with very limited or no results. Nonetheless, the British did relent in the face of new threats from Arab nationalism and Nasserism. They accepted sheikhly rule but recognised the dangers inherent in unmodified sheikhly government. The Foreign Office understood very well that in any Arab patrimonial state, the ruler was the key to good or bad government and progress or the lack of it.[4]

The Foreign Office understood that its position in the Gulf was the final vestige of British imperialism in the Middle East.[5] The trend elsewhere in the Empire was towards self-government but not in the Trucial States. The Foreign Office recognised that it had to take various steps to enhance British prestige and maintain regional stability. These measures included the establishment of the Trucial Oman Levies (renamed the Trucial Oman Scouts in 1956) in 1951, which was the first trained security force in the Trucial States. The Foreign Office also introduced a limited development policy in the Trucial States because it had to show the rulers and their subjects that it was taking positive steps to help them or they might look to the Saudis for assistance. The rapid and uncontrolled economic development in Kuwait and Qatar brought about by a windfall oil income made the British wary that this might occur in the Trucial States.

The Foreign Office also tried to improve the administration of the Trucial States and persuade the rulers to cooperate via the Trucial States Council that was formed in 1952. The Council achieved very little, but it was an example of the modest proposals that the Foreign Office could make. The rulers attempted to play off the British in their search for funds, and only Dubai made progress in improving its administration. In contrast, Abu Dhabi, under the rule of Sheikh Shakhbut since 1928, was a byword for sheikhly misrule. The ruler resisted all attempts to improve his administration and do anything for his people. Abu Dhabi was a notable example of the limitations of British influence in the Gulf.

The transformation of the Gulf in the post-war era

The demise of the British Indian Empire in 1947 led to the Foreign Office becoming responsible for the Persian Gulf in April 1948. The Foreign Office had little interest in the Gulf,[6] and, in 1945, Foreign Secretary Ernest Bevin held a conference of Britain's Middle East representatives.[7] The 1945 Middle East conference did not discuss the Gulf because it remained within the Government of India's sphere of interest. It was debatable whether the Foreign Office was best suited to take responsibility for the sheikhdoms. The Colonial Office would have been better prepared to provide administrative staff that had long experience of development in the colonies and managing indirect rule.[8] J. B. Kelly argues that the Foreign Office was never content with its role in the Gulf because of the imperial, rather than diplomatic, nature of the British presence. This was reflected in the titles of Britain's representatives, who performed tasks similar to collectors in India or a district commissioner in colonial Africa. The multifarious nature of the duties performed by British officials meant that this was a role best suited to former members of the Indian Civil Service or the Sudan Political Service. Some of the officials who served in the Gulf were originally members of these services, and their training and outlook made them well prepared to serve in the Trucial States. Britain's policy in the Gulf in the post-Second World War period became the sole preserve of Foreign Office officials. This was caused by the very limited knowledge of the area, which made the Gulf inaccessible, and ministers and Members of Parliament relied heavily on officials for information about the region.[9]

The decision to hand over control to the Foreign Office in 1948 set limits on the extent to which the British Government could guide the states in treaty relations with the Government of India. These limitations were hardly recognised in Whitehall. Ministers and senior officials in London, who had no experience of the region, were baffled by the Gulf and by why the sheikhs could not be won over by logical argument.[10] It took time for the limitations of the British position to be realised and for these fundamental weaknesses to be exposed. In the post-Second World War era, the states remained untouched by regional events, and it was hard to assess accurately economic and political developments. Nonetheless, American diplomats regarded British paramountcy in the Gulf as the final relic of British imperialism in the Middle East.[11]

The Foreign Office, notwithstanding its limitations, initially adhered to the Government of India's policy of non-interference in the internal affairs of the sheikhdoms, as long as British interests were not affected. Changing imperial circumstances led to a reversal of this policy. The transfer of power in India in 1947 and the growth of American influence in Saudi Arabia had a significant impact on Britain's strategic interests in the Persian Gulf.[12] The withdrawal from India seemed to undermine the *raison d'état* for the continuation of Britain's imperial role in the Persian Gulf, which had been premissed on the defence of India's frontiers and trade links.

Britain's interests in the sheikhdoms of Eastern Arabia increased in the post-war era. However, the Persian Gulf remained a secondary concern in British defence plans for the Middle East, which were focused on the defence of the Suez Canal in spite of drawn-out negotiations with the Egyptian Government about the future of British bases in the country.[13] In July 1948, the Eastern Department of the Foreign Office reviewed Gulf policy. Foreign Office officials debated whether it should continue with the existing policy of non-intervention or introduce a colonial policy based on direct administration. The Foreign Office believed that it should adopt a policy, which entailed expenditure on advisors and education. However, no British-controlled security force should be established, and the Political Resident would continue to rely on naval action as a last resort. The official mind recognised that this would not guarantee security inland or permit oil companies to prospect and exploit oil resources in the area.

British influence in the Trucial States increased in the post-war era as a result of the introduction of various legal measures, which included a series of Orders-in-Council that were made in 1946, 1949 and 1950 under the Foreign Jurisdiction Acts.[14] These legal methods formalised British territorial jurisdiction and all persons apart from Trucial States subjects were under the jurisdiction of British courts. In 1950, the rulers of the Trucial States granted their formal assent to the exercise of jurisdiction by the Foreign Office over British subjects and all foreigners. The Political Agent was Judge of 'Her Britannic Majesty's Court for the Trucial States'. The legal status of the Trucial States as 'protected states' was defined by Orders-in-Council that were promulgated in 1949 and 1953.[15]

The Foreign Office faced a dilemma in the Trucial States. It feared that if it did not intervene in the Trucial States, it risked the rapid deterioration of the sheikhdoms as a result of 'extremist influences', especially Arab nationalism.

However, the Foreign Office feared the accusation that it could be charged with failing to support the population and allowing the rulers to have unfettered control over the income from oil. The Foreign Office was also concerned that if it imposed direct administration, it would be 'accused of imperialism and of instituting a colonial regime in the Persian Gulf to make up for the losses of our position in Palestine and Egypt'.[16] Sir Rupert Hay, the Political Resident, dismissed these concerns, and his response exemplified the limited knowledge of the Gulf that characterised the Foreign Office at this time.

Hay argued that the Foreign Office's assumption that the Government of India had not tried to govern or administer the sheikhdoms and only intervened in their internal affairs to stop slave-trading and to prevent tribal wars was incorrect. Hay noted that the British had intervened in Bahrain to the extent of deposing its ruler in 1924 and, during the 1920s, the Political Agent had administered the island. On the Trucial Coast, the British had intervened to stop the slave trade, arms traffic and conflicts at sea, but it had not attempted to stop fighting on land. There had never been any 'cut and dried policy so far as intervention is concerned', and he doubted whether it was necessary to introduce one. Hay disavowed the Foreign Office's argument that the region was vulnerable to communism or nationalist influence. He argued that Whitehall was out of touch with the reality of the situation in the Gulf.[17] The rulers were keenly aware of external threats, and there was no indication of nationalism, with the exception of Bahrain, in the extremely mixed populations of the states. The Foreign Office adopted the third option that was discussed in July 1948, and attempted to encourage administrative reform, social progress and economic development. These efforts led to the reversal of the Government of India's hands-off policy in the Gulf.

Bernard Burrows, the Head of the Eastern Department of the Foreign Office, was the first visitor from a Whitehall department to the Trucial States, Qatar and Oman. Burrows' report on his excursion in May 1949 was a prescient analysis of the problems that bedevilled British policy in the region until the withdrawal in 1971. In 1949, the sheikhdoms of Eastern Arabia still had little connection with the Middle East or the rest of the Arab world, and there seemed to be little interest in developments elsewhere in the region. Burrows observed that it was hard to generalise about the area because of the wide range of physical, ethnological, economic and administrative conditions. Burrows, who, in 1953, became the first diplomat to be appointed Political Resident, anticipated that one of the main long-term problems was how potential oil income could be exploited for the benefit of the wider population and for each state. The absence of any administration, apart from in Bahrain, meant that it would be a mistake to introduce a democratic form of government until greater administrative efficiency had been achieved. There was also little prospect of any tendency towards the 'fusion' of the different states, with the possible exception of the Trucial States, on account of the jealousies between the rulers and because the centres of population were separated by the desert hinterland.

Burrows emphasised the strategic importance of the sheikhdoms, but Britain's position had suffered from the failure to keep up with changing developments, including the discovery and exploitation of oil resources. In spite of the withdrawal from India, the *raison d'être* for remaining in the Gulf had not changed. Communications with the Far East were of great importance, and airfields in the sheikhdoms still played an important role in civil and military air routes. The immense growth in oil resources provided an important market for British exports. Burrows also argued that the British had a humanitarian role to play in suppressing the slave trade, and if the sheikhdoms, which were the main market for slaves in the area, were absorbed by Saudi Arabia, it would be difficult to prevent this practice. If the Foreign Office handled the problems of the Trucial States and Oman, it would be possible 'to make a model of what the administration and social well-being of Middle Eastern territory can be'.

Burrows' report characterised the sheikhdoms as a somnolent imperial backwater, untouched by regional trends, notably the growing importance of Arab nationalism, that were affecting the Arab world at the time. Burrows' report was important because it provided the impetus for the development of coherent policy in the Gulf. Kuwait was a thriving boom town at the time, caused by a vast windfall oil income, but Burrows advised that much closer British guidance was needed to ensure the stability and development of the sheikhdom. In contrast, Bahrain was well administered by British officials, but the main concern was that the government would not be able to keep pace with the development of political consciousness. Qatar was perceived as a 'little Kuwait', but the British needed to exert their influence earlier than they had done in Kuwait so that development in Qatar would be effective. In the Trucial States and Oman, it was essential that the long-standing policy of not interfering inland be discarded, and influence had to be exercised inland to prevent the renewal of the slave trade and the development of oil resources.

Finally, Burrows detailed the anomalous character of the British role in the sheikhdoms:

> In general, it is important to we should bear in mind that this is by no means an
> ordinary Foreign Office posting because Britain's representatives have a wide

range of administrative, judicial and executive functions (e.g., they have criminal and civil jurisdiction over non-Arab foreigners who in Kuwait alone number 7,000). In fact, the Gulf posts are in a very small way at an intermediate stage between a normal diplomatic post and administration such as that of the Sudan of the ex-Italian colonies. If our representatives are to exercise these functions effectively, they must be able to give decisions quickly, and we ought to allow them the greatest possible discretion. The inhabitants of this area are far more impressed by the speed of decision and action than by its justice or accord with principle. That is to say, we must allow the Resident, and under him the Political Agents, to build themselves up a position of local authority and prestige in which they can influence events by their personality and their own decisions and not merely as cogs in a far away governmental machine which no Arab can understand.[18]

British objectives in the Gulf were clearly defined in 1953, when Burrows was appointed Political Resident. The Foreign Office issued Burrows with detailed instructions:[19]

(1) To maintain the traditional position of Great Britain in the Gulf and to continue to fulfil the obligations which they have assumed there. (2) The sheikhdoms of the Gulf have become of first importance to the United Kingdom and to the Sterling Area as a whole … exert sufficient influence in them to ensure that there is no conflict between the policies of the rulers and those of HMG. (3) Advance where appropriate the internal independence of the sheikhdoms. (4) Her Majesty's Government will not oppose any political or economic association or co-ordination between the sheikhdoms provided it is consistent with the aims (1) and (2). (5) The intrusion of the direct influence of other powers into British protected states is unwelcome. In particular the extension of the activities of the Arab League must be resisted. (6) Harmonise United States and British policy without, however, sacrificing the paramount British position. (7) Foster closest relations between British officials and the members of the ruling families, and keep in touch with opinion in all classes of society. (8) Give full attention to economic and financial matters since the expenditure and investment of the rulers' incomes is a matter of direct interest to HMG. (9) The standard of administration and justice in the sheikhdoms must be constantly improved. In particular, an advance must be made in the Trucial States. (10) The maintenance of good relations with Saudi Arabia is highly desirable and seek satisfactory solutions to frontier and sea bed disputes. (11) The oil companies must be free to develop their concessions and their relations with the states must be kept under close review at all times. (12) Maintain the facilities enjoyed by HM forces.

Burrows also received instructions that provided policy directives for the individual sheikhdoms. The Foreign Office stated that greater involvement in Kuwait's internal affairs was an economic and strategic imperative. Since 1950, Kuwait had become of 'prime importance to the United Kingdom and to the sterling area as a whole' because it was a major source of oil supplies and an important element in the UK's balance of payments. The Foreign Office stated that:

> Her Majesty's Government can no longer afford to confine themselves to the role authorised by the treaties and agreements in force and sanctioned by usage but must also interest themselves in all matters which affect the political and economic stability of Kuwait or which affect the interests of the United Kingdom in the widest sense.[20]

Not only had Kuwait become a significant source of Britain's oil supplies since 1950, but also 'expenditure on its large Sterling revenue unless properly directed is capable of inflicting the most serious damage on the Sterling area'.

As a result of these developments, the Foreign Office instructed Burrows that the subjects on which advice had been given should be expanded. A key requirement was that there should be a harmonisation of the ruler's internal and external policies with British interests. British requirements included: (1) the creation in Kuwait of sound and effective administration; (2) the terms of employment of British advisors and other British personnel; (3) the introduction of a proper financial system; (4) the development programme for Kuwait; (5) questions affecting the position and interests of British and United States oil companies; (6) the maintenance of good relations between British subjects in Kuwait and the local population; (7) the security of Kuwait and the prevention of the entry of undesirable elements.

British objectives in Bahrain were defined as: (1) to maintain the existing relationship between HMG and the ruler, based on treaty and usage; (2) to permit the continued orderly development of the administration; (3) to retain the present facilities enjoyed by HM Forces; (4) to ensure stable conditions for the production of oil; (5) to develop enterprises which will assist in sustaining the prosperity in the event of a substantial decline in oil revenue; (6) to create friendly relations between the ruler and his neighbours by the equitable solution of disputes involving territorial claims and the division of the seabed.

In Qatar, British aims were similar to those in Bahrain. In the Trucial States the objectives of British policy were defined as: (1) to maintain their position on the basis of existing treaties and usage; (2) to determine as soon as possible the boundaries between the Trucial States and Saudi Arabia in such manner as to establish the justifiable claims of the rulers against Saudi encroachment, and to determine the boundaries of the Trucial States' interests and with Muscat; (3) to foster good relations and mutual cooperation between the rulers, with the ultimate object of achieving some measure of federation; (4) to assist the oil companies in the exploitation of their concession on land and offshore; (5) to improve the administration of the states and, in particular, to bring about the expansion of health services, the abolition of slavery and the development of natural resources. The Foreign Office noted that the Political Resident would have the services of the Trucial Oman Levies, and that the Foreign Office would be responsible for policy matters relating to the Levies.[21]

British objectives in Muscat were defined as: (1) to retain as far as possible the relationship based on existing agreements between the UK and the Sultan of Muscat and to harmonise the Sultan's internal and external policies with the interests of Her Majesty's Government; (2) to retain the facilities in the Sultanate at present granted to HMG; (3) to secure recognition of the frontier between Saudi Arabia and the Sultanate as near as possible to the line defined by the Sultan in 1937; (4) to enable Petroleum Development (Oman) Limited to take full advantage of their concession (at the earliest moment) which HMG considers as severing the Sultan's territory up to the line defined by the Sultan in 1937. In pursuit of the last objective, the Foreign Office declared:

> That the Sultan of Muscat will be able to extend his authority peacefully and effectively over the tribes of the Central Oman and that Saudi influence will be excluded from that area. Her Majesty's Government are ready to assist the Sultan in this task but wish if possible to avoid direct involvement.

The Foreign Office decided to clarify the meaning of these lengthy instructions:

a) paragraph 1 means that we intend to stay in the Gulf; b) paragraph 2 is a reminder that constant effort is necessary to make our will felt and that we shall succeed only through success; c) paragraph 3 means that we may, where appropriate, surrender some of our capitulatory rights. It does not mean that we will encourage novel forms of government – a point which is deliberately omitted from the despatch. The second sentence of paragraph 7 shows that we will not neglect elements outside the Ruling Families; d) paragraph 4 means that we will not encourage federation and that in the unlikely event of it being desired we shall oppose it if it seems to conflict with our policies in general.[22]

These laudable objectives meant that the Foreign Office was determined to maintain and extend Britain's long-standing involvement in the Gulf. Furthermore, the Foreign Office sought to retain the treaty relationship with the sheikhdoms. These objectives were challenged by regional developments. A significant turning point was the Iranian oil crisis in 1951, which was caused by the Tehran government's nationalisation of the Anglo-Iranian Oil Company (AIOC).[23] Wm. Roger Louis notes that AIOC was a source of national pride in the UK,[24] and its refinery at Abadan was the largest in the world.[25] The evacuation of Abadan in October 1951 had huge economic and symbolic implications.

Sir Rupert Hay, the Political Resident, argued that it undermined Britain's position in the Gulf. Hay also contended that without the crisis, the Saudis would not have invaded the Buraimi Oasis in 1952.[26] The Iranian oil situation had significant implications for Britain's position in the Persian Gulf, which included the threat posed by the Saudis to the Trucial States. The Foreign Office introduced a development policy in the Trucial States in order to alleviate the overwhelming poverty that characterised the states, and also to maintain British prestige, which was a key feature of the Foreign Office's policy in the Gulf in the post-war era.

The Trucial States were fundamentally transformed during the 1950s. The region became open to the outside world on an unprecedented scale, and travel beyond the sheikhdoms became more common. The rulers went to India for medicine, and to Cairo and Lebanon on holiday, the merchants to Europe and the Far East in search of business opportunities, and even members of tribes travelled to Kuwait in search of work. The population was seeing more of the world as a result of these changes, and they were able to witness development elsewhere and begin to question their comparative 'backwardness'. Furthermore, migrant workers, such as teachers, introduced foreign ideas on an unparalleled scale.

The most important change in the Trucial States was the imposition of public security in the interior.[27] The tribes became more settled and a significant shift in power occurred. Until the 1950s, the tribes had been the preponderant force in the Trucial States. In their heyday, they could hold the rulers, merchants and people to ransom, and a ruler was only powerful if he commanded the loyalty of the tribes. Penetration of the interior by British officials and oil companies altered the pattern of tribal domination. The tribes steadily lost their power and, as the rulers, gained it with British support.[28] Some of the tribes migrated to work in oil fields or became an unemployed proletariat in the towns of the Trucial States. In contrast, the rulers were more powerful, their territories became more profitable and their internal frontiers were settled. This was because the British allowed them to extend their influence, but they were not necessarily grateful towards the British. By the late 1950s, they were increasingly dissatisfied with British protection and the restraints that had been imposed on them. For example, they were no longer allowed to attack one another, but their stronger political position meant that there was greater pressure to rule. The rulers were mainly interested in power and wealth, and their 'fidelity to the Bedouin tradition of hospitality is the closest they come to taking an interest in their people'. The rulers were condemned 'as ignorant, incompetent men, ill-fitted to adapt themselves to changing conditions'. Their sons and heirs were also held in low regard, and it was argued that if they continued to neglect their subjects and spend most of their income on themselves, they would not remain indefinitely acceptable to their people. The dilemma for the British was how to encourage 'illiterate and backward rulers, still rooted in the worst of the Bedouin tribal tradition to move with the times and thereby remain acceptable as governors of their people'.[29] The British never overcame this predicament in the Trucial States.

The limitations of Britain's role in the Trucial States were also exposed by attempts to persuade the rulers to cooperate. In 1952, the Trucial States Council was established and was chaired by the Political Agent at Dubai. The Council included the seven rulers of the Trucial States, and Sir Rupert Hay thought that there was no hope of the states establishing any kind of political federation.[30] However, the introduction of a development programme during the 1950s did improve the attitude of the rulers towards the Council.[31] By 1961, the Foreign Office believed that attempts to get the states to federate should be eschewed.[32] The failure to establish an embryonic federation was caused by the long-standing disputes between the rulers, and the likelihood of cooperation faded with the prospect of Abu Dhabi becoming oil-rich.

The establishment of the Trucial Oman Levies

Britain's defence responsibilities in the Gulf were very limited and until the withdrawal from India in 1947, there had been a finite requirement to deploy forces in the region.[33] The retreat from India left a gap in the defence plans for the Arabian Peninsula because the British could no longer rely on Indian forces to defend the region.[34] In 1939, the Indian General Staff estimated that local forces in the sheikhdoms, apart from Bahrain, consisted of lightly armed retainers (*askars*) who protected the rulers' forts and the British residency at Bahrain.[34] By 1950, the combined forces of Bahrain, Kuwait, Qatar, Muscat and the Trucial States added up to no more than 1,000 men,[36] whereas the Saudi Arabian Army was thought to number 8,000 men in 1948.[37]

The Foreign Office was concerned that the withdrawal from India left a gap in the defence plans for the Persian Gulf because the British could no longer rely on Indian forces to provide forces on the cheap. The British had considerable experience of raising armed forces in the Arab world. They adopted two approaches of military assistance and reform. In Egypt, Iraq and Saudi Arabia, military missions were employed to improve the standard of training and leadership in these states' armed forces. The objectives of the military missions also included enhancing their operational capabilities and maintaining their political neutrality. The performance of the Egyptian and Iraqi armies in the first Arab–Israeli War in 1948 was wretched,[38] and shows that the military missions were unsuccessful. This was because the standard of training, logistics and leadership was woefully inadequate to meet the operational requirements of a limited regional war. The role of military missions indicates how difficult it is to have a positive long-term impact on the operational capabilities of indigenous armies. Moreover, military missions became politically unsustainable because they undermined the 'veneer of independence and sovereignty' of local governments.[39]

The second method the British adopted was much more successful. Rather than trying to improve the operational performance of armies top-down, direct command of combat units by British officers was routinely applied across the Empire. The British favoured this approach because it was cheaper than deploying British Army formations. The long-term objective of this system was to hand over command to locally trained officers, but this was a time-consuming process. Moreover, in the post-war era, the role of British officers in command of military formations became politically sensitive on account of nationalist opposition, which claimed that local sovereignty was being undermined.

The best-known example of this approach occurred in Jordan, where a small number of British officers trained and commanded the Arab Legion (renamed the Jordanian Arab Army from July 1956).[40] The transformation of the Arab Legion from a gendarmerie to a highly capable fighting force is usually associated with General Sir John Glubb (commonly known as Glubb Pasha), who served in Jordan between 1930 and 1956.[41] During Glubb's era, the Arab Legion became the best-trained and most highly regarded Arab army, which out-performed the other local forces during the first Arab–Israeli War.[42] The Arab Legion is a notable example of how it was possible to establish an army from scratch, and Glubb's approach was applied in the Trucial States, to the armed forces of the UAE and the Sultanate of Oman.

Shortly after taking control of the Gulf, the Foreign Office re-evaluated its policy. It proposed raising a small force in the Trucial States because it was no longer possible to rely entirely on the Royal Navy to maintain security, handle emergencies and defend expanding oil interests.[43] The Foreign Office and Sir Rupert Hay argued that a levy force might prevent the renewal of slavery, which was commonplace along the Trucial Coast, and that such a unit acting in unison with the Royal Navy would obviate the despatch of land forces to the Trucial States. Additional reasons for establishing a levy force in the Trucial States included the prevention of fighting between the rulers, such as the war between Abu Dhabi and Dubai in 1945–7, to maintain order inland and secure the region's ill-defined frontiers. A further role for a levy force was to provide an armed escort for the Political Resident and other British officials, who had been shot at by the population.[44]

The tentative decision to raise a levy force was a prominent example of the reversal of the Government of India's policy on non-interference in the domestic affairs of the sheikhdoms.[45] The Chiefs of Staff (COS) initially rejected the notion of raising a levy force in the Trucial States because they believed that in a crisis, forces could have been flown to the RAF station at Sharjah.[46] However, Bernard Burrows, the then head of the Eastern Department of the Foreign Office, rejected the COS's objections. He argued that in spite of the withdrawal from India, Britain's interests in the sheikhdoms were still based on commercial, humanitarian and strategic grounds.[47] Burrows further argued that the states faced several important issues, including the continuation of slavery, pervasive poverty and underdevelopment, and that Britain's moral right to be in the Trucial States would be impinged if she failed to address these issues. The Foreign Office also believed that it should encourage and support the rulers to promote good government, economic development and social progress. Burrows and other Foreign Office officials were influenced by regional developments such as the disastrous withdrawal from Palestine in May 1948 that had undermined British prestige in the Middle East. The Foreign Office was wary of the growing sway of Arab nationalism, which led Burrows to conclude that steps had to be taken on moral and political grounds to improve the lives of the inhabitants.

The only effective mechanism for eradicating slavery was the establishment of a levy force, commanded by British officers. There were several precedents in the Arabian Peninsula for establishing local security forces, including the Muscat

Infantry, which was raised in the 1920s, and the Aden Protectorate Levies (APL).[48] There were several promising sources for recruits, including Aden and Pakistan, all of which were rejected by Sir Rupert Hay on the basis of their unreliability. In May 1949, the Foreign Office conferred with General Glubb, the Chief of the General Staff of the Jordanian Arab Legion, who had considerable experience in raising and training Bedouin troops. Glubb argued that the Bedouin could be trained as soldiers, and that establishing a small unit of tribal troops would be more cost effective than flying British forces to Sharjah.[49]

Ernest Bevin, the Foreign Secretary, concurred with proposals in August 1949 to establish a levy force – initially called the Trucial Oman Levies (TOL) – in the Trucial States.[50] Nonetheless, the Foreign Office had to obtain the rulers' support to establish the TOL, and the legal advisor advised that the most effective way of achieving the legal right to establish the levies was the rulers' 'sufferance'. In order to maintain the rulers' internal sovereignty, the Foreign Office proposed that the sheikhs must be notified in advance of the intention to establish the levies, and that Hay would overcome any objections.[51]

The Foreign Office followed Glubb's advice about establishing a levy unit, and the Arab Legion agreed to send fifty men, commanded by one of its British officers, Major Michael Hankin-Turvin.[52] Initially, the Arab Legion contingent was ordered to recruit and train 100 men, but establishing the TOL proved to be a complex process.[53] Glubb's original proposal to establish the levies would have cost £55,000 but the Treasury only provided £35,500.[54] This meant that the Arab Legion contingent had to be cut to thirty-four men and one officer. Even so, not enough locals could be recruited and trained, which undercut the TOL's effectiveness.[55] Various other hurdles beset the establishment of the TOL.[56]

The Saudi King, Abd al-Aziz Al Saud (commonly known as Ibn Saud), objected to the dispatch of the Arab Legion contingent to the Trucial States.[57] This was because he was a long-standing rival of Jordan's King Abdullah I,[58] and Ibn Saud was concerned about Hashemite encirclement.[59] The Foreign Office considered Ibn Saud's objections in 1949, but Hay mistakenly rejected the idea that the Arab Legion contribution would antagonise the Saudis.[60]

By the early 1950s, relations with the Saudis had declined because Ibn Saud had established closer relations with the United States, and Saudi Arabia's growing oil income meant that the Saudis were no longer beholden to the Foreign Office for financial support.[61] The British Ambassador at Jeddah reported that the Saudi King argued that raising the TOL was a turning point in relations with Saudi Arabia[62] and that the TOL gave the Saudis a convenient pretext to attack British policy in the Gulf. It was apparent that Ibn Saud would never be reconciled with the establishment of the TOL.[63] Raising the levies presented the Foreign Office with a diplomatic dilemma. Either the Foreign Office could abandon the TOL initiative and reduce the size of the Arab Legion contingent as a way of mollifying Ibn Saud, or instructors could be found elsewhere. The Foreign Office decided to simply ignore Ibn Saud's objections,[64] despite concern that the withdrawal from India made the British more reliant on Saudi goodwill.[65]

As a result of the Treasury's parsimony, and Saudi objections, the Arab Legion detachment only arrived at the RAF station at Sharjah in February 1951.[66] Recruiting and training a modest force of 100 men was hindered by the poor health of potential recruits, and Glubb's conviction that the Bedouin were natural soldiers was called into question in the Trucial States.[67] There was no tradition of raising an armed force in the Trucial States, and the Bedouin recruits were hard to train and discipline.[68]

The process of training the TOL recruits was also undermined by a mutiny that occurred in the Arab Legion contingent.[69] The Arab Legion's contribution to training the TOL was regarded by the Foreign Office as unsuccessful. This was compounded by the refusal of officers to be seconded to the Trucial States because of the deleterious impact postings would have had on their prospects for promotion.[70] This meant that it was difficult to find enough officers and other ranks to serve in the TOL. As a result of these political and military circumstances, the TOL was totally inadequate to defend the Trucial States. However, the Chiefs of Staff argued that the force was valuable because it provided a short-term insurance against having to fly troops to Sharjah in an emergency.[71]

Attempts to establish the TOL provide clear indications of the problems of establishing an armed force from scratch. However, the establishment of the TOL did have political benefits because the Foreign Office was able to show the rulers that it was willing to defend them against Saudi subversion.[72] Moreover, the TOL for the first time did provide a modicum of security in the desert interior of the Trucial States. Hitherto, the hinterland of the Trucial States had been characterised by raiding and wars between the rulers. The TOL provided clear evidence of the reversal of the long-standing policy of non-interference in the internal affairs of the Trucial States.[73] Although the TOL was meant to operate with the consent of the rulers, in reality it was the private army of the Political Resident, and became the arbitrator of disputes between the rulers and the tribes of the Trucial States.[74] An example of this expansion of British influence occurred in 1955, when Sheikh Rashid, the ruler of Dubai, requested the TOL to prevent his overthrow by his uncle.[75]

By 1952, it was clear to the Foreign Office that the TOL was too small to have a significant impact. Sir Roger Makins, a Deputy Secretary in the Foreign Office, visited the Trucial States in March 1952. Makins made various proposals about the future of the Trucial States, including the expansion of the TOL. Makins believed that there was a strong case for expanding the TOL to 200 men so that it could play a greater role in maintaining internal security and prevent the slave trade, and because it provided clear evidence of British intentions to defend the Trucial States.[76] General Sir Brian Robinson, the Commander in Chief of British Middle East Land Forces (MELF), exceeded Makins' proposals. Robinson also visited the Trucial States in the spring of 1952 and argued that the Foreign Office needed to pay the Trucial States far greater attention, and he proposed that the TOL needed to be increased to 500 men.[77]

The origins of the development policy

The creation of the TOL provided clear evidence of the Foreign Office's determination to become more involved in the Trucial States.[78] In August 1949, Bevin chaired a conference of Foreign Office Middle East representatives.[79] This meeting concentrated on the economic and social development in the Middle East as a means of countering the threat of Arab nationalism to British interests. The conference made brief references to the sheikhdoms, which remained of scant interest to the Foreign Office, and the requirement for social progress. In December 1949, an official committee, which was composed of representatives from several Whitehall departments, produced a detailed report about the economic conditions that prevailed in the sheikhdoms. The report argued that there was little long-term hope for economic development in the Trucial States, apart from the provision of public services, agricultural development and investment in hospitals and schools. The memorandum reached the banal conclusion that the Trucial States were 'an unusual and remarkable problem'.[80]

The prospects for economic development in the Trucial States were very limited, a problem that was compounded by Eastern Arabia's extreme climate and shortage of water, which limited the potential for agricultural development. Moreover, the population of the Trucial States, which was estimated to be around 80,000 in the early 1950s, was characterised by the dearth of education and the continuation of a subsistence economy, based on the sea and agriculture.[81] The absence of economic progress in the Trucial States in the early 1950s resulted in a large number of people leaving the states to work in the expanding oil industry in Qatar and Saudi Arabia.[82]

Although the population of the Trucial States was small and overwhelmingly poor, there were variations in wealth between the sheikhdoms. Dubai was the most economically developed of the Trucial States due to its role as the regional entrepôt.[83] In December 1950, the Foreign Office funded the first hospital in the Trucial States, which was built in Dubai. In 1954, the British Political Agent, who had been based at Sharjah, was relocated to Dubai, and played an important role in trying to devise a comprehensive development programme for the Trucial States.[84]

The Foreign Office was wary about encouraging development programmes in the Gulf because of the substantial increase in wealth that occurred in Qatar and Kuwait during the early 1950s, caused by a windfall oil income.[85] By 1950, Kuwait's greatly expanded oil wealth was having long-term consequences on its traditional maritime economy.[86] Kuwait's development programme was initiated in 1951 with a budget of $400 million, to be spent over the following decade.[87] During the early 1950s, there was a construction boom and a greatly increased government expenditure on social services and education. However, Kuwait's rapid economic growth was characterised by rampant corruption and cost overruns, which were influenced by the government's limited administrative ability.[88] Furthermore, the rapid process of development led to tension between Kuwait's merchant classes, who feared being sidelined by the ruling Al Sabahs.[89] By the mid-1950s, the Kuwaiti government had already spent $30 million on development, and one American diplomat referred to the 'feverish' pace of progress.[90] Kuwait's development programme during the 1950s provides clear evidence of the kind of economic and political problems caused by a rapid and sustained increase in income. These lessons were replicated in the Trucial States, and the United Arab Emirates, following the growth of the oil industry in the 1960s.

In contrast with the Kuwait's oil-driven economic growth during the 1950s, the Trucial States had analogous problems to those faced in India by the Government of India.[91] Hay argued that the internal sovereignty of the sheikhdoms should be encouraged. However, he contended that the Trucial States were so poor that the Foreign Office was obliged to keep them under close guardianship of a 'colonial' character for the foreseeable future.[92] Likewise, Bernard Burrows, the first member of the Foreign Office to become Political Resident after Hay's retirement in 1953, argued that the British government could have done more to develop the Trucial States in the past.[93] He believed that there was scope for a small-scale development programme in the Trucial States and rejected the contention made by some Foreign Office officials that the government should forgo its commitments to the rulers of the Trucial States. Such a policy would have reduced the Foreign Office's ability to guide events in Bahrain, Kuwait and Qatar. Burrows also contended that the Trucial States were not a 'derelict area' of 'which we should be glad to be rid, but with some care and continuity we can make something of them'. He added that regardless of the absence of communications, medical facilities, education and water resources, the states 'are more solid entities than at first sight might be believed'. Burrows was well aware that the development requirements in the Trucial States were immense, but he argued that a small amount spent on development schemes 'would obtain disproportionally larger results of goodwill' with the population and rulers.[94]

The very low level of economic and social development in the Trucial States meant that economic and social progress was bound to take place slowly.[95] Foreign Office officials were sceptical about the ability of the rulers to improve the lives of their subjects.[96] A key objective of the Trucial States' development programme was the expansion of education, which entailed a dilemma for the Foreign Office. The growth of education, which is a fundamental objective of any development initiative, relied on teachers from Egypt and Jordan, which meant that, for the first time, the population of the Trucial States became vulnerable to Arab nationalist sentiment.

Nonetheless, Sir Roger Makins argued in 1952 that there was limited scope for development in the Trucial States, apart from expenditure on education and health care. Alongside his proposals for expanding the TOL, Makins further argued that the Foreign Office had to make a small contribution towards the development of the Trucial States for political reasons. He also observed that Britain's contribution to the development of the Trucial States could not be carried out on the cheap.[97] The Foreign Office supported Makins' proposals to spend a small amount on development in the Trucial States in order to maintain British prestige.[98] However, his proposals about expanding the TOL and spending a small sum on development schemes were overtaken in the autumn of 1952 by the Saudi occupation of the Buraimi Oasis, which lies on the Abu Dhabi–Oman frontier.

The implications of the Buraimi Crisis[99]

Saudi attempts to proselytise their Wahhabi faith and plunder the Trucial States originated in the early nineteenth century.[100] Saudi efforts to expand their influence in the Trucial States, usually by the collection of *zakat* (alms tax),[101] were prevented by the Government of India but never extinguished.[102] The frontiers of Eastern Arabia remained indeterminate and, in 1933, the Saudi Government awarded the Standard Oil Company a concession to explore for oil in Eastern Arabia.[103] During the 1930s, the Foreign Office attempted to negotiate with the Saudi government about the demarcation of the region's frontiers. The talks failed, and during the course of the Second World War negotiations were in abeyance. In the aftermath of the war, oil prospecting increased, and in 1952 the British and Saudi governments signed a 'Standstill Agreement'. This agreement was meant to halt oil exploration in the region, but bilateral talks failed.[104]

In August 1952, a Saudi official named Turki bin Ataishan occupied the Buraimi Oasis.[105] The Saudis maintained that they had long-standing ancestral claims to the oasis, which was an important crossroads that was thought to contain oil reserves.[106] The Foreign Office consistently rejected the Saudi claim to Buraimi, and defended the oasis on behalf on the Trucial States and the Sultan of Oman.[107] It adopted a steadfast policy on the future of Buraimi because it argued that if it failed to defend the oasis, British prestige would be undermined.[108] The Foreign Office was also concerned about growing oil interests, and it was convinced that the Saudis had occupied Buraimi at the behest of the Arabian-American Oil Company (ARAMCO).[109]

The Buraimi situation was more than just a dispute about an important oasis because it led to a disagreement between the British and American governments. The United States believed that the British were the hegemonic power in the Persian Gulf,[110] and that the British presence was the final relic of imperialism in the Middle East. In contrast, the Foreign Office was determined to defend its allies and establish a joint oil policy with the Americans.[111] Glen Balfour-Paul, who served in the Gulf during the 1960s, argued that the Buraimi Crisis was a 'lurid demonstration' that the conduct of foreign policy 'was not, for Britain, all cakes and coffee'.[112]

In response to the Saudi occupation of Buraimi, the TOL was ordered to occupy the part of Buraimi that lies within Abu Dhabi's jurisdiction and stop any attempt by the Sultan of Oman to dispatch a tribal force to retake the oasis.[113] The Buraimi Crisis highlighted the TOL's limited capability to defend the Trucial States. This was because the TOL was too small, numbering no more than 100 men in the spring of 1953.[114] The British also faced a long-running obstacle in finding enough officers who spoke Arabic and who were willing to serve in the Trucial States.[115] The expansion of the TOL in 1953 was called into question by a long-running dispute between the Foreign Office, the Treasury and the War

Office about who should pay for the TOL and which department was responsible for military operations in the Gulf.[116]

The Foreign Office was forced to adopt a cautious policy on Buraimi because it was concerned that the Saudis might refer the issue to the United Nations, which would focus unwanted attention on Britain's anomalous position in the Gulf.[117] The Foreign Office believed that the Saudis had prevailed in the first round of the dispute, and that they were a serious threat to the integrity of the Trucial States.[118] Consequently, there was widespread support in Whitehall for the immediate increase of the TOL to 500 men.[119] The Foreign Office mistakenly believed that it would take years to train new recruits,[120] and instead 'Operation Boxer' was initiated. This involved the deployment of RAF aircraft and armoured cars from Iraq to Sharjah, and the dispatch of 300 Aden Protectorate Levies (APL) to the Trucial States.[121] The objective of Operation Boxer was to provide clear evidence of British intentions to defend the Trucial States, rather than take direct action against the Saudis.[122] Operation Boxer was a show of force that depended on RAF aircraft flying reconnaissance missions over Buraimi, but it is doubtful whether the Saudis would have been able to move its forces on any scale over long lines of communications and in such a hostile environment.[123]

The decision to dispatch the APL was a failure because they were responsible for a variety of crimes. These included bribery and the sale of weapons,[124] and in November 1953 three British soldiers were murdered by APL troops at Buraimi.[125] The British and Saudi governments agreed to arbitrate the dispute over Buraimi, but the threat of Saudi subversion in the Trucial States meant that the British had to retain forces in the region. The Chiefs of Staff were determined to prevent the permanent deployment of British forces in the Trucial States because they argued that it was uneconomical and troops could have been flown to Sharjah from Cyprus, Malta or the Suez Canal Zone within forty-eight hours.

The financial and political benefits of increasing the TOL's establishment came to the fore in 1953, when the TOL was transformed. The Saudi threat to the Trucial States provided the pretext to expand the TOL during 1953. However, the perennial complications of recruiting and training a heterogeneous force that included men from the Trucial States, Dhofar, India and Pakistan hindered the rapid expansion of the TOL.[126] These difficulties were compounded by the problem of finding sufficiently experienced British officers and other ranks to serve in the TOL.[127] By the spring of 1954, it included 10 British officers, 6 Arab officers and 500 other ranks. The Levies were a light infantry force, based at a regimental headquarters at Sharjah, and four infantry squadrons (companies) that were spread across the sheikhdoms.[128] The squadrons were tasked with patrolling the desert hinterland, including around Buraimi, which led to regular exchanges of fire with Saudi forces.[129]

The increased significance of the Trucial States led the British to introduce a system of higher command in the Persian Gulf, and the establishment of a military headquarters in Bahrain. Brigadier John Baird, who had served in the military mission to Saudi Arabia, was the first Senior Army Officer in the Persian Gulf (SAOPG), who was responsible for advising the Political Resident and directing military operations in the region. Baird shared the widely held view that more British forces were needed in the Persian Gulf. In December 1954, he proposed that the TOL's establishment should be increased to 500 men by forming a new rifle squadron and increasing the strength of each squadron from 94 to 150 men. Baird also suggested that for the first time, the TOL should be issued with heavy weapons, including 3-inch mortars.[130]

The Foreign Office was concerned about the Saudi threat to the Trucial States because of the United States' decision to sell the Saudis bombers and tanks, which were part of a military assistance programme.[131] The British believed that American support for the Saudis threatened the Trucial States, and would upset the regional balance of power. The American decision to supply arms to the Saudis was influenced by Cold War concerns, especially after the Soviet Union supplied Egypt with a large quantity of artillery, tanks and combat aircraft.[132] The American arms package meant that the Saudi armed forces were the largest and best equipped in the Arabian Peninsula.[133] The War Office challenged the Foreign Office's concerns as it argued that the supply of heavy equipment to the Saudis posed no practical threat to the Trucial States because of the desert that traverses the region. Furthermore, the War Office doubted whether the Saudis had the logistical capability to conduct operations over long and vulnerable lines of communication.[134]

The Chiefs of Staff assumed that the Royal Navy's Persian Gulf squadron and exercises that involved flying troops to Sharjah were required to deter the Saudis.[135] Defence planners wanted to avoid the permanent basing of British forces in the Trucial States for financial and health reasons.[136] This led the Chief of Staff and the War Office to support further expansion of the TOL for financial and prestige reasons. In May 1955, the TOL had increased to 22 British officers and other ranks, and 535 other ranks. The British contingent was responsible for commanding and training the TOL's rifle squadrons.[137]

The TOL received its first operational test in October 1955, when it participated in 'Operation Bonaparte', the name of the British operation to remove the Saudis from Buraimi.[138] The British decision to forcibly remove the Saudis from Buraimi resulted from the failure to arbitrate the future of the oasis.[139] The Foreign Office accused the Saudis of trying to bribe members of the arbitration panel that had been established to adjudicate the status of Buraimi.[140] Two TOL squadrons, supported by RAF fighters, were responsible for evicting the Saudis.[141] The decision to take decisive measures had significant implications for Britain's relations with the United States and the Saudis. In the aftermath of the Suez fiasco in October 1956, the Saudis broke off diplomatic relations with the British until 1963. Furthermore, the Eisenhower Administration was strongly critical of the handling of the Buraimi dispute.[142]

The removal of Saudi forces from Buraimi reduced the military threat to the Trucial States, but they remained vulnerable to Saudi intimidation and propaganda.[143] Notwithstanding the successful eviction of Saudi forces from Buraimi, the TOL was still regarded as inadequate because of the expansion of its area of operations.[144] The Saudi threat to the Trucial States led the Chiefs of Staff to recommend the expansion of the TOL and the provision of mortars and anti-tank weapons. The growth of the TOL was supposed to overcome the limitations of the Royal Navy's role in the Gulf, and prevent the posting of British forces in the Trucial States for financial reasons. The Chiefs of Staff assumed that the TOL would be able to defend the Trucial States while British forces were flown in from Aden, where an infantry battalion was located.[145]

Expanding the TOL also had significant political advantages. In contrast with Egypt, which had the largest British base in the Middle East and was a lightning rod for anti-British agitation, the military presence in the Trucial States was minimal. Therefore, increasing the TOL's strength entailed significant political advantages because locally recruited forces would attract far less attention than British units, which were also expensive to maintain. There was, therefore, an overwhelming case for expanding the TOL, but the cost in 1956–7 was £300,000, almost ten times the Foreign Office's total expenditure in 1951. The Chiefs of Staff estimated that an increased TOL would cost £520,000 per annum from 1958 onwards.[146] The TOL remained by far the most significant area of expenditure for the Foreign Office until the withdrawal in 1971.

However, expanding the TOL was not straightforward. Brigadier Baird and the Foreign Office recognised that it was difficult to find enough British officers to serve in the Trucial States. In 1955, General Sir Gerald Templer, the Chief of the Imperial General Staff, proposed renaming the TOL.[147] Templer argued that one of the problems associated with recruiting officers was that the TOL was associated with RAF levy units in Aden and Iraq, which had negative connotations for potential British Army recruits.[148] The War Office agreed to a change in name to Trucial Oman Scouts in November 1955, and the renaming occurred in March 1956.[149] In the summer of 1956, Baird reported that this innovation had the desired effect and it was becoming easier to recruit officers.[150] The expansion of the TOS meant that a rifle squadron served on operations in Oman in 1957,[151] although the British Residency at Bahrain did report disaffection within the TOS ranks.[152] The TOS continued to play an important internal security role in the Trucial States until the British withdrawal in 1971.[153]

The establishment of the TOS was not the only attempt to set up a security force in the Trucial States. In 1956–7, a small police force was established in Dubai, which numbered thirty men in June 1957. The Political Agent at Dubai, Peter Tripp, persuaded Sheikh Rashid bin Saeed Al Maktoum, the ruler of Dubai, to raise a police service in order to overcome increased lawlessness and the threat of subversion in the largest town on the Trucial Coast.[154] The TOS played an important role in this process, and the first commander of the Dubai Police was seconded from the TOS, and the Scouts trained the police recruits. The ruler of Dubai agreed to contribute £7,500, but the Foreign Office was forced to pay the rest because the ruler's resources were so paltry.[155] The War Office rejected proposals that the police operate outside of Dubai town because it feared that it would be unable to perform these duties. Moreover, officials in Whitehall were concerned that they would not be able to exercise the same level of influence over the police,[156] and Bernard Burrows did not think that a police force for the Trucial States was necessary at the time or in the foreseeable future on account of hostilities between the states.[157] Over the following decade, police and security forces expanded in Bahrain, Qatar and the Trucial States, but by 1967 they were still considered to be rudimentary.[158]

The expansion of the development programme

The Buraimi Crisis also transformed the Foreign Office's approach to the economic and social development of the Trucial States.[159] Saudi attempts to subvert the Trucial States were effective because there was little tangible evidence of the material benefits of British protection of the Trucial States.[160] Saudi propaganda led the Foreign Office to accept that it had to show the rulers and the population that the British Government was willing to do more than protect the Trucial States. Foreign Secretary Sir Anthony Eden, who showed great interest in the Trucial States, persuaded the Treasury to authorise the spending of £10,000 on several projects.[161] This included expenditure on education, the Al Maktoum

Hospital in Dubai, the dredging of Dubai Harbour and a water survey in the Trucial States.[162]

The Foreign Office was inspired more by political motives than by the inherent merits of spending money on development in the Trucial States.[163] Nonetheless, the Treasury's grudging agreement to allocate £10,000 led the Foreign Office to form a more concerted development programme for the Trucial States in the 1954–5 financial year, that would have cost £25,000.[164] The Treasury agreed to this proposal, contrary to its better judgement, because the Foreign Office made a strong case for arguing that the enhanced development scheme was intended to counter Saudi subversion in the Trucial States.[165] The Treasury's policy of spending as little as possible in the Trucial States was influenced by the desire to avoid ongoing expenditure and had significant implications. The introduction of improved health care and education was slower than might have been possible.[166]

The allocation of £25,000 for development schemes was totally inadequate. In response, Peter Tripp, the Political Agent at Dubai, compiled a five-year development programme. He proposed a wide range of projects, which included the expansion of the Trucial States Council that had been established by the British in 1952 to encourage the rulers to cooperate and take some responsibility for development. Tripp's programme conceptualised the expansion of projects that had already been initiated, including agricultural research, education, public health and water surveys. Tripp's plan also proposed spending money to improve policing and the civil courts in the Trucial States. Tripp was very critical of the rulers because, he argued, they were only interested in their own 'comfort and well-being', and furthermore, he said, nothing short of revolution would break the status quo. He added that if the Foreign Office failed to take action, Egypt or Saudi Arabia would do so. Tripp also argued that the Trucial States' poverty meant that the Foreign Office had to make a clear commitment to the them, and if this was not done, it was possible that Britain's prestige would be undermined.[167]

Sir Bernard Burrows rejected Tripp's criticism of the rulers, but he concurred with Tripp's development plan. Burrows argued that the Trucial States' 'poverty, backwardness and lack of political cohesion constitutes a weakness in the position we hold here'. Burrows also contended that Egyptian radio propaganda posed a real threat to the stability of the Trucial States,[168] and the most effective way to reinforce British prestige was to implement a long-term development programme, rather than relying on the Treasury to allocate funds annually.[169]

Tripp's development plan would have cost £428,000, but the Treasury refused to fund it on the basis that government departments had to cut costs.[170] The

Treasury's argument that the Trucial States development scheme was unaffordable was questionable. This was because the British Government was willing to spend large amounts of money in order to protect its political and strategic interests. The Treasury was willing to fund the expansion of the Trucial Oman Scouts because it was in Britain's interests to do so. Expenditure on the Trucial States development programme was a miniscule proportion of the £30.8 million that was spent in the Middle East in 1956–7. In 1957, Britain's treaty relations with Jordan were terminated, leading to a £12 million reduction in expenditure in the Middle East.[171] This meant that, in theory, money was available to fund the development programme, which increased in cost between 1956 and 1958 from £31,000 to £85,000.[172]

The Treasury's short-sighted policy of declining to adequately fund the Trucial States development programme was a consistent problem for Foreign Office officials serving in the Gulf.[173] Burrows argued that the 'niggardly' expenditure on development undermined British prestige, and that the Foreign Office urgently needed to show its good intentions.[174] He reported that the rulers were becoming determined to acquire development aid, and if the Foreign Office failed to support them, they would be forced to seek support from Egypt's President Gamal Abdel Nasser, not because they supported his anti-British stance, but because he promised to aid them.[175]

Britain's prestige in the Gulf was undermined following the Suez debacle in October–November 1956. The reaction to the Suez Crisis varied in the Gulf, with unrest in Bahrain and Kuwait,[176] where the US Consul argued that serious damage had been done to British prestige.[177] In the Trucial States, the population was agitated by British action at Suez, and Burrows reported to the Foreign Office that there was consternation amongst the rulers over the invasion.[178] However, he reached the conclusion that the British 'got away with it fairly lightly' in the Gulf.[179] Edward Baker, the British Bank of the Middle East (BBME) branch manager at Dubai, reported on anti-British hostility in Dubai, and how *Sawt al-Arab* (Voice of the Arabs) had 'poisoned the minds' of the townspeople and the Bedouin. The BBME closely cooperated with the Political Agency and the Trucial Oman Scouts with information about demonstrations in the towns.[180] It had a monopoly in Dubai, which lasted until 1963 and meant it undertook roles that were beyond those of a retail bank. The bank's contribution towards Dubai's economy included donations to charities, and it helped fund development schemes, such as a harbour and roads. The BBME granted Sheikh Rashid, who became ruler in 1958, lending facilities because he was trusted to spend the money wisely on the development of the sheikhdom.[181]

The Joint Intelligence Committee (JIC) accurately assessed that events in Egypt would not shake the rulers' long-standing attachment to their treaties with the British.[182] The US State Department's Bureau of Intelligence and Research (INR) estimated that, although the Arabian Peninsula remained at the centre of Britain's interests in the Middle East, economic and social changes in the region would make the British position increasingly precarious over the following decade.[183] In February 1957, the CIA produced a prescient analysis of the British position in the Gulf.[184] The CIA observed that since the Second World War, the British had taken steps to consolidate their position in the Gulf and deal with emerging political and economic issues. It believed that the British were moving towards a federation, which would promote the political stability of the sheikhdoms and provide for economic development. The evidence clearly shows that the Foreign Office's attempts to federate the Trucial States were unsuccessful. Nonetheless, the CIA correctly observed that the British were facing growing challenges to their pre-eminence, the most serious of which was the growth of nationalist movements in Bahrain and Kuwait. The vast growth of the income from oil had disrupted traditional patterns and caused an increased disposition to nationalist, pan-Arab and pan-Islamic movements from other parts of the Arab world. Egyptian radio propaganda had encouraged the belief that as protectors of the status quo, the British represented the main obstacle to political change. Reformist movements, such as those in Bahrain, increasingly identified their campaigns against the rulers and the British. Nasser and the campaign for 'Arab unity and solidarity' heavily influenced them.

The CIA also correctly commented that the British were confronted with increasing expansionist pressures from Saudi Arabia against the Trucial States. The Saudis were motivated by their Wahhabi fervour, suspicion and resentment of the British presence in Iraq and the Persian Gulf, and by the conviction that valuable oil deposits existed along its ill-defined frontiers. The CIA believed that the British had certain advantages and handicaps in the Gulf. The British benefited from the absence of political activity in the sheikhdoms, which meant they were not vulnerable to nationalist and other ideological forces that were highly influential elsewhere in the Middle East. The ability of the British to appeal to the ruling sheikhs to support them against their local enemies through the provision of support was still great. The sheikhs were still drawn to the British because of their desire to retain control over their oil resources, and their inability to operate oil installations without the assistance of foreign consultants. The rulers were also motivated by the desire to maintain their authority and avoid being dominated by neighbouring states, especially the Saudis. Finally, the rulers were suspicious of the intentions of Arab nationalist leaders such as Nasser, who threatened the basis of sheikhly rule.

Despite the growth of anti-British sentiment in Bahrain, political organisation in the Trucial States was rudimentary. The most serious handicap the British faced as a result of the Suez Crisis was that it lent new impetus to Nasser's appeal for Arab solidarity. However, the CIA's argument that the Suez Crisis had dealt a serious blow to British efforts to direct social unrest into evolutionary progress in Bahrain and Kuwait is hard to sustain. Notwithstanding these unprecedented challenges, the CIA reached the conclusion that the British position in the Sultanate of Oman and the Trucial States 'appears to be reasonably secure over the next few years'. There was little indication of significant support for Nasser and opposition to the rulers of the Trucial States, and it was likely that they would retain their ties with the British. This was because the rulers would continue to judge their British connection by the Foreign Office's ability to support them.

The evidence strongly supports this analysis of the Trucial States, but the CIA failed to identify the nuanced relationship between the British and their sheikhly protégés. The outlook for the British in Bahrain, Kuwait and Qatar, which were economically of far greater value than the Trucial States, appeared to be uncertain. There was no indication that the stability of the ruling sheikhs or their ties with the British were in danger. However, the British were criticised for their failure to establish relationships with local movements that would enable an orderly adjustment to economic, political and social pressures that would inevitably build up. More significantly, the Suez Crisis gravely weakened the prospects of achieving these objectives. In Kuwait, there were signs of growing unrest despite increased expenditure by the ruling family on welfare programmes. In Bahrain, the British seemed to have lost touch with emerging nationalist and reformist movements.

The British presence in the Gulf was heavily dependent on the rulers who were incapable of meeting internal demands for reform. There was no agreement within the Foreign Office about Britain's role in the Persian Gulf. One perspective argued that long-standing political and strategic reasons for the British presence in the Gulf had disappeared, following the demise of the Indian Empire. Sir Roger Stevens, the British Ambassador at Tehran, described the Gulf as a 'double-ended cul-de-sac'. He argued that Britain's role in the Gulf was regarded as a menace by the neighbouring states, such as Iran, and questioned whether the British would hold their position for much longer.[185] Sir Michael Wright, the British Ambassador at Baghdad, concurred with this perspective, which Burrows dismissed.[186] Burrows argued that the strategic importance of the Gulf to the British was very clear. The Political Resident contended that there was no need for systemic change in the handling of relations with the rulers and that the Foreign Office should allow the sheikhdoms to develop internally.[187] Selwyn Lloyd, the Foreign Secretary, concluded that the government's policy should lie between these two extremes but with a bias in favour of the established policy because the rulers accepted it. Lloyd also argued that the government should eschew a 'grand design' for the whole Gulf, but British policy should be regarded as an integral whole, no part of which could be weakened or resigned without affecting the rest.[188]

In the aftermath of the Suez Crisis, the British consolidated their position in the Gulf.[189] The Foreign Office reiterated its key interests, which included unfettered access to oil reserves on reasonable terms and the importance of oil-produced sterling balances. Imperial lines of communications that traversed the Persian Gulf to the Far East[190] and the Cold War requirement to keep the Soviet Union out of the Gulf were also regarded as crucial strategic interests.[191] Nonetheless, the Foreign Office failed to overcome the insuperable dilemma it faced in the Gulf States. The Foreign Office remained responsible for the foreign relations of the sheikhdoms, but it had no formal power to intervene in their internal politics, which limited its ability to implement a development programme and improve the administrative competence of the sheikhly regimes. Foreign Office diplomats such as Burrows and his successors could only advise the rulers. This meant that the Political Resident and other British officials serving in the Gulf were in a position of responsibility without any power.[192] It was widely but erroneously assumed that British officials could dictate terms to the rulers but, in practice, 'no British official, frustrated by his lack of direct and immediate responsibility, can do anything but laugh bitterly at the power attributed to him'.[193]

The Suez Crisis led Burrows to argue that the Foreign Office needed to intensify its involvement in the Gulf, and the Trucial States in particular, in order to prevent any further diminution of British prestige.[194] The expansion of the development programme was a notable example of this process. Although the Foreign Office's expenditure on development fell short of Tripp's proposals, the development budget increased annually from 1957 to 1959. Between 1953 and 1959, the Foreign Office spent £250,000 on development schemes, and British officials reported significant improvements.[195] These included the construction of more dispensaries, which made access to health care more accessible, the expansion of the Al Maktoum Hospital in Dubai and improvements in agriculture through the expansion of the agricultural trials station at Ras Al Khaimah.[196]

The Trucial States development programme emphasised the dilemmas the Foreign Office faced in the Gulf in its attempts to promote economic and social development. One of the most significant long-term objectives of the development scheme in the Trucial States was an attempt to improve the level of education. Schools in the states relied heavily on teachers from Egypt and Jordan,[197] and Hay reported that there was little indication of pan-Arab sentiment in the Trucial States, compared to Bahrain or Kuwait.[198] However, as access to education increased, it was certain that criticism of the patriarchal system of shiekhly rule that prevailed in the states was bound to increase. The British Council representative in the Gulf commented that the rulers wanted their subjects to be educated because it 'enhances their dignity more than do a hundred armed retainers siting listlessly at the gates of his castle'.[199] Peter Leinhardt noted that Sheikh Shakhbut and Sheikh Rashid bin Said Al Maktoum, the rulers of Abu Dhabi and Dubai, were slow to embrace education because they feared that an educated population would be more likely to question the nature of sheikhly rule.[200]

The expansion of education was a source of great concern to the Foreign Office because it portended a significant threat to the British position in the Gulf and to sheikhly rule.[201] The basis of this unease was the radio propaganda that was disseminated by *Sawt al-Arab* (Voice of the Arabs),[202] which promoted a Nasserist perspective that challenged British imperialism and the antiquated nature of sheikhly rule.[203] Elizabeth Monroe argued that Arab nationalism had scarcely prevailed in Bahrain and was only beginning in Kuwait. She commented that the situation in the Gulf was convenient for Nasser for deflecting attention from his failure to achieve domestic reform in Egypt. Monroe, who had considerable experience of reporting on the Middle East for *The Economist*, believed that the Buraimi situation and the anachronistic nature of the sheikhdoms were 'convenient topics on Cairo Radio'.[204] Colonel John Slade-Baker, the *Sunday Times* correspondent in the Middle East, wrote that there were two forces at work in the Gulf. He argued that the first was 'self-interest, which pulls in our direction as it is realised that it is only Great Britain that can and will guarantee their incomes and territorial integrity'. The second force was pan-Arab sentiment, which was influenced by the resentment 'felt at being regarded as second class citizens in their own country by foreigners who possess economic and political advantages which they do not. In their hearts they dislike our control of their foreign affairs, although they realise the necessity for it, and the fact that they are in a foreign sphere of influence'. Slade-Baker believed that it was only a matter of time before the situation in the Trucial States became dangerous on account of demands for constitutional reform and as a result of regional developments.[205]

Peter Tripp maintained that the development scheme contributed towards a process of 'psychological change' in the states, and that 'for the illiterate of the Trucial States the radio is their only window on the world'. He also argued that for the semi-literate, Arab propaganda 'is an intoxicating mixture of fact and fiction, tending to discredit honoured tradition and historical ties'.[206] Nonetheless, *Sawt al-Arab* was widely listened to in the Gulf and remained a source of great concern to British officials.[207]

The JIC adopted an optimistic assessment of the impact of Arab nationalism in the Gulf. It acknowledged that Arab nationalism was a powerful emotional force in the Gulf, but argued there was little indication of a significant nationalist movement that had any chance of overthrowing the sheikhly regimes.[208] Moreover, the JIC argued that the Trucial States were far less vulnerable to nationalist impulses, compared to either Bahrain or Kuwait.[209] Although intelligence assessments did acknowledge that in the long term, Arab nationalist sentiment would increase,[210] demand for education in the Trucial States grew significantly by 1960, leading to the concern that 'the products of the new schools must be given an outlet for their (admittedly modest) capabilities' by modernising the 'paternalist pattern of sheikhly rule'.[211] British officials were well aware that it was impossible to restrict the growth of political activity indefinitely. Nonetheless, Sir George Middleton, Political Resident between 1958 and 1961, asserted that political and diplomatic protection played an important role in upholding sheikhly rule. Middleton believed that the British would be criticised if they failed to cajole the rulers to broaden the basis of their governments.[212]

Sir Bernard Burrows claimed that the rulers were grateful for the Foreign Office's expenditure on development programmes, but he consistently reported that they had no conception of the importance of efficient administration.[213] He also commented that the rulers did not feel obliged to make any contribution towards development because the Foreign Office was willing to fund it without making any demands in return. Likewise, Peter Tripp believed that the development programme, which he had devised, 'encouraged a process of psychological change since, although very little has changed materially, more people in the area have been made aware of the need for the possibility of progress, despite the limited resources available'. He added that the rulers 'have been shown up, almost without exception, as ignorant, incompetent men, ill-fitted to adapt themselves to changing conditions'. Tripp was a consistent and vocal critic of the rulers. He argued that they would become unacceptable to their subjects if they failed to meet the demand for effective government. The inherent weaknesses of the rulers reinforced the limitations of the British position in the Trucial States and augmented the dilemma the British faced in trying to encourage 'illiterate and backward' rulers, 'still rooted in the worst of the Bedouin tribal tradition ... to move with the times and thereby remain acceptable as governors of the people'.[214] In contrast with Tripp's critique of the rulers, Burrows argued that: 'we are left, as often before, in an uneasy middle position between reformist elements with whose desire for administrative improvement we sympathise but who have no similar attachment to us'.[215]

The development programme in the Trucial States slowly improved the administrative and social situation, but the Political Resident could do little more than encourage the rulers to become more involved in development and improve their administrations.[216] Donald Hawley, who became Political Agent at Dubai in 1958, argued that, although the development programme had benefited the Trucial States, there was little tangible evidence of progress, compared to their oil-rich neighbours.[217] The states remained destitute and lacked basic infrastructure, including electricity, telephones, a clean water supply and paved roads. Hawley also observed that administration hardly existed and that the rulers still spent too much of their meagre income on themselves.[218] This inherent administrative weakness meant it was difficult for the development programme to have a significant impact.[219] The British Council representative observed that 'the corrupt regime in Saudi Arabia' led to a feeling of complacency about economic and social development, and that the sheikhs would continue to rule because they believed they had the right to do so.[220]

Burrows ended his tour as Political Resident in the autumn of 1958. In his valedictory dispatch, he argued there were grounds for 'cautious optimism' concerning the future of the Trucial States. Although Burrows had been a consistent supporter of the development programme, he emphasised that more could have been done to persuade the rulers to improve the administration of their sheikhdoms. Burrows also commented on the dilemma the Foreign Office faced in the Trucial States between establishing relations with emerging elements of influence and at the same time freeing the Foreign Office from its dependence on the sheikhs. He argued that the choice was not between autocracy and democracy but between a 'modernised tribal system of paternalistic though sometimes wayward despotism and military dictatorship'.[221]

These dilemmas were a perennial concern for successive Political Residents, and Sir George Middleton commented that: 'we can persuade, advise or cajole, but we cannot command'. He argued that the British Government could either yield to the sheikhly system of rule in the Trucial States or interfere more, which would risk allegations of imperialism.[222] The Foreign Office understood that it could not rely solely on the rulers of the Trucial States indefinitely, and it became very concerned about the growth of external influence in the Gulf.[223] In 1958, proposals were made that Foreign Office diplomats serving in the sheikhdoms should make every effort to become less conspicuous.[224] Events elsewhere in the region further undermined British influence.

The coup d'état in Iraq in July 1958 led to the destruction of the Hashemite monarchy and the 'old social classes' who had dominated the politics of the country since the end of the First World War.[225] Rashid Khalidi notes that the impact of the Iraqi Revolution on the Arab world was complex, and the states where revolutions did not occur, such as in Oman and the Gulf sheikhdoms, were of great importance. This was because they marked the first defeats of the 'Arab revolutionary tide' and became the centre of conservative opposition to the Arab revolutionary regimes.[226] Although Britain's long-standing influence in Iraq was swept aside by General Abd al-Karim Qasim, the prime minister of republican Iraq (1958–63), the Foreign Office gave no thought to disengaging from the region for a variety of economic and political reasons.[227] All the same, the Foreign Office understood that steps had to be taken to reduce the overt presence in the Gulf States.

Middleton proposed that the titles of British officials in the Gulf should be changed since they were 'an unfortunate survival of the British Raj in India because of their obviously imperial connotations'.[228] American diplomats in the Gulf also believed that the British role in the Trucial States was the final expression of imperialism in the Middle East, and that the British stuck to a 'stack of cards theory', which meant if one of the sheikhdoms fell, the rest would follow. The State Department regarded the British position as pragmatic and believed that there was no viable alternative to the *Pax Britannica* in the Gulf.[229] Nonetheless, the Foreign Office deprecated American attempts to promote political reform and argued that there were common interests in the Gulf.[230]

Shortly after becoming Political Resident in 1958, Middleton commented on the situation in the Trucial States and remarked that the population 'live in a time of innocence', on account of the traditional way of life that prevailed in the sheikhdoms. Middleton argued that the Foreign Office could either acquiesce in the continuation of sheikhly rule or it might intervene more but risk the allegation of imperialism. He believed that the development programme had made significant progress despite the shortage of funds, and argued that there was a clear correlation between advances in development and the political tranquillity that prevailed in the Trucial States. Middleton contended that if the Treasury declined to spend a small sum on the Trucial States, British officials would find it harder to maintain political stability in the face of growing Arab nationalist sentiment. Oil was belatedly discovered in Abu Dhabi in 1958, which meant that the sheikhdom would be able to fund the development programme. Nevertheless, Middleton further argued that it was in the Foreign Office's interest to continue funding development schemes in the interim because the Resident would be able to influence how the money was spent. These concerns led him to propose a second five-year development programme in 1960.[231]

Conclusion

In the post-Second World War era, Britain's role in the Persian Gulf, and in the Trucial States in particular, was fundamentally transformed. This was the result of changing economic, political and strategic circumstances. In contrast with the Government of India's policy of non-interference in the internal affairs of the sheikhdoms, the Foreign Office intervened on an unprecedented scale. However, there were significant limitations to the extent of British influence in the sheikhdoms that were caused by the treaty relations with the sheikhs. The Foreign Office was responsible for the external relations of the rulers but it was hindered by the extent to which it could interfere internally. The Political Resident and the political agents could advise the rulers about a broad range of economic and political issues but they were unable to impose their views. The inherent limitations of the British role were observed in a retrospective memorandum written in 1966, which commented on Britain's role in the Gulf since 1948. Peter Tripp, the author of the paper, argued that the Foreign Office had 'assumed the responsibilities but failed to take the power and have suffered the consequences ever since'.[232] Nonetheless, the maintenance of British prestige and stability were notable characteristics of the Foreign Office's policy in the Trucial States.

The establishment of the Trucial Oman Levies in 1951 was a clear example of the Foreign Office's determination to defend the Trucial States, and prevent them from being undermined by the Saudis. Although the Levies were a small force, commanded by British officers, they did contribute towards the internal stability of the sheikhdoms. Moreover, the Levies were important because they formed the basis of the United Arab Emirates' security forces. In contrast with developments in the Middle East, the Trucial States remained politically quiescent, which meant that coercive measures were unnecessary.

However, the sheikhdoms' low level of economic and social development was a much greater challenge because the Government of India had made no attempt to develop the sheikhdoms. The Foreign Office promoted a development policy in the Trucial States for several reasons, including moral imperatives. But the decision to spend small sums was heavily influenced by British fears that the Saudis might subvert the sheikhdoms by offering assistance, along with the Saudi threat to ill-defined frontiers of the region. The Foreign Office persuaded the Treasury to allocate small sums for development on political grounds. However, the Treasury was very reluctant to do so, and this was perhaps a key weakness in the Foreign Office's approach to developing the sheikhdoms.

The Foreign Office's attempts to develop the Trucial States were quite successful, and by 1960 some progress had occurred. The Foreign Office's role in the Trucial States was anomalous because it was responsible for development problems, which had little to do with conventional diplomacy. Nonetheless, the standard of the small number of British officials who served in the Gulf was very high. Some of the diplomats in the Gulf had previously served in India and the Sudan, which meant they had experience of similar development problems.[233] In the post-war era, the Foreign Office went to great lengths to train its Arabist officials in the culture, history and languages of the Middle East.[234] Its 'camel corps' became the elite of the diplomatic service, and their expertise had a considerable impact on the Gulf.

The British were, however, hindered by the rulers of the Trucial States, who were unresponsive to suggestions that they might modernise their administrations and take steps to improve the lives of their subjects. This presented the Foreign Office with a dilemma that was never effectively resolved. The Foreign Office wanted to downplay its role in the Gulf in order to counter Arab nationalist criticism of the British role in the Trucial States. Meanwhile, the Political Residents were instructed to encourage the rulers to introduce effective administration so that they could become responsible for their internal affairs. Little progress was achieved by 1960 because the rulers, notably Sheikh Shakhbut, were unwilling to introduce a limited administrative system. During the 1960s, the expansion of the oil industry in Abu Dhabi meant that the Foreign Office could no longer tolerate rulers who failed to adequately develop their states. Consequently, the British became much more interventionist in the internal affairs of the Trucial States.

3

The consolidation of British influence

The Conservative Government and the Trucial States, 1960–4

British policy in the Trucial States was made at the official level in the Foreign Office during Harold Macmillan's (1957–63) and Sir Alec Douglas-Home's (1963–4) premierships. Ministers were preoccupied with membership of the Common Market and the process of decolonisation in the remnants of the colonial empire. In the early 1960s, the Trucial States were immune from the 'winds of change' that defined Britain's imperial retreat and remained a backwater. The question was how long the British would be able to retain their predominant position in the Gulf. Economic considerations had a decisive impact on the government's willingness to relinquish control of the protected states in the Gulf.

During the early 1960s, the British position in the Trucial States faced significant regional challenges that included the Iraqi threat to invade Kuwait in 1961 and the growing importance of Arab nationalism as a subversive force. The Foreign Office successfully handled these unprecedented challenges to Britain's long-standing predominance in the Trucial States. The long-term objective was to create a situation in which Britain's obligation to protect the rulers of the Trucial States could be terminated without damaging the security of oil supplies and the political stability of the region.

The Foreign Office took various steps in the early 1960s to consolidate Britain's position in the Trucial States. These measures included the continuation of the economic and social development of the sheikhdoms. This policy was supposed to achieve certain objectives that included reinforcing British prestige in the Trucial States. The Foreign Office had to show the population of the Trucial States that there were benefits from the British presence. It also introduced a policy known as 'retrocession', which entailed the gradual transfer of powers to the rulers. The slow pace of development in the Trucial States during the 1960s hindered this policy.

One of the notable characteristics of the long British role in the Trucial States was that it solidified the position of the ruling families of the sheikhdoms. Furthermore, the absence of a viable alternative to the rulers meant that the British reinforced the sheikhly system of rule. By the 1960s, the Trucial States were starting to emerge from centuries of somnolence, which was caused by the development of the oil industry in Abu Dhabi and Dubai's growing importance as the Trucial States' entrepôt. The five smaller or petty sheikhdoms remained economically and politically insignificant, but the rapid growth of oil income entailed a radical transformation of the sheikhdoms. The development of oil economies in the Trucial States posed insuperable challenges for the British. The windfall oil income meant that the protected states had to establish an effective administrative system from scratch and devise development programmes. The experience in Kuwait in the 1950s showed that there were many obstacles to be overcome.[1]

These issues were replicated in the Trucial States as a result of the development of the oil industry in the 1960s. Oil was discovered in Abu Dhabi in 1958 and the first exports were in 1962. Sheikh Shakhbut bin Sultan Al Nahyan, the ruler of Abu Dhabi, declined to spend his windfall oil income on the development of a government machine, which was vital for the future of the state. The Foreign Office's handling of Sheikh Shakhbut was a notable example of the extent to which the British were determined to intervene in the internal affairs of the sheikhdoms in order to secure their interests.

The 'last ditch of British imperialism'[2] in the Middle East

The last decade of Britain's imperial role in the Gulf States was characterised by endless debates about the future, and the impact of domestic economic and political considerations that greatly influenced government policy. British strategy in the Trucial States and the Gulf was dominated by increased intervention in the internal affairs of the sheikhdoms. In February 1960, Macmillan's Cabinet was presented with a document titled 'Future Policy Study, 1960–70', which estimated that radicalism would threaten the rulers and the British position in the Gulf. The report argued that the *Pax Britannica* would appear increasingly anachronistic if no alternative to the rulers could be found. The objective of British policy in the Trucial States was to create a situation in which the treaty commitments to the rulers could be terminated without damaging the security of oil supplies or undermining stability. The rulers should be encouraged to modernise their regimes to prevent revolutionary pressures overcoming the sheikhly system of rule.[3]

In November 1960, the Arabian Department of the Foreign Office produced a lengthy paper that discussed future policy in the Persian Gulf over the next ten years.[4] Access to oil justified the British presence in the Gulf. Kuwait was the most significant oil producer at the time, and the retention of its sterling balances was a crucial economic concern.[5] The Treasury, led by Reginald Mauldling, argued that oil justified the small military presence in the region.[6] The UK's economy depended heavily on Persian Gulf oil because two-thirds of Britain's total oil imports came from Kuwait, Iraq, Iran, Qatar, Bahrain and Saudi Arabia, with about a third coming from Kuwait alone. Alongside oil, the Persian Gulf was also important to the British as a source of investment capital. Kuwait's investments in the UK were on such a scale as to be an important element in the British reserves and balance of payments.[7] There was also heavy public and private investment in the oil production complex in the Gulf.[8] The Gulf States were also strategically important because the region was a bulwark against the spread of Soviet influence in the Middle East, and imperial lines of communications traversed the region to the Far East.[9]

The Foreign Office regarded the *Pax Britannica* in the Gulf as archaic. The objective over the following ten years was to create a situation in which Britain's commitments could be terminated, without doing damage to the security of oil supplies. The British had to show that they favoured administrative and social reforms, but improving the economic and social circumstances of the states was an insuperable challenge. The feudal nature of the sheikhly regimes 'seemed poor advertisements for British administration', and the Foreign Office could not avoid responsibility 'for the inequities of those we protect'. The rulers of the states were vulnerable not only for their reactionary attitudes, but also for being allied to the British. The Foreign Office observed in November 1960 that: 'in the eyes of most of the world, the system is tarred with the same brush as colonialism proper and is certain to perish in the near future'.[10] Sir George Middleton, the Political Resident, reached a similar conclusion, and argued that: 'our position in the Gulf is fragile and anachronistic'. In spite of the shortcomings of British protection, the hands-off approach to the Trucial States prevented them from being absorbed by their neighbours, such as Saudi Arabia. Middleton argued that the future of the Trucial States was likely to be determined by external influences rather than internal forces. The British could not withdraw quickly on account of their reliance on Gulf oil. Moreover, the rulers were Britain's 'friends by tradition, perhaps by inclination, certainly because their regimes could not long survive without our presence'. Middleton also stated that the smaller sheikhdoms were economically and politically unviable, and that when the current rulers died, the British should promote their absorption by Abu Dhabi or Dubai.[11]

A combination of circumstances made it very difficult to achieve these objectives. By the early 1960s, the British were more committed politically and militarily in the Gulf than at any time since 1945. There were long-standing differences of perspective between government departments in the early 1960s about the value of the British presence. The Treasury argued that the oil-producing states had to sell their oil and world supplies were ample. This meant that it would be possible to obtain oil at reasonable prices, whether or not the British were in the Gulf.[12] The Foreign Office and Ministry of Power argued that withdrawal from the Gulf would so endanger the existing pattern of oil production that the consequences as regards both the availability of Gulf oil and the price at which it could be obtained would be detrimental. The Foreign Office also argued that withdrawal would leave a political vacuum that would lead to breaches of treaty obligations, which might affect Iran's pro-Western orientation.[13]

Edward Heath, the Lord Privy Seal and a minister in the Foreign Office, visited the Trucial States in January 1961. Heath's tour marked the increased significance of the Trucial States.[14] As Donald Hawley notes, this was the first ministerial visit to the Trucial States and nothing comparable had occurred since Lord Curzon's durbar at Sharjah in 1903.[15] Heath's tour of the Trucial States involved meetings with the rulers, who warmly welcomed the Foreign Office's interest in their affairs.[16] The extent of Britain's ongoing interests in the Gulf States was detailed in instructions dispatched to Sir William Luce, who became Political Resident in May 1961. Luce's fundamental tasks as Political Resident were: (1) to ensure the UK's continued access to Kuwait's oil on the present terms and satisfactory arrangements for the investment of Kuwait's sterling investments; (2) to assist in the steady development of the Persian Gulf States, economically, administratively and politically under the leadership of the present ruling families; (3) to avert communist subversion or other developments which would increase the Soviet threat to the Middle East and to the East–West and North–South communications through it; (4) to provide suitable conditions for the maintenance of British bases in the area.[17]

Luce, who had previously served as Governor and Commander-in-Chief of Aden (1956–60), was highly regarded. Glen Balfour-Paul, who served in the Gulf during the 1960s, referred to him as 'the last of the great imperial proconsuls'.[18] Luce played a central role in the direction of British policy in the

Trucial States. During his tenure, two incompatible trends characterised British policy. The Foreign Office made strenuous efforts towards the independence and unification of the sheikhdoms, but the unprecedented increase in British intervention in the internal affairs of the Trucial States 'conjured up all the hoary metaphors of paternalism'.[19] Luce was highly influential in his attempts to establish a coherent policy in the Gulf, and he remained the conduit of British policy in the region. Nonetheless, during his tenure, there were unprecedented internal and external challenges. Contrary to the publicly stated policy that the British did not intervene in the internal affairs of the sheikhdoms, the Political Resident remained omnipotent.

Arab nationalism and the Iraqi threat of Kuwait

One of the most significant challenges that Luce faced was the growth of Arab nationalist sentiment in the Trucial States. Arab nationalism was the most dynamic force in Arab politics, and Nasser remained its foremost leader and symbol. He was the first Arab leader to successfully defy the great powers and destroy the old ruling class in Egypt. The pinnacle of Nasser's political fortunes occurred in 1958, with the establishment of the Egyptian–Syrian United Arab Republic (UAR), which lasted until 1961. Some educated notables such as Easa Saleh Al-Gurg were clearly attracted by the Egyptian leader's socialist credentials,[20] but the extent of Nasser's appeal in the Trucial States is open to question.

The biggest challenge to the British position in the Trucial States and the Gulf as a whole in the early 1960s was the Iraqi threat to invade Kuwait, which became an independent state in 1961.[21] In June 1961, General Qasim,[22] who came to power following the bloody coup in Iraq in 1958, threatened to annex Kuwait.[23] The putative Iraqi menace forced the British to abide by their defence commitments to the Emirate.[24] Taylor Fain argues that the Iraqi threat to Kuwait was 'illusory'. Nonetheless, the British initiated 'Operation Vantage', which led to the deployment of 5,000 troops to Kuwait in order to deter the Iraqis.[25] The Kuwait crisis highlighted the limitations of Britain's control over the situation in the Gulf, and as one American diplomat noted, the Persian Gulf 'is the last sensitive nerve of the British Empire. It is both a vital resource to Britain and a focal point for vestiges of imperial sentiment'.[26] The Americans adopted a low-key and peripheral policy on the Gulf. They were content for the British to take the leading role in the region.[27] American officials routinely visited the Trucial

States from their consulate at Dhahran in Saudi Arabia, and the State Department received detailed accounts of the situation in the protected states.[28] American consuls were unsparing in their criticism of the Foreign Office's policy in the Trucial States, and argued that there was growing local dissatisfaction with the British.[29]

The Trucial States were scarcely affected by the situation in Kuwait because literacy was so low that Arab nationalist propaganda had little potential audience.[30] Nonetheless, Britain's intervention in Kuwait led to a re-evaluation of the Foreign Office's policy in the Trucial States. Luce argued that British military assistance for Kuwait shocked the rulers of the Trucial States and 'brought home to them forcibly the value of the *Pax Britannica* in the Persian Gulf'. Nonetheless, Luce believed that the main reason for the expansion of Britain's involvement in the Gulf 'has been our inability so far to devise any other policy other than the exercise of military power to protect our interests in the area and to meet our treaty and moral obligations'. He added that the anomalous character of Britain's role in the Gulf made it difficult to disengage because 'we are not the masters in this house. We have no power to set and pursue our own policy or to determine the course of events'. The policy of non-interference in the Trucial States meant that the British never officially had the power to plan and promote the economic, political and social development of the states in such a way as to create viable entities, and to bring about a smooth transition from British protection to independence. Luce was pessimistic about the ability of the Trucial States to become sustainable states and remain independent after the cessation of British protection. He also argued that the establishment of a federation 'breaks down on the hard facts of geography and population'.[31] His prediction about the future of the states proved to be wayward, but he played a central role in the establishment of the UAE in 1970–1.

Luce was a fervent advocate of the British presence in the Gulf, and argued that the region 'is an island of comparative stability surrounded by a sea of uncertainty'.[32] Relying on the rulers of the Trucial States, who benefited from British protection, made them a liability because they were out of step with the republican regimes in the Arab world. The Foreign Office recognised the weaknesses of the ruling sheikhs but could not see a viable alternative to maintaining regional stability. Luce's suggestion that other powers, such as the United States, should have been encouraged to take a greater interest in the Gulf was fanciful since it contradicted a basic principle of the treaties with the rulers, and because the Americans had no interest in becoming involved in the Gulf. American diplomats were critical of the *Pax Britannica* in the Gulf but were determined not to take any steps that might have given the rulers the idea that they could turn away from the British in favour of the USA.[33]

Robert Walmsley, the Head of the Foreign Office's Arabian Department (1961–3), challenged Luce's defence of the status quo. He argued that no attempt had been made to set out systematically British policy in the Persian Gulf.[34] The Americans continued, on their side, to endorse Britain's paramount position in the Gulf, and also accepted the premise of the 'indivisibility' of British defence commitments to Kuwait and bases on the littoral of the Arabian Peninsula. However, the State Department argued that the British commitment to Aden was becoming the Achilles heel of the 'indivisible' Persian Gulf defence chain.[35] Nonetheless, the Americans were relentlessly critical of British paramountcy in the Gulf and Aden since it 'represents an outmoded and archaic system of political arrangements' that had to evolve if basic Western interests were to endure.[36]

In August 1962, the State Department produced a memorandum on oil in the Middle East that argued that the status quo would be altered by internal and external forces. These included the influence of Arab nationalist ideologies that challenged the sheikhly regimes. Several of the peripheral states, such as Iran and Saudi Arabia, had territorial ambitions as well, and they were waiting 'to pounce on the weaker sheikhdoms in the event of a British disengagement'. The State Department concluded that it was likely that the British would be able to maintain their preponderant position in the Gulf for the next five years, with the likelihood of a 'gradual erosion of influence'.[37] The Foreign Office accepted these conclusions on the grounds that this document provided critical support for the British.[38]

Sir William Luce responded to the American memorandum by arguing that: 'our position here is not tottering nor it is in danger of rapid erosion by any internal influences. It remains acceptable to most of the people of the area and particularly those in power, and provided we play our cards skilfully, I see no reason why it should not remain so for many years.'[39] He believed that there were no internal challenges to sheikhly rule in the Trucial States, and that the main threat came from Nasserism, on account of its subversive and revolutionary force.

In 1963, the CIA argued that the growth of nationalism in the Gulf States, apart from Kuwait, was slow, largely due to their innate backwardness, remoteness and large non-Arab population. Nonetheless, Arab nationalism in the sheikhdoms was not regarded as 'immediately imperilling Western interests', but it posed a growing long-term threat. According to the CIA analysis, Kuwait and the other sheikhdoms were experiencing the early stages of popular demands for change.[40] In 1964, the CIA estimated that revolutionary nationalist pressure on the monarchical regimes remained strong, and that their survival depended on their ability to maintain a balance between firmness and concessions on the domestic front. Nasser was regarded as the 'prime symbol of revolutionary success', who possessed a powerful propaganda and subversive apparatus that was used against governments that were inimical to his interests.[41]

The Arab summit in Cairo in January 1964 showed that Nasser was the most important spokesman for Arab solidarity. He was the most formidable Arab leader of his generation, and his belief in major social, political and economic change in Egypt and the Arab world had widespread appeal. Nasser looked upon 'unity', 'dignity', 'socialism' and 'the end of imperialism' as central themes in the regeneration of Arab society.[42] Radio propaganda was a pervasive mechanism for transmitting Nasser's revolutionary message to the Trucial States because *Sawt al-Arab* was widely listened to by a population that remained overwhelmingly illiterate.[43] The Foreign Office responded by establishing *Sawt al-Sahil* (Voice of the Coast) in 1964, which was located at the TOS camp in Sharjah, to counter the influence of Egyptian and Iraqi radio propaganda.[44] *Sawt al-Sahil* became an important tool in British information operations in the Trucial States because it provided impartial news and programmes to the population.[45]

The JIC, the British inter-agency body responsible for intelligence analysis, initially adopted a sanguine approach to the security threats in the sheikhdoms in 1964.[46] None of the customary vehicles for subversion, including political parties and newspapers, existed in the Trucial States. Defence forces that were loyal to the rulers were regarded as a vital factor in the maintenance of stability. Nasser considered the sheikhly rulers as 'archaic collaborators with the imperialists'.[47] His aim was to drive the British out of the Gulf, but he had considerable financial interests in the uninterrupted passage of Gulf oil through the Suez Canal.

Luce wrote from Bahrain in February 1964 that the only way to counter Nasserism was an Anglo-American strategy to contain its spread in the Arabian Peninsula. This objective could have been achieved by mitigating the attraction of Nasserism among the growing educated classes. Furthermore, Luce hoped that if the rulers could be pressured to adopt administrative and economic reforms, Nasser's appeal could be assuaged.[48] These objectives proved to be illusory because the rulers refused to expand the basis of representation in their states. Luce also proposed the establishment of an 'Arabian Peninsula bloc' that was based on the geographic proximity of the states and their similar social and political systems.[49] He argued that the Saudis would be the lynchpin of this stratagem due to their size and wealth. The Foreign Office responded that there was no immediate practical value to these suggestions for the reason that they were 'pretty cloudy', and looked too far into the future.[50] The trouble with this scheme, which was meant to counter the revolutionary threat of Arab nationalism, was long-standing Saudi expansionism in Eastern Arabia and Oman. In July 1964, the JIC argued that the Saudis still posed a potential menace to the Trucial States and Oman.[51]

Other potential threats emanated from the Baathist regime in Iraq, which became increasingly preoccupied with the Persian Gulf in 1964. The Iraqi aspiration to acquire Kuwait did not disappear when the regime recognised the new state in 1961, and Qasim argued that the southern coast of the Gulf was an historical extension of Iraq. The State Department believed that Iraqi demands that the British withdraw from the Gulf were little more than a propaganda exercise.[52] By 1964, it became apparent that the Baathists were determined to exert their influence in the Trucial States through visits by officials and the invitations to the sheikhs to visit Iraq.[53]

The British were determined to prevent foreign powers from entering the Trucial States and, in 1964, the Foreign Office rejected requests by the State Department and the French to establish consulates in the sheikhdoms. The Foreign Office argued that the rulers were reluctant to permit foreign consular representation because they looked to the British Government to conduct their foreign relations. Furthermore, the Foreign Office contended that the rulers were concerned that they would be forced to accept representatives from the United Arab Republic and Iraq, which would increase their ability to promote subversion in the Trucial States.[54]

Relations with the rulers

During the early 1960s, British intervention in the internal affairs of the Trucial States greatly increased. The decade was marked by far-reaching economic and political changes. The Trucial States remained a patchwork of seven protected states that were rapidly emerging from centuries of obscurity and somnolence. The changing situation of the Trucial States resulted from improvements in communications, oil exploration and the gradual increase in political awareness. The discovery and exploitation of vast oil deposits in Abu Dhabi in 1958 meant that the small fishing village, with an estimated population of 11,500 in 1961, was starting to attract international attention.[55] By 1964, Abu Dhabi had the financial means to develop an administration but the personality of Sheikh Shakhbut significantly hindered development.[56] The Trucial States were still characterised by two anachronisms in the 1960s: their existence as small, fragmented feudal states and the nature of British protection over them.[57]

The Foreign Office claimed that it did not interfere in the internal affairs of the sheikhdoms because it was contrary to treaties with the rulers.[58] However, the vast Foreign Office records on the sheikhdoms contradict this assertion. The British were responsible for a wide range of civil codes since the early 1950s, but as the oil industry expanded in Abu Dhabi in 1962, the Foreign Office attempted to influence the rulers of the Trucial States to modernise their governments and introduce an effective development programme. The limitations imposed on the British in the Trucial States came to the fore during the early 1960s. The treaty relations with the rulers remained in force, meaning that the British were in no position to enforce major internal changes. The Foreign Office exercised few stern measures at the time and, instead, British officials relied on careful negotiation with stubborn rulers.[59]

The British faced the most acute dilemma in the Trucial States, where the shortcomings of the *Pax Britannica* were most evident. No attempt had been made to encourage local participation in anything, and unlike elsewhere in the Empire, no effort was made to train the population in how to run a government. Likewise, the small police forces in the Trucial States were British-officered and almost entirely made up of non-indigenous Arabs and mercenaries unlikely to rebel. The limitations of the benign British role were laid bare to American officials, who routinely visited the Trucial States from their consulate at Dhahran in Saudi Arabia.

In December 1960, Donald Hawley, the Political Agent at Dubai, wrote that there was little sign of change in the antiquated system of sheikhly rule.[60] The treaties with the sheikhs were 'anachronistically Victorian', but sheikhly rule seemed to work, and it was hard to envisage an alternative, nor was there any demand for one.[61] The Trucial States can be compared with the limited political reforms that occurred in Bahrain, but more importantly with Kuwait. Under Sheikh Abdullah bin Salim Al Sabah, who ruled between 1950 and 1965, Kuwait was transformed from an inconsequential city state under an autocratic ruler to a rich and independent welfare state.[62] Sheikh Abdullah's 'unique achievement' was the handing over of the absolute powers of his predecessors to a limited parliamentary government, without undermining the precarious equilibrium of Kuwait's political system.[63] Kuwait's transformation resulted from the historical differences that distinguished it from the Trucial States. The Kuwaitis were shipbuilders and pearl divers, trading with Iraq and India, which meant that they developed knowledge of the outside world.[64] Kuwait was geographically closer to important Arab states, and relations between the ruling family and merchants were more equitable than in the lower Gulf.[65]

In the Trucial States, there had been no constitutional development and the rulers had no interest in advocating representation. The *majlis* system still worked, which gave subjects access to their rulers, and this relatively democratic process was sufficient reason to prompt a cautious attitude towards popular representation.[66] Dubai remained the exception since it was the most prosperous of the sheikhdoms on account of its port, entrepôt trade and gold smuggling.[67] The Trucial States had a combined population of between 80,000 and 100,000, and Dubai was the most populous sheikhdom with a population of 40,000 in 1961.[68] Significant groundwork had been done in the 1950s for future development in Dubai, including the drawing-up of a town plan, the establishment of a rudimentary administration, the opening of an airport and installation of a telephone system. James Craig wrote that Dubai's prosperity was the result of Sheikh Rashid bin Said's 'hard, realistic, unsentimental shrewdness'. Sheikh Rashid was quick to learn and to trust his advisors, and in contrast with the other rulers, who 'sat idle, cautious and suspicious', he saw the possibilities of Dubai's position.[69]

In contrast to Dubai, the smaller sheikhdoms such as Sharjah were characterised by stagnation and decay because there was no prospect of oil being discovered. Most of the populace lived in the towns along the coast, and the population was predominantly Arab, with a growing number of migrants from Iran and the Indian subcontinent. Politically, the Trucial States remained peripheral in major regional trends, the most important of which was the impact of several competing models of Arab nationalism. The rulers of the sheikhdoms still looked to the British for advice and assistance in their internal affairs. There was no sign of the sheikhs sinking their differences, and federation in 1961 remained 'an iridescent dream or, at best a truncated and ineffectual affair subject to constant intrigue and plotting'.[70] A variety of centrifugal forces precluded effective collaboration between the sheikhdoms. The Trucial States lacked the basic attributes of 'stateness', such as established frontiers and governments, and therefore remained village states that had been the main political unit for centuries. Intertribal competition and jealousies continued and reinforced traditional separatism.[71]

Some of the states were fragmented internally, as distinct from the division of the Trucial Coast into seven sheikhdoms. This internal fragmentation caused disputes between the states regarding sheikhly 'sovereignty' over pieces of territory. The separatism that characterised the Trucial States was the paramount political factor in any consideration of unification, and it was hard to envisage the elimination of a situation in which each sheikh in 1965 was a 'ridiculous little cock crowing on his own private dung hill'.[72] The rulers could be expected to maintain the status quo in which each was paramount in his sheikhdom. The surrender of prestige and economic advantages had little appeal. The rulers of the smaller states might have been more amenable to unification, but the rulers of Abu Dhabi, which, as previously stated, was becoming the most powerful sheikhdom on account of its rapidly growing oil income, had little interest in unity.[73]

Nonetheless, the British took decisive steps to protect the Trucial States from invasion and to maintain the peace within the sheikhdoms. The Trucial Oman Scouts were the main instrument of this policy because they were responsible for suppressing the historical tendency of the rulers to fight each other for regional supremacy and the tribal tradition of raiding.[74] The Foreign Office did attempt to promote cooperation between the sheikhdoms through its support of the Trucial States Council. By the early 1960s, little had been achieved and Sheikh Shakhbut, the long-standing ruler of Abu Dhabi, was very reluctant to utilise his newly acquired oil wealth for the benefit of the poorer sheikhdoms.[75]

The Foreign Office's relations with Sheikh Shakhbut were extremely challenging, and in December 1959, Edward Henderson, the Political Agent at Abu Dhabi, reported that there had been a complete breakdown in confidence. Henderson believed that Shakhbut was sincere but his biggest problem was his absence of education, which made reading documents very difficult. Furthermore, Shakhbut lacked advisors and lived in isolation because his family were in awe of him. According to Henderson, Shakhbut thought that British intervention was undermining his authority, and that steps needed to be taken to win his confidence.[76] Donald Hawley argued that Shakhbut did not welcome oil wealth, and he observed that, as a sheikh 'of some nobility, he hated the idea of development which would destroy the centuries old way of life of his people and pollute the clear freshness of the desert'.[77]

One of the most significant challenges British officials faced was trying to persuade Shakhbut to develop Abu Dhabi, and to introduce a government system that was essential to manage the sheikhdom's windfall oil income. A notable example of this problem occurred in 1961, when Peter Lienhardt, an Oxford anthropologist, was invited to become Shakhbut's advisor because he was an authority on the sheikhdoms.[78] Lienhardt disagreed with the ruler about the importance of spending money on health care and education.[79] According to the Foreign Office account, Shakhbut accused Lienhardt of disloyalty and 'in veiled terms, of taking bribes'.[80] After three months in Abu Dhabi, Lienhardt resigned, and his successor and consultants were apparently treated in a similar vein.[81]

In 1962, Abu Dhabi exported its first shipment of oil and Shakhbut earned £375,000.[82] By 1964, the ruler's income reached £8 million.[83] Shakhbut was widely referred to as a miser,[84] and known for storing his wealth under his bed.[85] Henderson argued that Shakhbut was mean because of his historic lack of money.[86] Shakhbut also had a reputation for distrusting advisors, and was receptive to suggestions that he was being 'cheated, betrayed and being played around with'. This made him vulnerable to contractors and entrepreneurs who claimed they could fulfil contracts on the cheap.[87] Edward Baker, the BBME representative at Dubai, described Shakhbut's tendency of keeping currency in tins buried in the ground. Although the BBME had a monopoly in the Trucial States, Shakhbut was extremely sceptical about using the the bank's facilities to deposit his income.[88]

Notwithstanding the insuperable challenges that British officials, bankers and consultants faced in dealing with Shakhbut, he was regarded as 'a man of considerable charm, who commands considerable respect by sheer force of character'.[89] In contrast with his predecessors, who were killed or deposed, Shakhbut had managed to rule Abu Dhabi since 1928, but his leadership was regarded as arbitrary and erratic.[90] Nonetheless, he did achieve a modicum of security that his predecessors had not achieved. Before the onset of Abu Dhabi's windfall oil income, the British acknowledged his conservatism and careful spending.[91]

American diplomats were also scathing about Shakhbut's eccentricities. Arthur Allen, the consul at Dhahran, was convinced that Shakhbut did not want any more development, and that he was 'pretending to chase the development chimera solely because he thinks it keeps the British happy'. Allen was critical of the British, who, he argued, had done nothing about Shakhbut, and he believed that they had qualms about overthrowing the ruler in the absence of any evidence that his relatives wanted to assist in his removal.[92] The CIA characterised Shakhbut as 'an ignorant, backward Bedouin who cannot be changed. He cares only for himself and his family, and sees in any change the seeds of lessening of his authority. His oft-quoted philosophy is "keep a dog hungry and he will follow you. Feed him and he will ignore you"'.[93]

Uzi Rabi challenges the official description of Shakhbut's spending habits because he argues that he was generous outside of Abu Dhabi.[94] In 1966, Shakhbut gave King Hussein of Jordan a gift of £200,000 towards flood relief work, and made further acts of generosity towards the King during a visit to Amman.[95] Rabi argues that Shakhbut was psychologically ill equipped to comprehend vast government expenditure, which would expose the sheikhdom to rapid social change and corrupt the people. In the past, his rule had focused on the limited needs of the populace and the maintenance of the traditional balance between tribe, coastal town-dwellers and the inhabitants on inland oases, such as at Buraimi and Liwa.

Shakhbut's attitude may have been his response to what he might have regarded as unwarranted British interference, and the demand that he develop the sheikhdom faster than he would have liked. The chiefdom in Abu Dhabi had been maintained, notwithstanding the Saudi threat, and Shakhbut was determined not to allow oil wealth to alter Abu Dhabi's traditional way of life. His resistance to pressure to modernise Abu Dhabi was a rational reaction to the potential loss of control of his sheikhdom.[96] The development of the oil economy in Kuwait during the 1950s highlighted the potential pitfalls. Likewise, the Al Thanis, the ruling family of Qatar, received over £7 million in 1960 from a 50:50 profit-sharing agreement with the Qatar Petroleum Company. They were renowned for their extravagance, which threatened the economic stability of the country, and for their failure to distinguish between personal and government income.[97]

The imminent onset of a vast oil income called into question Shakhbut's suitability to remain in power. Abu Dhabi had no administration and no educated class from which a local administrative staff could be recruited. Colonel Sir Hugh Boustead, the Political Agent at Abu Dhabi (1961–5), constantly struggled to get Shakhbut to build a sound administrative system but with very limited success.[98] Archie Lamb argues that Shakhbut resented Boustead's 'shaikhly attitude', which had significant implications.[99] The ruler deprecated being dictated to by Boustead, who consistently failed to persuade him to mend his ways.[100] Shakhbut did not respond well to critical articles that appeared in the London press in the spring of 1964,[101] and his standing with the British was undermined by his reputation for mistreating experts who were assigned to establish the rudiments of an administrative system in Abu Dhabi.[102]

Shakhbut did the British no positive harm because he did not prevent the oil companies from bringing oil into production. Moreover, he did not impede the operations of the Trucial Oman Scouts, and he was not responsible for oppressing his people.[103] The Foreign Office's handling of Shakhbut was a notable example of the extent to which the British were determined to intervene in the internal affairs of the sheikhdoms. Luce and Boustead played a central role in a long-running campaign to depose Shakhbut. They started planning Shakhbut's overthrow in April 1962. The Political Resident argued that there was no hope of Shakhbut being capable of ruling Abu Dhabi to any acceptable standard. Luce concluded that the continuation of Shakhbut's rule 'into a new era will bring about a disastrous state of affairs in Abu Dhabi'. There was no chance of averting a disaster by 'working upon Shakhbut by cajolery, warnings or any other means'. The only alternative was to remove Shakhbut and replace him with his younger brother, Sheikh Zayed. However, it would be 'politically most unwise for HMG to take overt action' because the British would be accused of interfering 'for our own imperialist purposes', and Sheikh Zayed would be regarded as a British puppet.[104] Luce set out a clear plan to remove Shakhbut that was based on securing Sheikh Zayed's agreement to replace his brother.

The overthrowing of Shakhbut was based on questionable grounds. The Foreign Office acknowledged that it had no right to initiate a coup d'état that had no precedent in the Gulf since the removal of the ruler of Bahrain in 1923.[105] Sheikh Isa bin Ali was deprived of control of his government but not deposed because he was accused of following a 'notorious course of corruption, oppression and misgovernment'. In contrast, Shakhbut had not oppressed his people, nor had he been disloyal to his agreements or shown hostility to the British. The Foreign Office was also concerned about the impact that overthrowing Shakhbut would have on British prestige because international criticism, especially at the United Nations, would be unavoidable.[106] It was therefore essential that Shakhbut's family take, or appear to take, the initiative.

Sir William Luce's attempt to overthrow Shakhbut in 1962 failed because the ruler succeeded in rallying his family against Sheikh Zayed. In October 1963, Luce observed that Abu Dhabi was likely to become the richest state in the world in terms of per capita income. He argued that Shakhbut was incapable of using this wealth, and that there would be no orderly administration. The Political Resident noted that the British would be held responsible for this situation and 'nothing they will say will absolve them from this responsibility'. Luce also argued that the businesses that had tried to operate in the sheikhdom had been thwarted by the ruler's 'avarice, capriciousness and unreliability', and that failure to act against Shakhbut was regarded as weakness 'or even a mysterious desire to support Shakhbut'. Luce's determination to remove Shakhbut at all cost was influenced by the requirement to send a clear message to the other rulers that there was a limit to British toleration of inept rule.[107] The plan to remove Shakhbut in 1963 failed, although it was supported by the Prime Minister Sir Alec Douglas-Home and the Foreign Secretary Rab Butler, because his brother

Sheikh Khalid refused to cooperate with it, and Sheikh Zayed was not prepared to act alone.[108]

Luce was in no doubt that it was in Britain's interests and in the interests of the people of Abu Dhabi 'to get rid of Shakhbut'. In May 1964, the Political Resident made another attempt to remove Shakhbut because he dismissed a Jordanian judge who was responsible for retroceding jurisdiction in traffic cases, and he refused to conclude a 50:50 agreement with the Abu Dhabi Petroleum Company (ADPC).[109] This meant that the first quarter oil payment was only £250,000, whereas under the oil agreement it would have been £1.5 million. Luce argued that Shakhbut, as a result of 'sheer obstinacy and stupidity', deprived Abu Dhabi of £2.5 million in the first half of 1964. He also believed that Shakhbut's misrule would lead to a violent revolution in Abu Dhabi, and his conduct undermined British prestige on the grounds that it was assumed that the Foreign Office was responsible for the ruler's actions.[110]

There is no evidence to support Luce's assertion that Shakhbut's behaviour might have led to a revolution, but nonetheless the Political Resident reprised his plan to depose Shakhbut in October 1963. The Foreign Office acknowledged that the case against Shakhbut was 'formidable', but there were strong arguments against taking action. Shakhbut's brothers were unlikely to follow through, security in Abu Dhabi was bad and failure would have calamitous implications for relations with the ruler. Shakhbut was undoubtedly a poor ruler but he did not squander his wealth like the Al Thanis, and as one diplomat noted, 'if we once start to organise depositions, even by family consensus, where are we to stop?' The major British interest was in oil and the operations of the oil companies continued unimpeded and were very profitable. The Foreign Office argued that none of Luce's plans were acceptable, and it was critical of the approach taken by Boustead and Luce, who were originally administrators rather than career diplomats. Frank Brenchley, the Head of the Arabian Department (1963–7), argued that a diplomat who had observed misrule elsewhere might have been more detached about Shakhbut's misrule and 'less inclined to rouse his obstinacy by pressing him to develop his state faster than he himself thinks necessary'.[111] Nonetheless, the campaign against Shakhbut continued apace, and in October 1964, Luce argued the case for removing Shakhbut would be reinforced if it could be demonstrated conclusively that he obstructed the creation of a federation of the Trucial States, which the other rulers wished to bring about. Luce contended that overthrowing Shakhbut was the only way in which the British could discharge their moral responsibility for remedying the ruler's misrule and disregard for his people. He offered the prospect of a 'comparatively progressive and enlightened regime', under a ruler (Sheikh Zayed) who had the interests of the people at heart.[112]

Luce intermittently raised the question of overthrowing Shakhbut, but Patrick Gordon Walker, the Foreign Secretary of the new Labour Government, commented that: 'I will need a lot of persuading that this James Bond scheme is a good one.'[113] The Foreign Office was sceptical about removing Shakhbut because they believed the legal and political argument was weak.[114] In December 1964, Luce tried to persuade Gordon Walker to initiate a coup. Gordon Walker thought it was unviable to overthrow Shakhbut because the risks were too great. However, the Foreign Secretary did agree to an alternative plan that Sheikh Zayed should take advantage of Shakhbut's absence from Abu Dhabi and launch a coup d'état. According to this scheme, the Political Resident would immediately confer recognition on Sheikh Zayed and military support would be provided. The advantage of this approach was that the British would be responding to Sheikh Zayed's initiative.[115] Shakhbut was belatedly overthrown in a bloodless coup in August 1966.

The Arabian Department and the Trucial States

In November 1964, Sir William Luce reminded the Foreign Office that the policy of the government in the Trucial States was still based on long-standing agreements with the rulers. The current approach was very recent and came about as a deliberate act of policy, and as a consequence of regional influences. These included the threat from Egypt and Iraq, whose ultimate aim was to remove British influence in the Gulf. Internally, the growing educated class resented sheikhly rule and was attracted by Arab nationalist sentiment. Luce argued that in response to these changing circumstances, the rulers needed to adapt their methods of government by judicious economic and social development. Relations with the rulers were therefore very important but they could only be encouraged 'through extortion and persuasion'; however, there was nothing inherently wrong with sheikhly rule. Nonetheless, there was a manifest requirement for a change in policy based on gradualism rather than a clear break with the past.[116]

Luce contended that in the future, relations with the sheikhdoms should be based on shedding aspects of Britain's special position that were not essential to maintaining influence. Subtle changes in British authority would reduce the scope for international criticism that was growing at the United Nations.

However, the Foreign Office's ability to bring pressure to bear on the rulers and persuade them to reform their administrations remained unchanged. The Trucial States were regarded as a major problem, and their administrations were still rudimentary, their populations small and ill-educated. The objective of British policy was to enable the rulers to stand alone in close association with Saudi Arabia, which was contentious by virtue of the ongoing frontier disputes, especially at the Buraimi Oasis, that remained unresolved.[117] Moreover, the British only resumed diplomatic relations with the Saudis in 1963, following their cessation in 1956 in the aftermath of the Suez Crisis. The rulers therefore remained at the centre of British policy for the reason that there was no viable alternative. However, pressure could be exerted and recalcitrant sheikhs removed.

Luce was responsible for the introduction of a policy of modernisation and retrocession in 1963.[118] Retrocession meant the shedding of quasi-administrative functions that had been acquired since 1948.[119] The British exercised jurisdiction over all citizens of non-Muslim countries and all Muslim Commonwealth citizens resident in the protected states.[120] Jurisdiction developed on the basis of custom and usage, but Orders-in-Council under which the British functioned in the Trucial States were sometimes made on the basis of written agreements with the rulers.[121] There was no pressure on the part of the rulers to retrocede powers, and until the discovery of oil, it was perceived as unimportant to develop a legal system. Sheikhly justice prevailed in the Trucial States that was purely discretionary and did not safeguard basic human rights. The process of retrocession depended on the appointment of qualified judges and the existence of a written corpus of law.[122]

In January 1964, the Foreign Office argued that retrocession should be hastened, but it was inevitable that 'heavy and sustained pressure' on the rulers would be required to secure their cooperation in the transfer of powers.[123] In Dubai, Sheikh Rashid appointed a Jordanian legal advisor to draft laws for the Trucial States. In Abu Dhabi, British jurisdiction in traffic cases was transferred for an experimental period to a traffic court.[124] Some progress was also made in Bahrain and Qatar, but retrocession was slow because it depended on the rulers acquiring responsibilities as fast as their administrations could manage change. The American Consul at Dhahran argued that retrocession was 'a euphemism, like "under-developed nations"' because it was not forced on the British by local demands but it meant the disappearance 'of what amounts to capitulatory rights, an anachronism in today's world, but a necessity up to the present', owing to the lack in these sheikhdoms of people trained in modern law.[125]

The modernisation and retrocession of jurisdiction was associated with a development policy and attempts to federate the Trucial States. As has been previously discussed, the Foreign Office established the Trucial States Council in 1952 in order to set up a framework for cooperation in the protected states.[126] The Foreign Office dedicated considerable time and effort to the federation of the Trucial States. In April 1961, Sir George Middleton argued that federation remained doubtful and the Trucial States Council was unlikely to achieve this role.[127] The likelihood that the rulers would cooperate was far-fetched because their attitude was determined by self-interest and mutual animosities.[128] The Bahrain Political Residency argued that federation should have been eschewed for five years because the chances of success had faded with the prospect of Abu Dhabi getting rich.[129] Sheikh Shakhbut had no interest in cooperating,[130] and a federation without Abu Dhabi's vast oil wealth would be meaningless. Concerted British pressure on Shakhbut had little impact, and by July 1966, Luce acknowledged that Abu Dhabi's refusal to participate in a federation and share its oil wealth had frustrated any chance of success.[131]

The Foreign Office's inability to achieve a federal Trucial States highlighted an inherent facet of the British position in the Trucial States: responsibility without power.[132] The British had no legal authority to intervene in the internal affairs of the sheikhdoms, but were attacked by hostile critics for the rulers' shortcomings. Walter Schwinn, the American Consul at Dhahran, was scathing in his analysis of the Foreign Office's failure to federate the Trucial States, and wrote that: 'had the British acted more positively in the past to create a federation among the Trucial States, even at the cost of arm-twisting, the present situation might have been avoided. As matters now stand, federation of all the Trucial States seems likely to remain an iridescent dream, or, at best, a truncated and ineffectual affair subject to constant intrigue and plotting.'[133] The Foreign Office achieved some success in establishing a development policy in the Trucial States.

The economic development of the Trucial States

During the last decade of Britain's imperial role in the Trucial States, the Foreign Office initiated a variety of policies that were designed to hand over powers to the rulers. The long-term objective was to prepare the Trucial States for independence. The economic development of the Trucial States originated in 1955, when a very modest programme was introduced. Some progress was made in the Trucial States, but the drawing together of the sheikhdoms by establishing common services failed. By 1960, advances had been made in the economic and social transformation of the Trucial States.[134] The most important areas of expenditure were in education, health care and agriculture, and the Foreign Office argued that development expenditure paid important political and social dividends.[135] As a result of spending money on development, the British were able to show that they were taking into consideration the welfare of the population, something the Government of India had conspicuously failed to do. The rulers continued to make no contribution towards the development scheme. Sheikh Shakhbut promised to allocate 4 per cent of Abu Dhabi's prospective oil income to development, and it was expected that the sheikhdom would bear the financial burden.

In 1960, the Foreign Office proposed a second five-year development programme for the Trucial States.[136] The scheme had a total expenditure of £1,005,000, and it had two political objectives. The first was to assert the Foreign Office's role as the architect of the programme. The second political purpose was to use the plan as the principal instrument for bringing about the federation of the Trucial States. The Treasury regarded the Foreign Office's estimate to be wayward because the first five-year plan only spent £334,000 out of the £430,000 that had been allocated.[137] As a result of this significant shortfall, the Treasury rejected the Foreign Office's programme because it was disproportionate. The significant underspending suggested that the Foreign Office had overestimated what could have been achieved, and the scale of expenditure per capita was much higher than in neighbouring Oman, which had a population of 550,000 compared with 80,000 in the Trucial States. The Treasury decided to grant £100,000 per annum over the following five years.[138] However, it did agree to a small increase in expenditure, but the significant shortfall in the budget led to suggestions that international organisations, such as the UN development agencies, and charities, including the Ford Foundation, might be approached to meet the shortfall.[139] The Foreign Office rejected external funding because it was concerned that it would lose its predominant position in providing aid. Furthermore, the introduction of international experts might accelerate changes that were not in Britain's interests, and foreign funding would not free the Foreign Office of its contribution. The Foreign Office therefore concluded that the Kuwaitis were a better alternative since they were interested in maintaining the status quo in the Trucial States.[140]

Restricted finances meant keeping in place schemes that had proved successful, and which represented the greatest prestige value. The objective of expenditure on agriculture was to consolidate earlier success, but public health provision remained the greatest area of expenditure. There was considerable criticism in the Trucial States about the modest scale and low standard of the health effort because the population remained overwhelmingly destitute.[141] The expansion of education was hindered by the shortage of money, and the British Council representative in the Gulf argued that the standard of teachers imported from Egypt and Kuwait was low.[142] Notwithstanding the limitations of the development programme caused by the Treasury's parsimony, the scheme was supposed to achieve a variety of important political objectives. The development programme was intended to show the rulers and their subjects the benefits of the British connection, and that stability could be maintained not only by the small military presence but also by improving the lives of the population. The Foreign Office also felt that it would be able to rebut charges of exploiting the Trucial States and to reinforce Britain's position in the Gulf by spending money on development. However, the limited amount of funds suggested to the population that the development programme was little more than a token effort.[143] The Treasury belatedly agreed to increase expenditure to £200,000 in December 1963, and the Foreign Office hoped that the rulers might be encouraged to cooperate, which failed on account of their perennial disputes. Notwithstanding the increase in developing expenditure, the figure was a small proportion of British spending in the Trucial States.[144] Between 1960 and 1964, the Foreign Office spent £6.5 million in the Trucial States, of which the Trucial Oman Scouts accounted for £6 million.[145]

The impact of development expenditure varied in the sheikhdoms, and the Foreign Office realised that it would not be able to retain control of development indefinitely.[146] Dubai remained the most prosperous sheikhdom, whereas the Political Agent at Dubai reported in early 1963 that there was no commercial activity in Ajman, Umm al Qaiwann and Fujairah.[147] However, the education programme was improving, with new schools being built, and the trade school at Sharjah was regarded as a notable success.[148] The development of the oil industry in Abu Dhabi suggested that in due course, money would be forthcoming from the sheikhdom to fund development in the other Trucial States. In August 1962, a telephone system and a new water-distillation plant were opened, but development in Abu Dhabi was very slow. In October 1965, Archie Lamb, the newly appointed Political Agent at Abu Dhabi, reported that nothing had changed since 1961.[149] He painted a bleak picture of the sheikhdom and reported that it was still a 'shanty town and a shambles', and that the key impediment to change in Abu Dhabi was the personality of the ruler, Sheikh Shakhbut, who had thwarted British advisors and consultants.[150] British consulting firms, such as Sir

William Halcrow and Sons and Brian Colquhoun and Partners, were appointed in 1963 to offer advice and to supervise the completion of construction work, including building a jetty and an airport.[151] The development programme was a notable example of the expansion of the British role in the Trucial States, and it also highlighted the limitations of British political and commercial influence.

The forthcoming affluence of Abu Dhabi called into question whether continued expenditure on development could be justified. Abu Dhabi's income increased from £2.3 million in 1963 to over £8 million in 1964, but capital expenditure only grew from £325,000 to £1.4 million in the same period.[152] James Craig, the Political Agent at Dubai (1961–4), noted it was difficult to know precisely what the rulers earned and spent because sheikhly rule required continuous benevolence. The rulers were involved in both expenditure on philanthropic causes and sporadic development, which was impossible to itemise. Nonetheless, Craig estimated that the income of the other rulers, with the exception of Dubai, was inconsequential.[153]

In May 1964, the Treasury became increasingly sceptical about the economic case for supporting the sheikhdoms, and pressure was exerted on the Foreign Office to demand that the rulers make a substantial contribution to the development scheme. The Treasury also argued that spending large sums on the Trucial States was justified when the states were impoverished, but it could no longer be sustained in light of Abu Dhabi's oil income. Moreover, the Treasury argued that it was perverse to continue paying for the Trucial Oman Scouts when Sheikh Shakhbut of Abu Dhabi, who benefited from their protection, would soon be receiving millions of pounds of oil income.[154] The Arab League's offer of substantial development assistance in 1965 led to a reversal of this approach for political reasons, which included the importance of maintaining British prestige at all costs. The economic prospects of the smaller sheikhdoms remained bleak, which is why they were the focus of British development expenditure.

Conclusion

The Foreign Office directed British policy in Trucial States during the long-running Conservative Government of 1951–64. There was minimal ministerial intervention in the making of British policy because the Trucial States and Gulf region were an imperial backwater and the final vestige of British imperialism in the Middle East. The Kuwait crisis in 1961 led to uncharacteristic ministerial intervention. Sir William Luce and the Political Agents in Abu Dhabi and Dubai acted on instructions that were sent from the Foreign Office, and were responsible for the consolidation and deepening of British influence in the Trucial States. Nonetheless, it was clear to the Foreign Office that the *Pax Britannica* could not continue indefinitely, and it was clear that withdrawal would occur by 1975. However, the change in government in London in 1964 led to a fundamental reappraisal of British policy in the Trucial States.

The Trucial States were scarcely affected by Arab nationalist sentiment in the early 1960s. Nevertheless, the region became the focus of radio propaganda that challenged the established order in the Trucial States. It became increasingly difficult for the Foreign Office to prevent the spread of Arab nationalist thinking in the Trucial States because of the growing number of Arab expatriates living in the sheikhdoms. The Trucial States were therefore gradually affected by regional trends, and in 1965, the Arab League made efforts to open an office in the Trucial States. The Foreign Office went to extraordinary lengths to preclude external forces in the Trucial States.

The Foreign Office's attempts to introduce a development policy continued during the early 1960s, but the programme was hindered by a shortage of funds. The development scheme was important because the Foreign Office had to show the population of the Trucial States that the British presence was beneficial. However, there was no question of introducing any political reforms in the Trucial States, and sheikhly rule remained the favoured form of government. British officials increasingly intervened in the internal affairs of the Trucial States because of the development programme, but the rulers remained immune from British attempts to reform their governments. Sheikh Shakhbut was a notable example of a ruler who was determined to protect his prerogatives and feared the development of the oil industry. The Foreign Office's attempts to overthrow Shakhbut in the early 1960s failed, and he was deposed in August 1966.

4

Responsibility without power

The vicissitudes of British policy in the Trucial States, 1964–7

British policy in the Trucial States was influenced by a variety of domestic economic and political considerations. Hitherto, the Foreign Office had directed British policy in the Trucial States, but between 1964 and 1967, Harold Wilson's Labour Government intervened on an unprecedented scale in the making of British policy. The Labour Government was riven with internal disputes about the value of the remnants of Empire, and domestic political considerations had a fundamental impact on the Wilson Government's policy East of Suez. The economic and strategic value of long-standing British commitments in the Persian Gulf was of secondary importance to the Labour Government.

The Trucial States were different from other examples of retreat from Empire because there was no indigenous demand for Britain's withdrawal. The most important economic and strategic justification for the continuation of the *Pax Britannica* was the growing importance of Gulf oil, and the maintenance of regional stability. The long-term objective was to create a situation in which Britain's obligation to protect the rulers could be terminated without damaging the security of oil supplies and the political stability of the region.

The Foreign Office faced other challenges in the Trucial States during the Wilson era. One of the notable characteristics of the long British role in the Trucial States was that it solidified the position of the ruling families of the sheikhdoms. By the 1960s, the Trucial States were starting to emerge from centuries of torpidity thanks to the development of the oil industry in Abu Dhabi and to Dubai's growing importance as the Trucial States' entrepôt. The five smaller or petty sheikhdoms remained economically and politically insignificant, but the rapid growth of income from oil entailed a radical transformation of the Trucial States. The Foreign Office faced significant challenges in its relations with the rulers of the Trucial States, who were reluctant to cooperate and, with the exception of Dubai, unwilling to take the necessary steps to develop their states. The Foreign Office's handling of Sheikh Shakhbut was a notable example of the extent to which the British were determined to intervene in the internal affairs of the sheikhdoms in order to secure their interests. In August 1966, Shakhbut's brother, Sheikh Zayed, deposed him, with full British support.

The Foreign Office and Ministry of Defence continued to fund the Trucial Oman Scouts because it was in Britain's strategic interests to maintain an effective fighting force in the Trucial States. Nonetheless, the establishment of the Abu Dhabi Defence Force (ADDF) in 1965 challenged the TOS's pre-eminent role in the Trucial States. The British could not prevent the rulers from forming their own armies, but they did play an important role in raising local security units. The Foreign Office was instrumental in the development of the police and intelligence capabilities of the Trucial States. The objective of these forces was to police the towns of the Trucial States and to counter potential subversive threats.

The development of oil economies in the Trucial States posed insuperable challenges for the British. The windfall oil income meant that the protected states had to establish an effective administrative system from scratch and devise development programmes. The experience in Kuwait in the 1950s showed that there were many obstacles to be overcome.[1] The Foreign Office also continued to spend money on the economic and social development of the Trucial States between 1965 and 1967. This policy was supposed to achieve certain objectives that included reinforcing British prestige in the Trucial States. The Foreign Office increased expenditure on development in 1965, in response to the Arab League's proposition to spend £1 million in the Trucial States. The Arab League's offer was the greatest potential threat to British predominance in the Trucial States, and the Foreign Office was determined to take all necessary steps to maintain British paramountcy. In 1965, the Foreign Office played a role in the deposition of the ruler of Sharjah, who welcomed the Arab League's intervention in the Trucial States.

Domestic influences on policy in the Trucial States

Domestic political forces back in Britain heavily influenced the Foreign Office's policy in the Trucial States and the Persian Gulf between 1965 and 1967. One of the most significant questions about the British role in the Trucial States, and in the Gulf in general, concerns the motives and timing of the decision to withdraw from East of Suez.[2] The continuation of British predominance in the Gulf was called into question in 1964, when the Labour Party came to power. During the election, Harold Wilson made much of the Labour Party's anticolonial tradition and denounced the Conservative folly in preserving the expensive trappings of power. He promised to reassess these 'entanglements' in light of Britain's limited resources. Wilson had championed Britain's East of Suez disposition, and feared Conservative criticism of any reduction in Britain's global status. He was influenced by the Labour Party tradition that asserted Britain's role as a world power, and he was reluctant to abandon positions of influence until they became untenable.[3] Saki Dockrill argues that when Wilson became Prime Minister in 1964, his government 'was subconsciously at least already prepared' for the decision to withdraw from East of Suez in 1968.[4] Members of the Cabinet were hostile to the East of Suez concept. Denis Healey, the Defence Secretary, described it as an 'anachronism', and George Brown argued that withdrawal was 'inevitable and essential'.[5] Gregory Gause is undoubtedly correct in arguing that the combination of budgetary constraints, opposition by the left in the Labour Party and a consensus of opinion that Britain must look to her future in Europe rather than in the Empire, placed growing pressure on Wilson's two governments in 1964–6 and 1966–70.[6]

Wilson's premiership was weakened by a succession of financial crises between November 1964 and June 1966 that led to deflation, cuts in government expenditure and heavy borrowing. The Treasury demanded that the defence budget be limited to £2 billion, resulting in the most far-reaching change in Britain's world role since the withdrawal from India in 1947. This meant that large-scale defence cuts were required, including the revocation of an election commitment that Britain would retain forces East of Suez.[7] The Labour Government planned to maintain the British presence East of Suez, and the Defence White Paper that was published in February 1965 stated that it would be 'politically irresponsible and economically wasteful' to withdraw.[8] Tore Petersen argues that the Labour defence reviews 'were part of Labour's plan to divest Britain of its bases East of Suez'.[9] In June 1965, Healey visited the Middle East, and he argued that there was a case for sending an additional infantry battalion to the Gulf.[10] In November 1965, the Defence and Oversea Policy (OPD) Committee, the highest-level policy committee chaired by the Prime Minister, concluded that the British military presence in the Gulf had been a major factor in keeping the peace, but the British should not envisage remaining in the region indefinitely. Defence facilities were needed to ensure security in

Bahrain, maintain Britain's ability to come to Kuwait's assistance and prevent any external threat to the protected states.[11] It was also concluded that British forces would remain in the Persian Gulf after the withdrawal from Aden.[12] It would not be possible to carry on in the Gulf after the withdrawal from Aden without the build-up of forces in the region to ensure the commitment to defend Kuwait.[13]

In November 1965, the Defence and Oversea Policy Committee decided that British forces would be retained in the Persian Gulf after the withdrawal from Aden.[14] In January 1966, the Chiefs of Staff produced a detailed account of the minimum forces and facilities that would be required in the Persian Gulf. The principal units were three frigates/destroyers, two infantry battalions and supporting arms and seven squadrons of aircraft.[15] The small increase in forces was acknowledged in the Defence Estimates that were published in February 1966, which stated that the withdrawal from Aden would occur in 1968.[16] The Labour Government announced that Britain would withdraw from Aden and the protectorates by 1968, but British forces would remain in Bahrain and Sharjah in the Trucial States.[17] This led to an increase in forces during 1967, from 3,677 to 6,234, which were based in Bahrain and Sharjah, and cost £10 million.[18] The Foreign Office was concerned that withdrawal would have unwelcome consequences in the Gulf, where the rulers were anxious that they would not be abandoned in the face of popular pressure and terrorism.[19] The retention of Aden was not essential to the position in the Gulf, provided that there was an increase in forces in the area to compensate for the withdrawal.[20]

In December 1965, the Arabian Department of the Foreign Office made it clear to the Labour Government that Britain's political and military position would not last beyond the mid-1970s. Britain's retreat from the Gulf was inevitable, and the most efficacious way of achieving stability was Saudi suzerainty or sovereignty over the sheikhdoms. Unless the British took steps to achieve an alternative pattern of stability, it was likely that the Saudis would be content to leave Bahrain and Qatar as satellites but would turn the Trucial States into a vassal. Alternatively, the British could use their remaining years in the Gulf to promote cohesion amongst the sheikhdoms.[21] The rulers of the Trucial States, and the Sultan of Oman, regarded the Saudis as a significant threat to their sovereignty, which was reinforced by the Saudis holding firm on their territorial claims that included three-quarters of Abu Dhabi.[22] The notion that the Saudis might replace the *Pax Britannica* also contradicted the long-standing policy of excluding foreign powers from the Trucial States. A far more significant concern for the British was the civil war in the Yemen, and the prospect of Britain's withdrawal from Aden and South Arabia.

The scale of British forces in the Gulf, which increased from 3,500 to 7,000, had significant political implications.[23] The Joint Intelligence Committee argued that the decision to withdraw from Aden indicated to the rulers of the Trucial States that Britain's interest in the Middle East was declining. If guarantees of continuing British interest were not reassuring to the rulers, they would probably feel that one British 'betrayal' might lead to another, and they would be inclined to seek protection from another state in the region. The British would not oppose Saudi protection, but Egyptian propaganda was bound to exploit the announcement to withdraw.[24] The Ministry of Defence was concerned that the presence of British forces in Bahrain and Sharjah would lead to increased hostile propaganda against the British position in the Gulf and on the rulers. The establishment of effective counter-subversion measures was therefore an urgent requirement, but the extent of the subversive and terrorist threat to the Trucial States was open to question.[25]

The Foreign Office believed that if withdrawal occurred in 1969–70, it would undermine the Anglo-American alliance that was regarded as a fundamental British interest. The CIA observed in June 1965 that since the Second World War, the erosion of Britain's position in the Mediterranean, Middle East and Africa had increased the importance of the Arabian Peninsula in British strategic thinking. From an American perspective, the British position in Arabia was challenged by a variety of unprecedented stresses, which included the future of Aden and the Arab League's determination to drive the British from Arabia.[26]

The State Department commented that the Labour Party had traditionally been deeply anticolonial, but its leaders recognised the necessity of a strong British presence East of Suez. Senior Labour figures told US officials that a Labour government would 'at all costs' maintain British strength and influence East of Suez.[27] President Lyndon B. Johnson was advised that no matter who was in office in London, the UK faced deep economic trouble, but it was in American interests for the British to stay in the Gulf.[28] British policy was reiterated in a series of summits. Britain's global role was discussed when Wilson and Johnson met in December 1965 and July 1966. Wilson made it clear both to Johnson and Defence Secretary Robert McNamara that the British would withdraw from Aden but the position in the Gulf would be reinforced.[29] The deepening war in Vietnam meant that the Americans increasingly valued the British military presence in the Gulf.[30] In July 1966, Wilson assured Johnson that the British would remain in the Gulf until the mid-1970s.[31] The President was advised that the USA should not press the British to maintain their role in the future for financial reasons.[32] The Americans received similar assurances in October 1966 from George Brown, the Foreign Secretary, who stated that the British had every intention to stay in the Gulf following the withdrawal from Aden.[33] There was no likelihood that these discussions would have led to any change in the decision to withdraw from Aden or to the proposed increase in facilities in the Gulf.[34]

The British convinced their American interlocutors of their intention to stay in the Gulf, but there were other considerations that influenced the situation. A precipitous departure from the Gulf would provide opportunities for the United Arab Republic and the Soviet Union to meddle in the region. Furthermore, it would risk the Iraqi conquest of Kuwait, the Saudis assuming control of Abu Dhabi, and war between Saudi Arabia and Muscat over the Buraimi Oasis.[35]

The Defence Review and the withdrawal from Aden were the source of anxiety in the Trucial States about the future of their protected status.[36] Likewise, Mohammad Reza Pahlavi, the Shah of Iran, wanted the British to maintain the status quo in the Gulf because of his fear of Arab nationalism.[37] The Shah also despaired of the Trucial States rulers' inability to work together.[38] The CIA argued that the Shah was developing a more active and independent foreign policy that was based on his fear of Nasser's capability of fomenting a revolution in the Arab world.[39] The Shah believed that Arab nationalism, personified by Nasser, was aiming to dominate the Persian Gulf area. His concern was heightened by Britain's diminishing role in the sheikhdoms, which led him to bolster Iran's defences.[40]

Despite Nasser's costly intervention in Yemen between 1962 and 1970, the Shah perceived little diminution in Nasser's influence, and he had ambitions to replace the British in the Gulf.[41] By 1967, the rulers of the Trucial States were becoming increasingly nervous about developments in the region. The withdrawal of British forces from Aden and South Arabia was a severe shock to the rulers of the Trucial States, who feared they would be abandoned.[42] Several parliamentary statements made by ministers that the British would stay in the Gulf did not convince the rulers,[43] and the Arab–Israel War in June 1967 heightened tensions.[44] The withdrawal from Aden that year antagonised relations with King Faisal of Saudi Arabia, and the Trucial States rulers were concerned that the Yemeni Revolution might spread to the sheikhdoms. The Foreign Office's objective in the Trucial States was to enable the rulers to stand independently, either collectively or individually, and make a contribution towards stability in the region.[45] In July 1967, the Wilson Government announced that it would withdraw forces from South-East Asia, but the Gulf was not mentioned because the Foreign Office was working on a comprehensive memorandum on the future of British policy in the Gulf. In September 1967, the Foreign Office concluded that:

After our decision to withdraw militarily as well as politically from Aden by 1968, no one really believes that we shall be able (or even wish) to stay indefinitely in the Gulf. By the mid-1970s we must expect a world where almost all colonial and quasi-colonial traces have disappeared and the overseas deployment of British power has contracted further than at present. If we have not gone from the Gulf, the pressures on us to are likely to be very severe indeed.[46]

The Foreign Office also believed that the union of the protected states was still regarded as unworkable, and Saudi protection would be unpopular with the rulers. The Foreign Office envisaged that once British protection was withdrawn, Bahrain, Qatar, Abu Dhabi and Dubai would become independent states. The smaller sheikhdoms would be absorbed by Abu Dhabi and Dubai, and this policy depended on Saudi cooperation and Iranian understanding. In December 1967, Sir Stewart Crawford, the Political Resident at Bahrain (1966–70), proposed Abu Dhabi's separation from the other Trucial States and the domination of Dubai over the five smaller sheikhdoms. A union of the seven sheikhdoms was regarded as impracticable because it would have demanded administrative skills from the members that they did not possess. The main impediment remained the rivalry between Abu Dhabi and Dubai, and union would not have satisfied Sheikh Zayed's ambition for his own state. More significantly, it was not wanted by the rulers and could not be imposed on them.[47]

The Foreign Office's attempts to persuade the rulers of its intention to stay came to the fore in the autumn of 1967. Goronwy Roberts, Minister of State in the Foreign Office, toured the Gulf in November 1967 in order to reassure the rulers that the British had no plans for withdrawing, nor had they set any time limit.[48] Denis Healey made a similar statement in the House of Commons on 8 November,[49] but Glen Balfour-Paul argues that 'there was indeed little sign of any constructive policy emerging in London for the long-term security of the Gulf'.[50] Roberts' assurance to the rulers that the British political and military presence would be retained for as long as necessary was short-lived. Schisms within the Labour Party led to the dramatic reversal of this policy in January 1968.[51]

Domestic political considerations outweighed all other interests for Wilson's government in the autumn of 1967. Jeffrey Pickering argues that political transformations caused by the devaluation of the pound in November 1967 from $2.80 to $2.40 had a more significant impact on the East of Suez role than economic concerns. Short-term political considerations outweighed any serious discussion of Britain's East of Suez role.[52] On 30 November, Roy Jenkins replaced James Callaghan as Chancellor, which led the Treasury to initiate discussions about the withdrawal from the Gulf. Shohei Sato shows that Jenkins failed to comprehend the implications of leaving the Gulf, and that the Labour Government's decision to withdraw was a way of justifying the reversal of domestic policies.[53] The economic case for withdrawal was tenuous because the saving in the Gulf was a paltry £12 million in foreign exchange costs and £25 million in budgetary costs, per annum.[54] The cost of the Persian Gulf commitment was inconsequential compared with oil revenues, which were valued at £200 million, and sterling balances, which were worth between £400 million and £500 million.[55] Roger Louis is undoubtedly correct in arguing that Wilson's decision to end the British role in the Gulf was related to the sterling crisis. The withdrawal from Aden was a 'crisis of disillusionment of empire' that was caused by Wilson's desire to rescue the British economy by taking severe measures in order to protect the welfare state rather than shore up the remains of the Empire.[56]

The threat of the Arab League

The most significant threat to British predominance in the Gulf occurred in 1964 and 1965. *Sawt al-Arab* had criticised the treaties with the Trucial States and British imperialism in the Gulf since the 1950s. In March 1964, there was an increase in Egyptian and Iraqi radio propaganda directed against British 'imperialism' in the Gulf. Baghdad and Cairo radios claimed that the British and the Iranians were working together against Arabism in the Gulf. In April 1965, *Sawt al-Arab* started broadcasting a fifteen-minute daily programme entitled 'Whirlwind in the Gulf'.[57] *Sawt al-Arab* was a highly influential propaganda tool, and it was used to broadcast a wide range of programmes that attacked British imperialism in the Middle East.

In March 1964, the Arab League Political Committee announced that Dr Abdul Khaliq Hassouna, the League's Secretary General, would lead a delegation to the Gulf to discuss limiting immigration into the sheikhdoms. The Arabian Department of the Foreign Office acknowledged that increasing interest in the Gulf on the part of the Arab states was inevitable, and the rulers could not put off the Arab League because it would conclude that the British were trying to keep 'Arabism' out of the Gulf.[58] The Foreign Office therefore faced an unprecedented information and propaganda challenge to its traditional predominance in the Gulf.

In October 1964, an Arab League mission visited the Trucial States in order to establish formal relations with the sheikhdoms,[59] and to study methods to maintain their Arab character in the face of immigration.[60] The rulers of Dubai and Qatar openly expressed their fears that the Arab League mission was the first step in Egyptian and Iraqi penetration of the Gulf. They agreed that they would listen to the delegation but that they had no intention of allowing the Arab League to open an office in their sheikhdoms.[61] In contrast, Sheikh Saqr bin Sultan Al Qasimi, the ruler of Sharjah (1951–65), adopted a favourable attitude towards the Arab League. Sheikh Saqr promised the Political Resident that he would not enter into any commitments with the Arab League. However, he was accused of fomenting disturbances.[62]

In early 1965, it was clear that the Arab League's attempt to penetrate the Trucial States would be launched in the impoverished smaller sheikhdoms. The Arab League offered the rulers £1.5 million as the first instalment of a programme of aid totalling £5 million. The Arab League's objective was to establish an office and carry out a development programme that would be independent of the Trucial States Council. Sir William Luce observed that the danger of political activity and subversion was obvious to all the rulers, with the exception of Sheikh Saqr and his cousin Sheikh Saqr bin Mohammed Al Qasimi, ruler of Ras Al Khaimah, who was the main local sponsor of the Arab League.[63] Sheikh Sultan was motivated by his 'intense jealousy' of Sheikh Rashid and by his ambition to become 'the big man' of the Trucial Coast. Sheikh Saqr's support of the Arab League led to an 'acute expectancy' throughout the Gulf about how the British Government would handle the situation.[64]

The Foreign Office viewed the Arab League's intervention with considerable apprehension, and it adopted a tough policy because it was convinced that it was a long-term objective of Nasser's to 'liquidate the British position in the Gulf'.[65] In January 1965, Luce argued that the Arab League and Egypt were indistinguishable. He hypothesised that if an Arab League development office was established, the consequences for Britain's standing would be serious because it would allow the Egyptians to establish a permanent base for subversion and political indoctrination. The British were concerned that if the rulers accepted Arab League economic assistance, it would be an invaluable vehicle to intimidate them.[66] Luce also contended that the most efficacious means of countering the Arab League threat was to enlist the support of the Kuwaiti and Saudi governments on the grounds that they had a mutual interest in preventing the Arab League from entering the Gulf. This approach would be reinforced by additional British and Qatari financial assistance.[67] The Shah and King Faisal expressed their alarm and anxiety that the Foreign Office should keep the Arab League out of the Gulf, and they hinted that if the British failed to do so, then they would be forced to intervene. The establishment of an Egyptian bridgehead in the Gulf would have undermined the confidence of both monarchs, and possibly affected Iran's alignment with the West.[68]

Sir William Luce described the disastrous consequences if the British Government ignored the situation.[69] The Political Resident argued that if the Foreign Office failed to prevent the establishment of an Arab League office, 'we shall look back on 1965 as the beginning of the end of our power to maintain stability in this area'. Luce advised that the rulers should pass a resolution in the Trucial States Council, welcoming aid from any source, but this assistance should be channelled through their own development fund. Sheikh Saqr, the ruler of Sharjah, remained wedded to the Arab League, but Luce erroneously believed that he would be able to 'frighten him into acquiescence'.[70] The Foreign Office was forced to adopt more direct methods, including the overthrow of Saqr in June 1965.

The situation in the Gulf reached its apotheosis in May 1965. Dr Sayed Nofal, the Assistant Secretary General of the Arab League, visited the Gulf and set about obtaining letters from the rulers of Sharjah and Ras Al Khaimah agreeing to the opening of Arab League offices in their states, and letters from the three smaller sheikhdoms agreeing to accept aid from the League.[71] Coincidentally, George Thomson, the Minister of State for Foreign Affairs, visited the Gulf and warned Sheikh Saqr that establishing an Arab League office in his sheikhdom was in breach of his treaty with the British regarding external affairs.[72]

Luce wrote that these developments were more dangerous and difficult than any previous peril, including the Iraqi threat to invade Kuwait in 1961, because they exploited disaffected elements within the Trucial States. He feared that if the Arab League succeeded, it would undermine the British position and create a power vacuum.[73] The rulers of Bahrain, Qatar, Abu Dhabi and Dubai looked to the Foreign Office to protect them from the Arab League.[74] Their confidence in the British was related to the extent and success of the Foreign Office's efforts to prevent the Arab League from penetrating the sheikhdoms.[75]

The CIA noted that the dissident sheikhs seemed determined to accept the Arab League's aid, and their recalcitrance violated the treaties with the British. It believed that the British were determined to stand firm but they seemed undecided how to prevent the Arab League presence in the sheikhdoms.[76] Luce and Glen Balfour-Paul, the Political Agent at Dubai, failed to persuade the rulers to decline aid from the Arab League. Luce argued that: 'we have now reached a situation which requires a decision of major importance to the future of our position and interests in the Gulf'. He contended that the other Gulf rulers and the Saudis regarded the situation as a major test of the Foreign Office's determination to 'resist the dangers of Egyptian penetration, and our prestige and ability to influence future developments will ... depend on the way we handle it'.[77] The Foreign Office took various steps to meet this unprecedented challenge to its predominance. The failure to persuade the rulers of the five northern sheikhdoms meant that the Foreign Office had to prevent Arab League personnel from entering the Trucial States. The British closed all the airfields in the Trucial States in May 1965, and domination of the sheikhdoms' external relations meant that the British controlled immigration into the Trucial States.[78] The British relied on administrative measures to deny visas to Arab League personnel. However, the legality of these measures was open to question.[79]

Sheikh's Saqr's refusal to follow British advice meant that steps were taken in 1965 to secure his deposition.[80] The Foreign Office's policy is hard to accurately assess because a variety of documents concerning its stance towards Sheikh Saqr are unavailable.[81] The Foreign Office believed that it could rescind Saqr's protection,[82] but it resorted to traditional mechanisms and Saqr's family asserted their rights and, on 24 June, replaced him with his brother, Khalid bin Mohammed.[83] The official account of Saqr's overthrow argues that he was deposed on the grounds of his neglect of his subjects, misgovernment of the sheikhdom, extravagance and his dissolute way of life.[84] Helene Von Bismarck is undoubtedly correct in arguing that the Foreign Office's account of its role in deposing Sheikh Saqr is unconvincing.[85] The Defence Review Working Party report of June 1967 commented that: 'we had no constitutional sanction and were obliged to organise his (Saqr's) deposition by indirect means'.[86] A TOS intelligence report provides additional details about how Saqr was overthrown and the British role in his deposition.[87] The CIA observed that there was little doubt that 'British manoeuvring' was behind Saqr's removal,[88] and President Johnson was briefed by the Agency that the 'ruler of Sharjah has been ousted certainly with British connivance. The other four are likely to take the hint.'[89] The overthrow of Saqr sent an unambiguous message that the British would not tolerate rulers who acted against British interests.[90] Shortly after being deposed, Saqr condemned the British on Baghdad and Cairo radio. He denied that his dismissal was the result of family differences, and accused the British of trying to isolate the sheikhdoms from the Arab League.[91]

The Foreign Office succeeded in preventing the Arab League from penetrating the Trucial States in 1965, and it also sent a clear message to the rulers that it would not tolerate flagrant violations of the treaties. Although the Political Resident averted a disaster, the Trucial States were now inescapably part of the Arab world and 'subject to the strains and stresses which that dubious privilege entails'.[92] Anthony Parsons argued that if Nasser, who was preoccupied with the civil war in Yemen, had launched an all-out propaganda campaign against the British and the sheikhs, the region might have become a second Aden.[93] The CIA believed that Nasser's standing was declining as a result of the UAR's expensive intervention in Yemen's civil war.[94] The UAR deployed 50,000 men to Yemen, which compounded domestic economic dislocation, and led to the requirement to spend a large amount of foreign exchange to buy food due to the stoppage of American aid. However, the Arab League's attempt to intervene did lead to an unprecedented increase in development aid in the Trucial States.[95] Nonetheless, the rulers failed to take advantage of this crisis, and a meeting of the sheikhs of Bahrain, Qatar and the Trucial States at Dubai in July 1965 achieved very little. The rulers declined to make any progress on federation, and the rulers of Abu Dhabi and Dubai were unwilling to pledge a fixed percentage of their oil revenues as an annual contribution to the Development Fund.[96]

Overthrowing Shakhbut

One of the most significant challenges successive Political Residents faced was how to handle rulers who declined to follow British advice. Shaikh Shakhbut, the ruler of Abu Dhabi, was a notable example of a ruler who frustrated the British. Until the development of the oil industry and the rapid economic growth that it entailed, the Foreign Office showed little interest in the conduct of the rulers. The onset of the oil economy in Abu Dhabi after 1962 transformed British attitudes because they were unwilling to tolerate Shakhbut's misrule. Furthermore, the Foreign Office could not condone rulers who defied their treaty commitments because it would undermine British prestige.

As we have seen, the Foreign Office started to plan Shakhbut's overthrow in April 1962, but it failed to make a coherent case for this manoeuvre. The argument for deposing Shakhbut was tenuous, and between January 1965 and August 1966, the extent of British plotting to overthrow him is unclear.[97] In November 1965, Archie Lamb, Boustead's successor as Political Agent, characterised Abu Dhabi as a shanty town, and saw Shakhbut as the main obstacle to change. Lamb noted that Shakhbut cooperated with the British because it was in his interests to do so. British protection solidified Shakhbut's rule, and he cooperated with the Foreign Office because he knew that without it, the Saudis would have taken control of Abu Dhabi. Lamb argued that Shakhbut's brothers failed to persuade him to adopt constructive administrative and financial policies during his final years as ruler. Shakhbut had absolute control over his family and subjects, and 'cajolery and persuasion' were the only methods available to the British.[98] In November 1965, Lamb prepared a memorandum on government organisation and financial control at Shakhbut's behest.[99] Although Shakhbut accepted proposals for the creation of a government in Abu Dhabi, Lamb and other British officials were suspicious of the ruler's intentions because of his focus on minor details as a delaying tactic. In early 1966, Shakhbut appeared to make progress in the establishment of an administration and the expansion of development projects.[100]

In July 1966, Sir William Luce retired from Bahrain and his departure was widely lamented. Anthony Parsons (Political Agent at Bahrain, 1965–9) commented that Luce's departure 'was mourned throughout the Gulf by Arabs and British alike'. He argued that Luce had 'secured the love as well as the respect of the rulers from Muscat to Bahrain and Qatar: his personal prestige and influence were great'.[101] Luce commented in his valedictory despatch that Abu Dhabi had been a constant worry during his tenure. He believed that the future of Abu Dhabi was the main problem the British faced in the Gulf, and it was more than just a question of Shakhbut's 'unbalanced and inept' rule. Abu Dhabi's rapidly growing income inevitably meant that the sheikhdom would be increasingly scrutinised, and that the British Government would be criticised for its association with such a 'disreputable and wholly inadequate regime'. Luce reiterated the case for removing Shakhbut on the grounds that he was a major obstacle in the way of British attempts to promote good relations and cooperation between the Gulf States. Shakhbut's refusal to cooperate with his neighbours was compounded by his poor relations with King Faisal, which meant it would be impossible to make progress on the intractable Buraimi Oasis dispute while the ruler was still in power.[102] Saudi influence in the Trucial States remained significant, and King Faisal thought that the sheikhdoms were 'historically, geographically and politically' Saudi Arabia's preserve.[103]

Sheikh Zayed was confronted with Abu Dhabi's future during a visit to the UK in the summer of 1966, and when he returned, tribal leaders apparently threatened to take matters into their own hands.[104] As a result of these developments, Sheikh Zayed was compelled to take action with British assistance. On 6 August 1966, Shakhbut was finally deposed by his family and replaced by Sheikh Zayed as ruler of Abu Dhabi.[105] Balfour-Paul, who was serving as Acting Political Resident at Bahrain, played a key role in Shakhbut's overthrow because Luce had just retired and Lamb was on leave.[106] The operation to remove the ruler took place in great secrecy, and Balfour-Paul was responsible for telling

Shakhbut that his family wanted him to abdicate. The TOS was instrumental in Shakhbut's overthrow because A Squadron was sent to Abu Dhabi, where it neutralised the ADDF barracks, took control of the telephone system and surrounded the ruler's palace. TOS officers escorted Shakhbut to the airport, where he was flown to Bahrain, followed by exile in Iran.[107] Subsequently, he was allowed to return to Abu Dhabi, and <u>he spent the rest of his life as a respected tribal elder at Buraimi.</u> *The Daily Telegraph*'s correspondent described these events in detail but his account was never published.[108]

The overthrow of Shakhbut was bloodless in contrast with his predecessors, and it showed that the TOS's role went beyond the maintenance of internal security and defending the Trucial States' boundaries. This episode also shows that the TOS was an instrument of British policy, although it was meant to be the army of the Trucial States. In June 1967, the Cabinet Office in London produced a detailed report on British policy in the Gulf. This document observed that the Foreign Office had no constitutional sanction to overthrow recalcitrant rulers but it had 'supported the deposition of the incorrigible Sheikh Shakhbut'. Moreover, it noted that: 'it is conceivable that we could repeat such operations in the future (particularly in the Trucial States where the main local security force, the Trucial Oman Scouts, is under our Political Resident's orders). But they are very much of a last resort and politically most embarrassing.'[109]

Shakhbut's overthrow concerned the other rulers. Sheikh Rashid, the ruler of Dubai, was extremely disturbed, despite his bitter feud with Shakhbut. He professed to see in Shakhbut's deposition a radical departure in Britain's policy of non-interference in the internal affairs of the sheikhdoms.[110] He was also alarmed that the TOS had been used to remove Shakhbut, but his concern might have been inspired by his displeasure at the emergence of Sheikh Zayed, who was influential through his charismatic personality and wealth.[111] Shakhbut's overthrow served its main objective, which was to show the rulers that misrule would not be tolerated. The Foreign Office declined to give Sheikh Rashid an assurance that the British were committed to maintaining him in power. Frank Brenchley, the Head of the Arabian Department, argued that it was not in the Foreign Office's interests that the rulers should believe the British would keep them in power against the wishes of their subjects, however badly they ruled.[112]

Sheikh Zayed's accession to power marked a significant transformation in the fortunes of the Trucial States. David Roberts, the Political Agent at Dubai, wrote that Sheikh Rashid was no longer 'in a different class' from the other rulers. They 'found in Zayed a potential source of bounty' that would allow them to enrich their impoverished sheikhdoms. Most significantly, the possibility that Sheikhs and Zayed might cooperate, in spite of traditional obstacles, offered the best hope that progress might be achieved towards wider cooperation between all the sheikhdoms.[113]

In November 1966, Archie Lamb wrote about Sheikh Zayed and Abu Dhabi's economic and social circumstances. Lamb portrayed Zayed in glowing terms, describing him as 'probably the European ideal of the romantic Arab Sheikh: youngish, good looking in the Bedu way, cheerful and generous, gallant to European ladies'. Lamb added that Zayed 'enjoys playing the part of an Arab Sheikh, "father of the people", and cannot resist showing off to European visitors his *majlis* when he is receiving greetings and petitions from his bedu subjects'. The most important question was, 'what sort of client have HMG in Sheikh Zayed?' Lamb believed that Zayed 'is certain to play a bigger and more positive part than his predecessor'. Lamb argued that Sheikh Zayed was conscious of his dependence on the British 'and his wish to give us a very special position in Abu Dhabi (his own preference would be an all-British senior administration) could be embarrassing politically if advantageous administratively to Abu Dhabi and commercially to the UK'. Sheikh Zayed had no interest in pandering to pan-Arab sentiment, and he regarded his future position as an 'Arabian, rather than Arab, ruler'. Lamb advised that Abu Dhabi should no longer be regarded as just one of the Trucial States because Zayed would not permit the Trucial States Council to play any role in the internal affairs of the sheikhdom. Abu Dhabi's predominant position meant that it should be regarded as an independent sheikhdom, whose size and wealth were greater than the other Trucial States. Lamb reported that Zayed was ready and eager to accept British advice and assistance, and it should be given because it was in Britain's financial and commercial interests. Furthermore, the rapid and successful development of Abu Dhabi was in Britain's short-term interests, and in the longer term, it would be beneficial if the sheikhdom played a role in a wider Arabian grouping.[114]

There was a variety of impediments that hindered development. Abu Dhabi remained a tribal society, and no advances had been made towards setting up a comprehensive education system. The tribes continued to support the rulers during the 1960s because of the 'good things in life with which he can provide', which included security against attack and the protection of their livelihood and, in a rich state like Abu Dhabi, money. The function of the ruler was to distribute the wealth of the sheikhdom to his subjects by offering cash grants and, indirectly, by providing jobs in the oil fields and on development projects. However, a key problem lay in education. It was estimated that it would take a minimum of six years before more than a 'sprinkling of Abu Dhabians can be called educated'. This meant that the Trucial States could not exist without foreign manpower and skills. There were no quick and easy solutions to the economic and social problems facing Sheikh Zayed. The role of the Foreign Office was to persuade him to adopt a phased development programme so that the needs of the sheikhdoms could be seen in advance, and to get him to accept expert advice on the economic and social development of the state.[115]

In 1967, progress had been made, and Sheikh Zayed was willing to follow the advice of his British advisors. All the same, he was criticised for his 'ingrained inability to announce unpalatable decisions'. Zayed believed that Abu Dhabi was the 'big brother' of the Trucial States, and his objective was to bind the five smaller sheikhdoms to him by financial support through the Trucial States Development Fund. He donated almost £2 million to the Fund, but he was opposed to interdependence between the Trucial States. His attempt to dominate the Trucial States, which was reinforced by 'an exaggerated view of his own diplomatic ability', increased his rivalry with Sheikh Rashid.[116] The Foreign Office encouraged Sheikh Zayed to develop his external relations, which resulted in embittering a border dispute with Qatar, and aggravated King Faisal because of the Buraimi Oasis dispute that remained unresolved.

Security forces and intelligence in the Trucial States

The Foreign Office took significant steps during the 1960s to enhance the police and security forces in the Trucial States. The Trucial Oman Scouts continued to be the most cost-effective mechanism for defending the Trucial States. The Scouts' most important and enduring role was the maintenance of peace and security in the Trucial States.[117] They were an internal security force tasked with guarding against and deterring an armed incursion of the Trucial States. It was gradually militarised, which concerned officials such as Donald Hawley, who believed that it must adhere to its policing role.[118] The TOS was based at a headquarters at Sharjah, and made up of five rifle squadrons, a support group, a training squadron supported by signals, transport, medical, education, ordnance and repairs services. The Trucial States were divided into squadron areas of responsibility and each rifle squadron patrolled its region, meeting as many inhabitants as possible, learning about local activities and dealing with tribal and other incidents. The function of the support group was to provide extra firepower with mortars and heavy machine guns to back up the rifle squadrons.[119] The

Scouts would routinely rotate around the Trucial States, known as 'Operation Roundabout', and took part in operations in neighbouring Oman.

The Scouts had successfully served on operations in Oman in 1957–9, and in December 1961, Luce argued that they should be available to support the Sultan's Armed Forces (SAF) in an emergency.[120] The Foreign Office supported Luce's views, but utilising the TOS in Oman was politically controversial because it undercut the argument that the Scouts were meant to be the army of the Trucial States.[121] More significantly, the Sultan of Oman was opposed to the Scouts' presence, and the SAF's increased operational capability meant that the TOS was no longer needed. The case for utilising the Scouts in Oman was also weakened by the rulers' opposition to the Scouts being employed to bolster an unpopular Sultan. Dispatching the Scouts to Oman also contradicted the British policy of encouraging the rulers to regard the Scouts as their force.[122]

The TOS was also very effective in preventing the long-standing tribal tradition of raiding and disputes between the states.[123] The maintenance of peace in the sheikhdoms was one of the most significant benefits of the British contribution in the Trucial States, and British officers and other ranks played a central role in commanding the Scouts. By 1960, the TOS had become an efficient and capable force, and it was the largest single item of British expenditure in the Trucial States. In 1960, the Scouts cost £958,081 and numbered 1,376 men. The TOS were useful because they provided tangible evidence of Britain's determination to defend the Trucial States, and it was much cheaper than deploying British ground forces. It was a cardinal principle that it was undesirable for British troops to become involved in internal security, except in extreme emergencies. It was the role of local police and security forces such as the TOS to handle internal security.[124]

In 1961, the Foreign Office sent a colonial policing expert to advise on the establishment of police forces in the five smaller sheikhdoms.[125] Luce rejected proposals that a police force should be established in the northern sheikhdoms because, he argued, they were nothing more than large villages and crime was minimal.[126] He believed there was no need for a police force in the smaller sheikhdoms, but he did argue that the TOS should establish a police wing that would operate in parts of the Trucial States where local police forces were absent in order to suppress traffic in slaves and weapons. Except in an emergency, the TOS police wing was forbidden to operate within any town that was the capital of a ruler or within their palaces without instructions from the Political Agent.[127] This proposal failed because the rulers would not allow the TOS police wing to operate in the towns. In contrast, the Dubai Police countered Omani rebels and smugglers in the town, which led the Foreign Office to support the establishment of police forces in the sheikhdoms.[128] The Abu Dhabi Police numbered 450 officers, who were recruited mainly from Buraimi. They were still ineffective because Shakhbut failed to pay their salaries.[129] The Dubai Police was a much smaller force, numbering 194 men, but was commanded by British officers and capable of maintaining security. The smaller sheikhdoms either had no police forces or they were little more than palace guards.[130]

The Scouts proved that they were capable of maintaining internal security in the Trucial States, including being dispatched to Abu Dhabi in 1963 to quell rioting oil workers.[131] The Scouts were sent to oilfields because the Abu Dhabi Police were totally ineffective and were neither trained nor equipped to handle riots.[132] The financial case for the continued funding of the TOS was hard to sustain, and the Treasury argued that there was no economic case for ongoing outlays, in light of Abu Dhabi's rapidly increased wealth.[133] The Treasury wanted Sheikh Shakhbut to make a contribution towards his defence, and in 1963, the ruler stated that he intended to establish his own army. His desire to raise an army meant it was very unlikely that he would make any contribution to the annual cost of the TOS.[134] The TOS was supposed to be the army of the Trucial States, but this notion was called into question in 1964, when Shakhbut established the ADDF. Shakhbut probably wanted to raise an army because he was concerned about his own security, and as a result of his growing oil income, he could afford it. Moreover, a small force was prestigious and would be valuable in handling disorder in Abu Dhabi's oil fields.[135]

The Foreign Office was initially very sceptical about supporting the establishment of the ADDF, but Luce recommended that it was in Britain's interests to assist Shakhbut in establishing a reasonably efficient force.[136] There were clear financial benefits, including the sale of weapons to Abu Dhabi, which is why the Abu Dhabi Political Agency rejected the arrival of arms salesmen because 'it might merely put ideas into the ruler's head, causing him to order expensive toys the army does not really need'.[137] There was nothing the Foreign Office could do to prevent Shakhbut, or any other ruler, from raising his own army or importing weapons. This led it to conclude that it should assist Shakhbut by selling arms and providing officers to train the ADDF.[138] The objective was to assure direct British influence, and to potentially reduce the size of the TOS once the ADDF was in a position to take over from the Scouts at Buraimi and in the oil fields.[139]

Shakhbut insisted that British officers command the ADDF and the TOS allocated two officers. By April 1966, only 158 men had been recruited, but considerable rivalry developed between the ADDF and the TOS.[140] The ADDF was a sheikhly force, which meant it could be paid and equipped 'almost at the whim of the ruler', whereas the TOS only received increases in equipment and pay once a detailed case had been submitted to Whitehall for approval.[141] The expansion of the ADDF depended entirely on the ruler's willingness to spend large sums, and it was hard to know when it would become operational.[142]

The TOS remained the most important security force in the Trucial States despite the establishment of the ADDF. In September 1964, James Craig, the Political Agent at Dubai, argued that the TOS had peacefully imposed stability and, without it, the states would have reverted to war and been exposed to external aggression.[143] However, the Scouts faced a variety of limitations. The War Office argued that the Scouts should be expanded to meet a wider range of operational requirements, but it was debatable how long the TOS could hold off a concerted attack from Saudi Arabia. Since its inception, a British officer had commanded the Scouts, and in 1966, there were 45 British officers and 111 other ranks, but there was a compelling case for reducing the number of British personnel. Experience in Jordan showed that British officers were potentially a lightning rod for nationalist agitation that called into question the sovereign control of armed forces. There was, therefore, a political requirement to reduce overt British control and train Arabs to command the Scouts. Arabisation was initiated in May 1962, and in 1964, Colonel H. J. Bartholomew, the Commander of the Scouts, argued that Arabisation should take place as quickly as feasible, and that the ultimate aim was to produce a force that was completely non-British.[144] This objective was never achieved and a British officer always commanded the Scouts.

The TOS also had a limited intelligence capability that was based on a handful of Desert Intelligence Officers (DIO), whose role was to obtain intelligence on dissident and subversive activities.[145] This glaring limitation came to the fore in 1964 and 1965, when the Trucial States were subjected to intense Arab nationalist propaganda and were potentially threatened by subversive activity. The Joint Intelligence Committee produced a series of assessments between 1965 and 1967 that reported on the extent of the subversive threat in the Gulf. In the Trucial States, the deposition of Sheikh Saqr, the ruler of Sharjah, in June 1965, had a salutary effect on internal security and on the other rulers, but there were signs that Arab nationalist sentiment was increasing.[146] The analysts in London assumed that the TOS would be able to counter internal subversion, but they were concerned about the vulnerability to sabotage of oil-production facilities and shipping.

These events brought home the urgent need to improve the intelligence organisation in the Trucial States.[147] The Trucial States were characterised by the absence of an effective intelligence and special branch capability. Two DIOs were responsible for the collection and analysis of intelligence on dissident and subversive activities and groups.[148] A Local Intelligence Committee already existed that included the Political Resident's political intelligence officer, an intelligence officer from each of the three Service headquarters in Bahrain, and the Resident's deputy as chairman. The weakness of this organisation was that all of its members were preoccupied with their professional duties and could not give sustained attention to the intelligence picture in the region.

In order to overcome this weakness, the Bahrain Residency proposed the establishment of a Gulf Intelligence Centre (GIC) to collect, collate, evaluate and disseminate intelligence.[149] The reorganisation of the organisation of intelligence was accepted in Whitehall, and at the end of 1965, the GIC was established and permanently staffed by professional intelligence officers, responsible to the Political Resident.[150] Luce was instrumental in the establishment of a special branch organisation in the Trucial States and in reinforcing Bahrain's existing counter-subversion capability.[151] Bahrain was the most vulnerable state, with its comparatively large urban and student population. The police and special branch in Bahrain were rapidly reorganised and re-equipped at the Bahrain Government's expense, and the Ministry of Defence helped to recruit officers.[152]

Luce proposed that a special branch should be established in Dubai, led by two British officers with a staff of thirty. He also argued that a special branch be raised in Abu Dhabi that would be responsible for domestic intelligence operations in the remaining Trucial States. In Abu Dhabi, the intelligence task consisted of keeping watch on subversives among the people and tribes of the sheikhdom, immigrants from the neighbouring sheikhdoms, labour organisations in the oil fields and of attempts to establish links between these groups. Raising an effective intelligence organisation was hindered by Shakhbut's unwillingness to pay for intelligence officers and a police force that was unsuited to this role.[153]

The expansion of intelligence organisations was reinforced by a variety of other proposals that were intended to enhance the domestic security organisation in the Trucial States. These included strengthening the Dubai Police, the establishment of a small police force in Sharjah and increasing the number of DIOs to five. The maintenance of internal security in the Trucial States and Bahrain required a wider range of measures. Luce argued that more needed to be done in the realm of domestic propaganda and to enhance the role of the British

Council in Bahrain. To achieve these objectives, an information officer was appointed to counter hostile propaganda against British interests and those of the rulers, and also to improve the image of the rulers in the outside world. The strengthening of police forces and special branches initially cost £26,500 in 1966, with a recurrent annual expenditure of £105,000.[154]

In May 1966, the JIC argued that the UAR and Iraqi intelligence services supported subversion and terrorist activities in the Gulf. Although their interests coincided, there was little indication of recent cooperation between them. There was a growth in subversive activity in the Trucial States, and the influx of a large number of foreign labourers in the construction of the oil industry risked a growth in subversive activity. Bahrain was regarded as the principal target for subversion, on account of its accessibility and the British presence. Successful attacks on expatriate police officers in March 1966 showed a new level of sophistication, and isolated cases of murder and sabotage were anticipated.[155]

Colonel Freddie de Butts, the Commander of the TOS during 1964–7, reported in May 1966 that there was a shortage of candidates suitable for officer training, and he doubted whether Arab officers commanding the Scouts' rifle squadrons could be impartial in disputes the TOS settled.[156] De Butts believed that Arab officers could be trained in Jordan, and it would be possible to gradually introduce new officers because there was no political pressure to Arabise rapidly. By 1967, the ratio of British to Arab officers was three to two, which meant it was very important to select suitable British officers.

The rulers and their subjects perceived the Scouts as 'al-Geish al-Inglise' (the English Army) because they were under the direct control of the Political Resident and closely associated with British forces based at Sharjah airfield. In order to prevent the TOS from being regarded as 'British auxiliaries', they were moved to a new camp outside Sharjah at the end of 1967.[157] The Scouts were run along the lines of a British Army unit, and de Butts noted that the Scouts' relations with the rulers were hard to define. If a ruler requested assistance, it would be provided after consultation with the Political Agent, but the Scouts would not provide assistance if it was contrary to British interests. In spite of their British image, the Scouts were well respected in the Trucial States as they were the single most important factor in maintaining internal stability.[158]

When the ADDF was established, it was envisaged that it would be possible to reduce the strength of the TOS by one squadron in April 1967, and possibly by another in 1968. The slow expansion of the ADDF, and the forthcoming withdrawal from Aden and South Arabia in 1967, undermined the case for reducing the TOS. The growth of subversion in the Trucial States called into question the viability and limited ability of local security forces.[159] These concerns reinforced the case for maintaining the TOS at its current strength.

The British had to contend with other problems with the Scouts. The Ministry of Defence, which was responsible for appointing new officers, found it increasingly difficult to select a new commander of the Scouts in 1967 because of declining Middle East commitments. This meant that fewer officers with the necessary seniority and experience were available.[160] There was also growing evidence of ill discipline amongst the Arab soldiers serving in the Scouts. No clear explanation for this problem was established, but morale fell and soldiers were leaving in order to serve in the better-paid ADDF.[161] The Foreign Office was consistently pressurised by the Treasury to cut costs by reducing the number of TOS squadrons.[162] Crawford argued that this was out of the question because 'we cannot administer this kind of shock now or in the near future'.[163] He also rejected the notion that some of the cost of the TOS should be transferred to the rulers, who would then pay in proportion to their income, since it would complicate control of the TOS.[164] The TOS remained the private army of the Political Resident, but in 1967, the British military presence in the Gulf grew when two infantry battalions, a headquarters and supporting arms were deployed to Bahrain and Sharjah. The arrival of British troops did not have a bearing on the role of the TOS because they were part of the defence plan for the region, rather than being responsible for patrolling the Trucial States.[165]

Inevitably, other rulers wanted to establish their own armed forces.[166] Sheikh Rashid, the ruler of Dubai, expressed interest in the autumn of 1967 in creating a defence force, which was regarded by the Foreign Office as regrettable but inevitable in the long term.[167] By the end of 1967, Sheikh Rashid had done nothing about establishing an army because he could not afford it. Every effort was made to discourage him since establishing an army in Dubai made no military sense, and it might exacerbate relations with Abu Dhabi. Instead, he was encouraged to expand his police force, which had proven to be capable of handling crime and security in the town.[168]

There were several problems in recruiting suitable Arab officers, which included the level of education in the uniformed branches of the Police and TOS. Expanding the size of the special branches was also hindered because the population believed they were formed to extend the intelligence coverage of the British. Another problem was that the salary scales of the Police compared unfavourably with pay in businesses, making it difficult to recruit educated officers. An additional impediment was Sheikh Zayed's demand that his own nationals be recruited into the Special Branch. The Foreign Office recognised that care had to be taken to show the population that the Special Branches were the guardians of law and order. This meant that the British connection with the Special Branches was downplayed, and the rulers had to be consulted about the suitability of candidates. However, the establishment of the TOS Special Branch, which was based on the existing DIO system, was regarded as a new departure for the Scouts because it marked their intervention in the towns. The TOS had significant advantages over the police forces since they could recruit personnel regardless of nationality, and it had the right to operate across state borders. The TOS Special Branch was recognised 'as a bird of the same feather; it is therefore necessary to disguise as far as possible the Special Branches' methods of operation'.[169] The most important focus for the TOS's operations were Ras Al Khaimah and Sharjah because they had a history of subversion. The head of the TOS Special Branch was therefore responsible for intelligence coordination in the Northern Trucial States. In spite of these efforts, establishing special branches in the Trucial States was not straightforward, and by December 1967, progress had been limited since recruitment was slow and cooperation between the states was difficult to achieve.[170] Nonetheless, the steps marked an important development in the establishment of an internal security organisation in the Trucial States.

In May 1967, the CIA estimated that in the Trucial States, there were stirrings of political activity in the towns where education was still limited and where expatriate Arabs were employed. The focus of political discord was confined to dynastic infighting and disputes over boundaries and oil rights.[171] Nonetheless, representatives of the Security Service (MI5) visited the Gulf annually to advise on counter-sabotage measures, but the state of knowledge on subversive groups was limited, making it difficult to make an accurate assessment.[172] The Security Service was reluctant to send a representative to the Gulf in 1966 because it believed that there was not enough work to justify permanent representation. However, the Political Resident and Chiefs of Staff supported the appointment of a permanent Security Service officer in the Gulf.[173] The JIC dispatched a Security Liaison Officer to Bahrain in early 1967 to provide the Political Resident with an enhanced intelligence capability.[174] By August 1967, the Trucial States Special Branches numbered seventeen officers, including five British specialists.

The Arab–Israeli War in June 1967 had far-reaching implications in the Gulf. Riots broke out in Doha and Dubai and extensive damage was inflicted but the police managed to handle the situation.[175] Two Arab officers serving in the TOS resigned, and the war played an important role in drawing the sheikhdoms into the Arab world.[176] Bahrain remained peaceful, which was attributed to the ruler's 'patriarchal influence' with his people, and the skilful way in which he handled the situation.[177] The JIC argued in October 1967 that the Trucial States were following Kuwait's lead into the mainstream Arab cause. The level of UAR propaganda and subversive activity was reduced, and Nasser's long-term objective of replacing the rulers with 'progressive' governments was unlikely to reach fruition. His remarkable defeat by the Israelis in June 1967 had marked domestic economic ramifications,[178] but more significantly, Nasser's standing in the Middle East was significantly diminished because his status as the leader of the revolutionary Arab states and the leading symbol of radical forces was called into question.[179]

Nationalist feeling in the Gulf was still sympathetic to Nasser, but his prestige amongst the educated minority was called into question as a result of the June War and the withdrawal that same year of Egyptian troops from the Yemen. The British believed in October 1967 that nationalist movements in the Trucial States, with the exception of Bahrain, were small, poorly organised and under local rather than external control.[180] The rulers showed that they were able to exercise effective authority over their states with virtually no recourse to force. The expansion of the state in the sheikhdoms undercut demands for political reform and for the rulers to make political concessions. The rulers also benefited from loyal security forces and an increasingly efficient police and special branch organisation. They also benefited from growing oil incomes and the expansion of development programmes that improved the standard of living.

The economic development of the Trucial States

The economic prospects of the smaller sheikhdoms remained bleak, which is why they were the focus of the British development expenditure. The Foreign Office was determined to retain control of the development budget, which focused on projects, including water supplies, electricity and roads, that had the widest public benefit.[181] The Trucial States Development Office and Fund were established on 1 March 1965.[182] The British understood that they had to compete with the Arab League, and the Ministry of Overseas Development, which assumed financial responsibility for the development scheme in January 1965,[183] proposed that an additional £1 million be allocated to the Trucial States, along with £290,000 from Bahrain and Qatar.[184] The Treasury challenged the Foreign Office's and Development Ministry's assumptions about efficacy of aid in an era of domestic economic stringency.[185] There was no economic rationale for increased expenditure in light of Abu Dhabi's rapidly increasing oil income. The Foreign Office also claimed that generous offers of aid from the neighbouring states would only be forthcoming if the British took the lead.[186] The Treasury's critique of the Foreign Office's assumptions should be seen in the context of long-running differences between departments about the value of the British role, particularly the military presence in terms of safeguarding oil supplies. The Treasury argued that since the oil-producing countries must sell their oil and world supplies were ample, the British could rely on obtaining oil at reasonable prices. In contrast, the Foreign Office argued that withdrawal would have severe consequences.[187] The Foreign Office perspective prevailed,[188] and the Defence and Oversea Policy Committee, which was chaired by the Prime Minister, authorised the allocation of an additional £1 million.[189]

In 1965, the development budget amounted to £500,000 and it increased to £600,000 the following year.[190] In spite of this significant increase in expenditure, which was augmented by £500,000 donated by Abu Dhabi, the programme was criticised for its slow pace.[191] However, a road linking Dubai and Sharjah was built, and during 1967, drinking water and electricity were brought to every centre of population in the Northern Trucial States, except Fujairah.

The most significant economic developments occurred in Abu Dhabi and Dubai. In 1967, Abu Dhabi accrued £30 million from oil production,[192] which increased to £111 million in 1971.[193] This staggering increase in income allowed the government to spend £40 million on development over a three-year period.[194] However, the system of government in the sheikhdom was rudimentary, and British advisors played an essential role in the development process. Oil was discovered in Dubai in May 1967, and British banks and construction companies were responsible for funding and building a deep-water harbour in the sheikhdom that cost £10 million.[195] By late 1967, Dubai's economy had grown at a startling rate, but the Ministry of Overseas Development was still proposing to spend an additional £1 million. The objective was to lay the foundations for future development wherever possible, on the basis of having common services across the seven sheikhdoms.[196]

By the end of 1967, progress on modernisation had been 'patchy' because the varying conditions in the Trucial States meant that a common administrative system would not work. Sir Stewart Crawford argued that the provision of advice towards improving efficiency, rather than the modernisation of the internal administration of the states, was the most important facet of the government's policy. Administrative efficiency was more likely to promote stability than any other feature of modernisation which the Foreign Office could promote. The introduction of 'popular government' in the states would 'have a profoundly disturbing effect', and the rulers were instead encouraged to associate their subjects with the sheikhly system of rule.[197]

Conclusion

The Wilson Government intervened on an unprecedented scale in the direction of British policy in the Trucial States and the Gulf region. Political differences within the government in London and worsening economic circumstances in the UK called into question the continuation of the British role in the Trucial States. The cost of the British presence in the Trucial States was minimal, in contrast to the vast increase in oil production in the Gulf during the decade. The British economy significantly benefited from Gulf oil and sterling balances deposited in London. The British departure from the Persian Gulf was inevitable. Until January 1968, the Foreign Office assumed that the withdrawal would occur by the mid-1970s because it would be impossible to justify the retention of British interests in light of changing international circumstances.

British policy in the Trucial States during the 1960s remained a model of successful low-cost imperialism. The Foreign Office maintained its key strategic and economic objectives, in contrast to the retreat from Empire in Aden and the Far East. It was possible to maintain the anomalous position in the Gulf because there was scant opposition to the British presence. Nonetheless, the Foreign Office faced a variety of challenges during the 1960s. The most significant threat to the stability of the Trucial States resulted from the unprecedented growth of Arab nationalist sentiment that was disseminated by radio propaganda and school teachers from Egypt and the Levant. Although Bahrain was affected by these developments, the Trucial States remained immune to these nationalist currents because political consciousness was very limited at the time, and political parties were absent. The Foreign Office, and most of the sheikhly rulers of the Trucial States, had a shared interest in preventing the spread of nationalist ideas and the Arab League from penetrating the region.

The Foreign Office's policy in the Trucial States remained benign, and the British only intervened when they believed that recalcitrant rulers were threatening their interests. The overthrow of the rulers of Sharjah and Abu Dhabi in 1965 and 1966 were notable examples of the extent to which the British were determined to secure their interests. The most significant British contribution to the stability of the Trucial States was the development of armed forces and domestic security organisations. By 1967, the Trucial Oman Scouts had evolved into a highly effective military organisation that was entirely funded by the Foreign Office and Ministry of Defence. A British officer always commanded the Scouts, and they succeeded in defending the frontiers of the Trucial States and conducting joint operations with the Sultan's Armed Forces. The TOS also played a central role in preventing tribal conflicts by conducting routine patrols of the sheikhdoms, thereby keeping the peace. The Scouts furthermore played a key role in the development of nascent security forces in the sheikhdoms, such as the establishment of the ADDF. The Foreign Office also funded the development of local police forces, and of domestic intelligence organisations that played an important role in countering subversion in the Trucial States. These developments were important because they allowed the British to contemplate withdrawal in benign political circumstances. In contrast to the other examples of decolonisation, the British were not forced out of the protected states.

The Foreign Office can be criticised for its failure to spend more on the economic and social development of the Trucial States. The intrinsic merits of a comprehensive development programme were a secondary consideration compared with the Treasury's determination to cut overseas expenditure. Furthermore, nothing was done to prepare the Trucial States for independence. Nonetheless, it was hard to justify on economic grounds the continuation of British aid in light of Abu Dhabi's rapidly increasing oil wealth. The Foreign Office also failed to persuade the rulers of the Trucial States to cooperate effectively in forming a union. This was an insuperable challenge for British officials because the rulers were determined to protect their sovereignty. The rulers were only forced by work together following the British decision in January 1968 to withdraw by the end of 1971.

5

All politics and no strategy

The withdrawal from the Gulf

The Labour Government's decision to withdraw from the Persian Gulf by the end of 1971 was influenced by a variety of domestic economic and political considerations, rather than by strategic calculations. There was no local demand for the British to leave the Gulf, and the rulers of the Trucial States were shocked by this dramatic reversal in British policy. The British were determined to retain their strategic interests in the Gulf region, which included access to cheap oil, the maintenance of regional stability and effective armed forces. The future of the Trucial Oman Scouts and the continuation of British command of the armed forces of the Trucial States were crucial requirements for the Foreign Office.

By the late 1960s, the Foreign Office had to contend with the growing influence of regional powers, including Iran and Saudi Arabia. The withdrawal was therefore influenced by Iran's dubious claim to Bahrain and the Gulf islands (Abu Musa and the Greater and Lesser Tunbs). In addition, the Foreign Office failed to resolve the Buraimi Oasis border dispute with Saudi Arabia prior to the withdrawal. The British decision to depart also forced the rulers of the Trucial States, Bahrain and Qatar to cooperate with one another on the future of the states. The Foreign Office had made strenuous efforts to persuade the rulers to cooperate through the Trucial States Council. Attempts to cajole them to work together failed on account of long-standing jealousies between the rulers and Abu Dhabi's growing influence in the region, which was the consequence of its oil wealth. The rulers of the other sheikhdoms feared Abu Dhabi's growing influence, but the British withdrawal forced them to cooperate on an unprecedented scale. The final years of British supremacy in the Trucial States were characterised by a marked decline in British influence with the rulers, and the process of departure brought to the fore a variety of complex issues that had to be resolved by the end of 1971. There was a high degree of uncertainty about the future political structure of the protected states during the final era of the *Pax Britannica* in the Gulf.

The Foreign Office continued to support the economic and social development of the Trucial States. The economic case for the provision of aid was tenuous because the extent of British assistance was insignificant compared with Sheikh Zayed's, the ruler of Abu Dhabi, determination to spend large amounts of his oil income on development schemes in the poorer Trucial States. The Foreign Office therefore spent money on development for political reasons, and British advisors played a central role in directing the development of the Trucial States since there was a dearth of locally educated people who could perform this role.

The response to the Labour Government's policy reversal

In January 1968, Goronwy Roberts, the Minister of State at the Foreign Office, toured the Gulf to inform the rulers of the protected states that the British would be terminating the protective treaties, and withdrawing their military presence by the end of 1971.[1] The commitment to pull out from the Gulf and South-East Asia was announced by Harold Wilson in the House of Commons on 16 January.[2] The end of the *Pax Britannica* in the Gulf was influenced by domestic political considerations, and Saul Kelly notes that the decision to leave in December 1971 was a compromise between the Treasury, which wanted to depart by April 1971, and the Foreign Office and Ministry of Defence, which wanted to hang on until March 1972.[3] The British departure from the Gulf had considerable strategic implications because it meant the end of the protection for the Trucial States and the defence commitment for Kuwait, and the Foreign Office would no longer be responsible for the foreign relations of the sheikhdoms.[4] The decision to depart was widely regarded as a 'scuttle',[5] and commentators were extremely critical of the government's policy. D. C. Watt argued that the policy was an 'outstanding illustration of all that is wrong in current British official decision-making processes', and the reversal of the Labour Party's official policy was 'a crowning exhibition of weakness in an area where visible strength counts for a good deal'.[6]

The decision to retreat, which clearly contradicted assurances given by the government two months earlier, had considerable implications for Britain's relations with the rulers of the Trucial States, Bahrain and Qatar. They were stunned by the government's volte-face, which was regarded as a betrayal of Britain's longstanding protection of the sheikhdoms. Sir Stewart Crawford, the

Political Resident, observed that the rulers' confidence was shattered because they had been told that the British would stay for as long as necessary to ensure peace and stability, and no attempt had been made to consult them in advance.[7] He also believed that the announcement would reduce the Foreign Office's ability to influence developments, and the British should abstain from exchanges between the rulers.[8] The rulers believed that their security had been rescinded without any viable alternative.[9] Foreign Office officials serving in the Gulf were dismayed by this reversal in policy, and Anthony Parsons, the Political Agent at Bahrain, contemplated resigning but the ruler, Sheikh Isa, persuaded him to stay.[10]

Immediately after Sheikh Zayed was informed of the government's decision to withdraw, he offered to cover the cost of British forces that were based in Bahrain and Sharjah.[11] Sheikh Rashid, the ruler of Dubai, reaffirmed Zayed's offer. Defence Secretary Healey's response to this suggestion provided a telling insight into the government's attitude towards the rulers. Healey commented in a television interview: 'Well I don't very much like the idea of being a sort of white slaver for Arab shaikhs', and 'I think it would be a very great mistake if we allowed ourselves to become mercenaries for people who would like us to have a few British troops around.'[12] The Foreign Office attempted to apologise to the rulers for this slight, but the damage had been done.[13]

The regional response to the British decision was significant, and confirms Saul Kelly's argument that the government's 'double-cross' of the rulers lifted 'the lid on the endemic rivalries in the region', which made Britain's military and political retreat much harder.[14] In January 1968, the reaction in Iran and Saudi Arabia, which were the most important and influential neighbouring states, was mixed. King Faisal was dismayed by the announcement, but he regarded the sheikhdoms as historically, geographically and politically a Saudi preserve, and his main objective was to keep subversion at bay.[15] The King hoped that after the British left the Gulf, he would be able to pressurise Abu Dhabi to surrender the Buraimi Oasis. He regarded reclaiming Buraimi as a question of personal honour. The Shah took the decision with remarkably 'good grace',[16] and regarded the British departure as an unprecedented opportunity to expand his influence in the Gulf and replace the British as the protecting power in the region.[17]

The Wilson Government's decision caused consternation in Washington because it contradicted British assurances about the retention of forces in the Gulf until the mid-1970s.[18] The Americans were astonished that Britain should contemplate withdrawing from a region where its economic interests were so significant, political relations with the rulers were cordial and the military costs were inconsequential.[19] Secretary of State Dean Rusk urged the British to continue their presence in the Gulf, or at least not announce a date for departing.[20] He explained the American view in the sharpest terms to Foreign Secretary Brown, who reported: 'I had a bloody unpleasant meeting in Washington this morning with Rusk.'[21] President Johnson sent Wilson two letters, in which he expressed his deep dismay about the government's policy, which he regarded as being 'tantamount to British withdrawal from World affairs.'[22] Despite America's deep dismay with the Wilson Government, the Gulf was not discussed when Wilson met Johnson in February 1968.[23] The Johnson Administration refused to replace Britain's security role in the Gulf on account of the war in Vietnam and Cold War commitments. Jeffrey Macris argues that the United States wanted to delegate the security of the Gulf to Iran and the Saudis, which would obviate the requirement to locate significant US naval forces in the region. This was the origin of the so-called 'twin pillars' strategy that characterised American strategy in the Gulf during the Nixon Administration.[24] Meanwhile, the State Department's policy was to encourage the British to maintain as much of their presence as they could, and to foster greater political and economic cooperation among the Gulf States. The Americans also wanted to avoid a regional arms race, and there were indications that the Gulf littoral states welcomed greater American involvement.[25]

The policy of the Labour Government also had implications for the Cold War, although the Soviet threat to the Trucial States, Kuwait and Oman was limited. This was because Soviet efforts to become involved in the affairs of the Trucial States had been limited in scope. However, the Russians maintained close relations with the Baathists in Iraq and the regime in Yemen. In 1968, the Soviet Navy started to conduct visits in the Gulf, which demonstrated the possibility of a larger Soviet presence in the region.[26] The JIC argued that after the withdrawal of British protection, there would be growing instability in the Gulf, with the possibility of coups in Kuwait or Saudi Arabia, which the Soviets would be able to exploit. The USSR might be able to utilise potential Arab anger at Western attitudes on the Arab–Israeli issue and the West's close relations with 'reactionary' regimes. Soviet activities in the Gulf were limited on account of the Gulf States' close commercial ties with the West and Muslim antipathy towards communism.[27]

The State Department's Bureau of Intelligence and Research (INR) argued that British policy was welcomed in Moscow with 'unconcealed enthusiasm' because the Soviets attempted to establish diplomatic relations with Bahrain, Qatar and the UAE. According to the INR analysis, the Soviets were willing to set aside their ideological qualms about 'breaking bread with the feudal families' in the sheikhdoms, with the long-term objective of acquiring naval facilities in the region. These efforts reflected the Soviet Union's desire to establish ties that had been denied by the British. The British departure offered a significant opportunity for the Soviets to expand their presence, which led the British and the Saudis to caution the rulers not to establish diplomatic relations with Moscow.[28]

Defence and security forces in the Trucial States

The decision to depart entailed a significant increase in subversion prior to the British departure. The Foreign Office was concerned that Iran, Iraq and Saudi Arabia would reassert their territorial claims on the Gulf States. The withdrawal also raised the prospect of renewed Iraqi aggression against Kuwait, because the Baathist regime still hankered after the recovery of what they regarded as a lost province. Britain had important economic interests in Kuwait, which included the investments by BP and Shell in Kuwait's oil production. The Kuwaitis also had large sterling holdings worth £250 million, and the country was a promising market for British goods. The continuation of the sheikhly regime in Kuwait was furthermore valuable because it assisted in the pursuit of British political objectives in the Gulf. The Al Sabah ruling family had shown a close interest in the affairs of the sheikhdoms in the lower Gulf, and had contributed towards development schemes in the Trucial States. Although there was some opposition to the ruling family, the police and armed forces appeared to be loyal to the regime.[29]

One of the most important issues to be addressed between 1968 and 1971 was the organisation of the union's defence and security forces. A significant British objective was to establish a unified military force, and effective police and intelligence services in the Trucial States. The Foreign Office was especially concerned about the future of the Trucial Oman Scouts. By the late 1960s, the TOS had proven itself an effective force that played a major role in the pacification of the formerly lawless tribes and in maintaining internal security in the Trucial States. The Scouts also had the unique ability to operate across the Trucial States, except in the towns, where they could only enter with the agreement of the rulers. The TOS remained the private army of the Political Resident, who was advised by the Commander of British forces in the Gulf.

The TOS performed a variety of other roles, including assisting the Sultan of Oman's Forces, the SAF, in the conduct of counter-insurgency operations. In December 1970, the TOS mounted 'Operation Breakfast', which involved flying

C Squadron from Sharjah to the Musandam Peninsula to curtail the movement of the Popular Front for the Liberation of Oman (PFLOAG) insurgents.[30] Until the end of the British era in the Trucial States, the TOS continued to handle tribal disputes. In the spring of 1971, the TOS was also responsible for policing the border between Ras Al Khaimah and Oman because the leaders of the Shihuh tribe were dissatisfied with the military occupation of their tribal dira (area).[31]

In April 1968, the TOS numbered 1,881 men, including 162 British personnel, and British officers commanded its main units, either on secondment from the British Army or serving as contract officers. The TOS was entirely funded by the Foreign Office and Ministry of Defence. In 1968, it cost £1,377,000.[32] In December 1966, a working party was established in Whitehall to review the roles and purpose of the TOS. This enquiry was postponed because of the Defence Review but was reactivated following the decision to withdraw. In June 1968, the group concluded that the British should cease all responsibility for the pay or control of the TOS after the withdrawal. However, it was vital to the stability of the Trucial States that the TOS should remain a viable force under British control. This meant that it was in Britain's strategic interests to continue to meet the expenditure of the force, and the rulers should be compelled to subsidise additional pay increases.[33] The working party concluded in 1968 that it was essential that the TOS should remain in being as a cohesive and viable force until the British retreat in order to obviate the requirement for British forces to operate within the Trucial States. The continuation of the TOS as an effective force was also essential because it would ensure stability, and that the withdrawal could take place peacefully.[34] In July 1968, the Labour Government's stated policy in the Gulf was as follows: 'we wish to see a steady evolution in the local arrangements for defence and cooperation'.[35]

The most significant challenge the TOS faced was the growth of the ADDF. The ADDF's proclaimed role was to 'defend the integrity of the country', and by August 1968, it had grown to 1,400 men, with a planned strength of 4,000. The expansion of the ADDF called into question the future of the TOS because its pay scale was 85 per cent more than the Scouts. This meant that skilled soldiers were being lost to the ADDF and the TOS risked being crippled,[36] which forced the Foreign Office to demand that the rulers contribute towards the cost of the Scouts. The establishment of rival armed forces in the Trucial States cast doubt on the future role of the TOS because the five smaller sheikhdoms could not afford to support it.[37] In July 1968, General Sir George Baker, Chief of the General Staff (CGS), visited the Trucial States. Baker observed that the professional standards of the TOS were higher than those of the ADDF. Nonetheless, the CGS recognised that the uncertain future of the TOS and the difference in pay with the ADDF had undermined morale in the Scouts.[38] In November 1968, this problem was overcome when the rulers agreed to contribute £350,000 to bring TOS pay scales up to the level of the ADDF.[39]

Sheikh Rashid, the ruler of Dubai, was alarmed by the expansion of the ADDF. By the end of 1968, the ADDF numbered 1,991, including 45 British loaned and contract officers. During the year, a sea wing was established and three British patrol boats were delivered. Furthermore, the nucleus of an air force was established when two Bell helicopters and transport aircraft arrived in Abu Dhabi.[40] In July 1968, Sheikh instructed Jack Briggs, the Commander of the Dubai Police, to establish a force of 500 men.[41] The Foreign Office made great efforts to dissuade him from establishing a Dubai Defence Force on the grounds that it would further undermine the TOS. Crawford proposed stationing a TOS squadron in Dubai territory in order to persuade Sheikh Rashid not to raise a defence force. But he made it clear to Foreign Office officials in July 1968 that he was 'afraid of' the ADDF because its size was beyond any reasonable operational requirements. He believed that the expansion of the ADDF was part of Abu Dhabi's policy of dominating the Trucial States, and he was not persuaded by the counter-argument that the ADDF was still being formed.[42]

Alongside the development of local armies, the Foreign Office took steps to enhance the police forces of the Trucial States. In February 1969, it sent a policing expert, L. A. Hicks, to the protected states to examine their police and special branch organisations.[43] Hicks ascertained that the police forces of the Trucial States varied in their competence and organisation. Sharjah had a police force of 57 men that was commanded by a British officer, who was planning on expanding the force to 108 men. However, the force was starved of funds, which inhibited progress, and Hicks recommended that £5,000 be immediately advanced to cover the cost of expansion. The Ras Al Khaimah Police was similarly underfunded, which meant that it was unable to function properly. Abu Dhabi had a police force of 650, commanded by Sheikh Mubarak, a nephew of Sheikh Zayed. The deputy commander of the force was British and was responsible for training, but Hicks found that Sheikh Zayed did not trust his relative and the police was being neglected. Furthermore, Hicks ascertained that the Special Branch had been separated from the control of the Police and it was not clear who was in command. Hicks advised that Archie Lamb, the Political Agent, should take steps to impress on Sheikh Zayed the importance of a strong and efficient police force, which would be able to play an important role in maintaining internal security. Hicks found that the police in Dubai was the most efficient in the Trucial States. They numbered 430 men, commanded by a British officer, Jack Briggs, who had the 'complete trust' of Sheikh Rashid. Hicks concluded that in light of the decision to withdraw, the British needed to devote attention to the police forces of the Trucial States.

The Foreign Office's objective was to establish a unified military after the British withdrawal, and in order to achieve this, a joint defence advisor, General Sir John Willoughby, was appointed. In April 1969, Willoughby submitted a report to the rulers that proposed establishing a Union army, based on the TOS. This brigade group would initially consist of two motorised infantry battalions, with an armoured reconnaissance squadron, a mortar battery and supporting arms and services. The report advised that the British Government should provide a training team to assist in the development of the Union army, and that foreign advisors would be needed for the foreseeable future.

The Willoughby report also proposed the establishment of an air force, which would be based on eighteen Hunter fighters, sixteen helicopters, four transport aircraft and Tigercat surface-to-air missiles. A small navy would also be established, based on the purchase of eight patrol boats.[44] Sheikh Zayed was allegedly critical of Willoughby's proposals because he was not aiming for a large enough force. Zayed told Edward Heath during his visit to the Gulf in April 1969 that the Willoughby proposals relied too much on the TOS. The ruler apparently stated that Abu Dhabi would have to expand its own forces to make up the gap.[45] However, Crawford contradicted this assertion when he reported that Sheikh Zayed accepted the Willoughby report, 'lock, stock and barrel'.[46] The future of the TOS and the Willoughby report were discussed when Sheikh Zayed visited London in June 1969. Zayed reiterated his desire to establish his own army and that the TOS should be incorporated into it at a later date.[47] The extent of defence cooperation with Abu Dhabi was marked by Sheikh Zayed's willingness to accept an SAS training team to train his bodyguard.[48]

The Foreign Office failed in its efforts to prevent the rulers from establishing their own security forces. Its attitude towards these nascent armies was governed by the principle of 'festina lente' (make haste slowly).[49] There were no grounds for objecting to the formation of indigenous armies and the procurement of weapons. Sheikh Saqr, the ruler of Ras Al Khaimah, also wanted to establish a security force to counter disputes between the Shihuh tribe and a German mining company.[50] Sheikh Saqr's interest in raising an army was influenced by other considerations, including his concern about the defence of his sheikhdom after the British withdrawal. Although the ruler was happy to rely on the TOS in the interim, he was also concerned about Abu Dhabi's growing influence. Sheikh Saqr appointed Major David Nield in the spring of 1969 to establish the Ras Al Khaimah Mobile Force (RAKMF), which was equipped with the same weapons used by the TOS.[51] The Foreign Office had no objection to Sheikh Saqr raising the RAKMF and to approaching the Saudi Government to fund the supply of arms, which were purchased in the UK. The only quibble the Foreign Office could raise was if the force was too large to meet the sheikhdom's security requirements.[52] The RAKMF received its first recruits in early 1969, with the objective of establishing a force of 150 men, who were trained by the TOS. However, by the end of the year, Sheikh Saqr was still attempting to raise money to fund the Mobile Force in Iran and Qatar.[53]

In August 1969, the Joint Intelligence Group in the Gulf produced an analysis of the security situation in the Trucial States, Bahrain and Qatar until the end of 1971.[54] It was believed that the breakdown of law and order was unlikely, even in Bahrain, which was the most vulnerable state. It was possible that riots and demonstrations on a small scale might occur, particularly in 1971, but it was improbable that subversive groups would take action, as long as British officers remained in command of security forces. It was doubtful that acts of sabotage would be directed against oil installations. However, the main concern was that the Trucial Oman Scouts could lose its effectiveness as a stabilising and impartial force, caused by the uncertainty about its future.

The year 1970 was marked as a turning point in the growth of subversion in the Trucial States, which was an indication of the limitations of British power. In July 1970, a bomb exploded in the ruler of Sharjah's majlis,[55] and he would have been killed if he had kept to his usual timetable.[56] The attempted assassination of the ruler led to the first coordinated operation by the Trucial States security organisations against subversive groups, and six members of the National Democratic Front for the Liberation of the Arab Gulf (NDFLOAG) were arrested.[57] There were indications of growing subversion in the Trucial States, which was characterised by secret meetings, leaflets and 'ominous reports from the Special Branches'. Much of this activity originated outside of the Trucial States, and Julian Bullard, the Political Agent at Dubai, noted that: 'I hate to see the northern Arabs invading the Trucial States with their bigotry, nepotism and greed.'[58] Crawford commented his valedictory dispatch in July 1970 that:

> Omens for the future are less encouraging. The police cover is thin; potential subversives are growing in number, especially with the increased flow of Palestinians into the Trucial States; the Iraq government is beginning to penetrate

the area, so far mainly by overt methods but undoubtedly with the intent of later promoting activities against the rulers and perhaps against our forces; there are signs that the various subversive groups may now be drawing together under the umbrella of a single organisation with a better chance of producing a coordinated effort than previous such attempts. It is reasonable to expect that some effort will be made by subversives, by methods which may include using sabotage, to support a claim that the withdrawal of British forces from the Gulf is taking place under local pressure, and we shall be lucky if no incidents occur.[59]

The future of the police and special branches was a key British interest, and Sir William Luce commented in November 1970 that: 'we should also continue to do all we can to help with the build-up, training and supply of equipment to local police forces and in particular to their security and intelligence branches'.[60] The Foreign Office recognised the subversive threat in the protected states. Antony Acland, the Head of the Arabian Department, commented that the police and special branches had disrupted dissidents, but the rulers were unlikely to survive unless they acknowledged public opinion.[61] In March 1971, the Foreign Office produced a detailed report on how the security forces in the Trucial States could be assisted after the British withdrawal. It assumed that the five Northern Trucial States were most vulnerable to subversion because their existing security forces were least developed. If subversion occurred in the poorer states, the Foreign Office argued, it would quickly spread to Abu Dhabi and Dubai, where the British had important economic interests. It suggested that a new department be established under the control of the Trucial States Council that would be called 'the department for co-ordination of police and internal security'. The Foreign Office envisaged that the existing programme of police support would continue until the end of March 1972 and would cost £125,557. It was envisaged that there would be a supplementary programme for 1971/72 and four more years of expenditure, which would cost £193,000 per annum.[62] The Treasury only agreed to fund additional expenditure for 1971/72 on the grounds that no new commitments could be made after the withdrawal unless a strong case was presented.[63]

The future of defence questions dominated negotiations during the last months of the British era. In June 1971, the COS examined how Britain's military influence could be retained after the withdrawal. Luce observed in his report on the Gulf that: 'the holding by British officers of key position in local forces is a stronger safeguard against military revolt than the presence of British battalions'. In the summer of 1971, there were 358 British loan personnel in the Gulf from Kuwait to Muscat, and the COS commented that their importance was out of proportion to their numbers. Retaining British personnel was economically the most effective way of preserving British influence, providing advice and maintaining efficiency. The COS also proposed that a Military Assistance Team (MAT) should be sent to the Trucial States to coordinate British exercises and to provide training and assistance to local forces.[64] The MAT arrived in Sharjah in December 1971.

In August 1971, Sheikh Zayed and Sheikh Rashid agreed to Willoughby's proposal for the gradual expansion of the TOS. The newly formed army required armoured cars and artillery at a cost of £28 million. This amount was deemed by the Treasury to be too costly and was significantly reduced. During the last months of the *Pax Britannica* in the Trucial States, the Foreign Office succeeded in guaranteeing the continuation of British control of the armed forces of the Union. Luce proposed that Colonel Freddie de Butts, the former TOS Commander, should become the Director Military Liaison Office (DMLO) and later Chief of Staff of the Union Ministry of Defence.[65] Luce noted that the appointment of a British officer responsible to the rulers was an essential achievement of Britain's military aims in the Trucial States. Shortly afterwards, the rulers of Abu Dhabi and Dubai without question agreed to Luce's proposals about military cooperation and the expansion of the TOS.[66]

The continued support for the police and special branches in the Trucial States was open to question because the extent of subversive activity was minimal. In September 1971, the State Department's intelligence analysis of the Trucial States concluded that the rulers had succeeded in countering subversion by utilising the special branch organisations that the British had established. Nonetheless, these forces were still finding it difficult to recruit local personnel. Locals were reluctant to apply for police posts because they did not wish to be considered 'British spies', and there were better-paid jobs in the oil industry.[67] The JIC closely observed events in the Trucial States and reached the conclusion that barring an Iranian occupation of the disputed islands or another Arab–Israeli war, it was conceivable that the departure of British forces would take place peacefully. However, if the Iranians did occupy the islands or if Arab–Israeli hostilities resumed, it might lead to action by subversive groups.[68]

The Trucial States remained quiescent and Sir Geoffrey Arthur, who became the last Political Resident in October 1970, handed over the assets and personnel of TOS to Sheikh Zayed, and at midnight on 22 December, the Scouts ceased to exist.[69] In January 1972, Arthur wrote a valedictory about the TOS, in which he observed that the transfer of responsibility was a formality because nearly all the officers and men remained: 'the familiar blue-grey shirt and red check head-cloth will still be seen in the Trucial States as evidence of an impartial force that owes allegiance to no single ruler'. Arthur added that: 'without the Union they cannot survive; but nor can the Union survive, at any rate in the short term, without them'.[70] The rulers agreed that the TOS should become the federal force of brigade strength. De Butts observed that: 'several wanted to copy the Abu Dhabi example and have their own small private armies as well. It made them feel safer now that the British umbrella was removed. I could only stand on the touchline and advise on shape and size'.[71] It was possible to retreat peacefully and hand over the TOS to Sheikh Zayed because the Trucial States were becoming increasingly prosperous, which forestalled demands for any reform of the sheikhly system of rule.

The Foreign Office and cooperation between the rulers of the protected states, 1968–71

The Foreign Office was concerned that there would not be enough time for the Trucial States, Bahrain and Qatar to establish a political structure that would enable them to survive on their own. The objectives of British policy during the final years of protection included strengthening the administrative system and security forces. The most complex aspiration was to encourage the protected states to establish a political relationship that would enable them to survive after British protection was rescinded. A final goal, which was not achieved, was the resolution of frontier disputes between the Trucial States and their neighbours.[72] The decision to withdraw had significant long-term consequences for British prestige in the protected states, and it undermined the Political Resident's ability to influence the rulers.[73] The Foreign Office also wanted to secure essential oil resources, which constituted about 50 per cent of British oil imports annually. The economic importance of the Gulf was a fundamental concern, and the protection of investments in the region and their contribution to the UK's balance of payments were regarded as key criteria.[74] The Foreign Office wanted to achieve a seamless political disengagement and military withdrawal from the Gulf.

The most important issue in handling the retreat was the political and structural relationship between the Trucial States, Bahrain and Qatar. Glen Balfour-Paul notes 'that if they did not hang together, some outside executioner would string them up separately'.[75] The most far-reaching impact of the government's policy was that it forced the rulers for the first time to cooperate.

Previous attempts to persuade the rulers to work together through the Trucial States Council and the Development Office had been unsuccessful. This was the result of long-standing mutual animosities and competing attempts to dominate the area by the most powerful rulers, notably by Sheikh Zayed, the ruler of Abu Dhabi. However, the rulers regarded the three or four years that had been allocated to sort out these complex arrangements as a 'derisory period'.[76]

They ostensibly had a strong incentive to cooperate because of the Trucial States' small population, and their need to work together in order to counter pressures from outside powers, most notably the Saudis, who had long-standing territorial claims against Abu Dhabi. Moreover, the threat of subversion remained a concern for the rulers, and they had a good reason to pool together their limited resources if they wanted to survive as independent states following the British withdrawal. The most important political question to be resolved was the future structure of the protected states. In December 1967, Sir Stewart Crawford recommended the separation of Abu Dhabi from the other Trucial States and Dubai's domination over the five smaller sheikhdoms.[77] This approach proved to be unworkable, and shortly after the British announcement, two plans emerged. The first initiative was agreed between Sheikh Zayed of Abu Dhabi and Sheikh Rashid, ruler of Dubai, for a union of the Trucial States.[78] The Abu Dhabi–Dubai federation aroused the suspicion of Qatar, which feared that Dubai might be detached from its traditional relations with the Al Thani ruling family. At a meeting in Dubai on 25 February, the Qataris responded by proposing a second plan, which envisaged a larger grouping that consisted of the nine protected states leading to the establishment of a Union of Arab Emirates (UAE).[79]

Balfour-Paul described this meeting as 'a mutation in their traditional feeling of apartheid bred by tribal differences and geographical separation', but the declaration was a 'spontaneous response of the Gulf governments to the alarms and excursions of the last two or three years'.[80] Sheikh Isa, the ruler of Bahrain, was nervous about the future of his regime. The Bahraini ruler's concern was caused by the British departure, Iran's territorial claim and the latent discontent of Arab nationalists in Bahrain. Sheikh Isa realised that the British decision was irrevocable, which meant that he had to find a substitute security arrangement. His attitude towards the UAE appeared to be ambivalent because Bahrain's involvement in a union of nine states would frustrate Iran's claim. Sheikh Isa also seemed to doubt the viability of a federation including all nine of the sheikhdoms. A more realistic alternative was to achieve independence, with membership of the Arab League and the UN.[81]

The Union came in existence on 30 March 1968, and it was unlikely to be a successful venture in Gulf unity.[82] The rulers' difficulties in turning the UAE into a meaningful political entity were numerous. They were divided by traditional suspicions and jealousies, which were compounded by significant disparities in wealth.[83] Sheikh Zayed was deeply dissatisfied with the creation of the UAE, and took steps to undermine it because he wanted to become the dominant ruler in the Trucial States. He distributed his rapidly increasing oil income to the tribes and rulers of the five poorer sheikhdoms.[84] His efforts to dominate the Trucial States were matched by his preoccupation with building up his security forces despite the fears of Sheikh Rashid. Sheikh Zayed was described in 1968 as an 'autocrat and man of the people, an illiterate who possesses abundant native wit, wise counsellor and intriguer and favoured with a personality and charm with which it is the fortune of few men to be blessed'. Jim Treadwell, the Political Agent at Abu Dhabi, argued that Sheikh Zayed remained an 'intriguer and muddled thinker', but his respect for the British was not diluted and he was quick to 'declare his dependence on us for advice and support'.[85]

Sheikh Isa also had little faith in the prospects of the Union, which he regarded as an obstacle to Bahrain's independence. However, his advisors initially did not share his scepticism, nor did his people, but disillusionment soon set in. This was caused by Iran's seemingly implacable opposition to Bahrain's inclusion in the Union, and the island's relegation to second-class membership in order to placate the Shah. The government and the people had expected Bahrain to be at the forefront of the Union but when it became clear that it would not work, they did not want to be the first to break it up. The Bahrainis were determined not to 'sin against the doctrine of Arab unity', which influenced Sheikh Isa's determination not to be the first to leave the Union.[86]

The Foreign Office's ability to influence the formation of the Union was subtle. Bullard argued that the Foreign Office could still intervene with decisive effect, for example when the rulers were told that it would be advantageous if the UAE sought military advisors from Britain. Nonetheless, Bullard claimed that Sheikh Rashid would support the Union more strongly if Dubai was not so prosperous, and the poorer rulers needed and wanted the Union.[87]

The rulers met again at Dubai in May 1968 and their talks were characterised by mutual recriminations.[88] The rulers were divided into two camps, with Abu Dhabi, Bahrain, Ajman, Fujairah and Umm Al Quwain in one and Qatar, Dubai and Ras Al Khaimah in the other. The first group insisted on the prior drafting of a constitution, whereas the second group wanted to agree on the location of a capital and the nomination of a president. The rulers were not adept at finding compromises, and their long-standing rivalries made them believe the worst of each other. By June 1968, the prospects for some form of unity were bleak, and the Foreign Office's policy was to try to help the rulers find compromises and to induce the Saudi Government to take a supporting role.[89] The Political Resident argued that the Foreign Office should continue to support the UAE and offer advice to the rulers because an open power struggle between them would have detrimental implications. Economic development and security depended on cooperation between the rulers. It would be difficult to find a solution to the future of the Trucial Oman Scouts, and the British feared the Saudis might take sides.[90] These concerns were discussed at the State Department in September 1968. The Americans expressed their support for the Foreign Office's approach and the need for the littoral states to find solutions for Gulf problems.[91]

In January 1969, Donald, who had served as Political Agent at Dubai in 1958–61, visited the Trucial States. Hawley wrote that little had changed in the rulers' attitudes since 1961, and that they 'evidently had not hoisted in the full implications' of the British withdrawal by 1971. Some of the rulers acted as if the decision had never been taken, although they were starting to think about the future. It was not easy for the older rulers 'to change acquired or inherited attitudes of mind towards their fellow rulers and towards HMG. The length of the British connection had undoubtedly made it a very strong one in the Trucial States.' Hawley reached the conclusion that a federation of the seven Trucial States would have a much better chance of survival than the federation of the nine. Moreover, the federation lacked impetus, and the rulers wanted more British advice and support.[92]

By January 1969, disagreements between the different camps were overcome on account of Kuwaiti intervention and some preparatory work on the Union had been achieved. The most serious impediment to the prospects of the Union was Iran's claim to Bahrain. Parsons argued that the Bahraini opposition had no interest in falling under the sway of the Shah, and that there was no chance of Iranian irredentism in Bahrain. The only solution to the Iranian claim was Bahraini membership of the UN, either as a independent state or as part of a union.[93]

British officials reported a significant increase in Iranian intelligence activity in the Trucial States in 1968, and Iranian agents were extremely effective in pressuring the rulers.[94] However, the Shah's visit to Kuwait and Riyadh in November 1968 produced no clear results for the protected states.[95] Kelly argues that the Iranian claim to Bahrain was spurious, and the Shah's aim was to disentangle himself from the Bahrain imbroglio and gain some benefit from doing so.[96] The British aided the Shah because they wanted a smooth exit from the Gulf, and they did not want to defend Bahrain's territorial integrity against the Iranians. More significantly, the rulers were unwilling to form an association with Bahrain that might have required them to support it against Iran.

An additional obstacle was Sheikh Zayed's ambitions, which included the expansion of the ADDF.[97] The British withdrawal had two major implications for Abu Dhabi's defence. It was unlikely that friendly forces would come to her immediate aid, in the event of external aggression. Britain's departure entailed a lessening of the stabilising influence the British military presence had brought to the Trucial States. In light of these circumstances, Sheikh Zayed decided that a larger force was required by the end of 1971. In September 1968, the ADDF consisted of one Ferret scout car squadron, three rifle squadrons and a Royal Guard squadron, one troop of 81 mm mortars, a combined headquarters squadron and signal troop, a combined transport and workshop squadron, and training squadron. The ADDF also had a Sea Wing with three 40 ft patrol craft. The Force had two main roles, which included guaranteeing the integrity of the state against external aggression and the maintenance of internal security.[98] The expansion of the Abu Dhabi Defence Force, which was still militarily irrelevant, greatly concerned Abu Dhabi's neighbours because it was larger and better equipped than the Trucial Oman Scouts.

The Foreign Office's ability to restrain Sheikh Zayed was still based on the authority of the Political Agents, but there were no effective sanctions to apply if he ignored their advice.[99] The outlook for the UAE in early 1969 was discouraging because the rulers showed little enthusiasm for it and there was little public interest. The Political Resident argued that the reasons for setting up the Union were still valid, including their small population, the requirement to 'hang together' against outside pressure from larger powers and the need to pool their unequal resources. Crawford believed that the Foreign Office should continue to support the Union because it was in Britain's interest to lay the foundations of an enduring and stable political system.[100] This objective could be achieved by a peaceful military withdrawal that would maintain the goodwill of the rulers and their subjects towards the British. A successful Union would lead to a commercial and cultural relationship after the withdrawal, and although there was uncertainty about the future, it was essential to support the Union quietly because it was backed by the other Arab states. The Foreign Office was wary of pursuing an active policy that advocated union because it wanted to avoid the appearance of 'an imperialist design'. To be successful, the Union had to be spontaneous, and if the British forced it through against the rulers' interests, it would probably fail.[101]

The problems the Foreign Office was facing in the Gulf were revealed in high-level consultations with the State Department in March 1969. The British believed that their American counterparts depended on the Foreign Office for reliable information on the Trucial States and Oman, and that they had 'scrupulously refrained from commenting on or grumbling' about the decision to leave the Gulf. The Foreign Office was 'in an impossible position' with the rulers because they were equally obligated towards them.[102] The American response was that they still required the British to carry the burden of defending the region, and that the future stability of the Gulf would best be preserved by the littoral states.[103] The US Government consistently stressed it had no interest in assuming the British role in the Gulf in meetings with Foreign Office officials.[104]

A meeting of the rulers at Doha in May 1969 failed to reach agreement over the main points being discussed, such as the location of the Union capital.[105] Sheikh Ahmed, the ruler of Qatar, blamed Bahrain for the failure and its attitude towards the Union.[106] Crawford argued that the UAE was going through a serious crisis of confidence caused by doubts about Bahrain, which revived long-standing animosities between the Bahraini and Qatari ruling families.[107] The Foreign Office continued to support the union of all nine protected states, but it was ready to support a union of eight, as long as it was acceptable to the rulers. However, a union that included Bahrain appeared to be unrealistic because the island's much larger population, but its limited wealth, made her a 'dominant but grasping partner'. The inclusion of Bahrain was also unappealing because of the sheikhdoms' political instability.[108] By the summer of 1969, it was becoming increasingly clear that a union that included Bahrain and Qatar was unlikely to reach fruition.[109] Nonetheless, the Political Resident believed that a union of nine 'looked the best bet',[110] but the Foreign Secretary instructed that no new steps should be taken about the future of the Union.[111]

Meanwhile, in Whitehall, steps were being taken to plan the military withdrawal from Bahrain and Sharjah. In summer of 1969, the Chiefs of Staff produced the first iteration of a Gulf rundown plan that involved the removal of 7,350 personnel and 1,660 dependents.[112] British forces' order of battle was founded on a naval base, an infantry battalion and three aircraft squadrons in Bahrain. A second battalion was based in Sharjah, plus an armoured car squadron and three aircraft squadrons.[113] The Chiefs of Staff and the Commander of British Forces in the Gulf envisaged a phased withdrawal by the end of December 1971, with warships remaining in the area. However, the plan was modified in the spring of 1971, in light of continuing uncertainty about setting up the union and the future of Bahrain and Qatar.[114] There was no discernable internal opposition to the British military presence in the Gulf, which aided the seamless departure of British forces.[115]

The future organisation of the protected states remained uncertain. In July 1969, Bullard, who was serving in the Political Agency at Dubai, wrote a detailed memorandum that addressed the potential alternatives for the protected states.[116] This is an important document because it outlined the rationale for the formation of the Emirati system that came into existence after the British withdrawal. Bullard argued that there were only two possible patterns, the union or confederation of the Trucial States, or a union or confederation of the Northern Six with Abu Dhabi as a separate mini-state. He further argued that a union of seven was the obvious alternative, after a union of eight or nine (including Bahrain and Qatar) had failed. The union of the Trucial States was the most likely solution because the states were geographically contiguous, and they already possessed elements of a unitary structure, including the Trucial States Council, the Development Office and the TOS. The movement of goods and services between the states was straightforward, and although there were still wide variations in the level of development between the states, their international status was the same. Moreover, their tribal structure and the sheikhly system of rule were very similar.

Bullard argued that the skills needed to run a union of seven were far less than for eight or nine members. Experience of trying to establish the Union had forced Sheikh Zayed and Shaikh Rashid closer together, and the forthcoming British departure meant that a union of seven 'was their best hope of salvation'. A potential stumbling block was the defence organisation of the states, and the future of the TOS. The separation of Abu Dhabi from the other states corresponded to the reality of the situation because the gap between Sheikh Zayed and the other rulers had considerably widened. Abu Dhabi's oil income, the gradual development of its system of government and the expansion of the ADDF suggested that it was distinct from the other Trucial States. The key question was whether Sheikh Zayed would continue his financial support for other sheikhdoms if he broke away, and whether they could survive without it. These ideas were controversial, and were rejected at the time because it was believed that a union of the seven had little chance of success.

The rulers met again in Abu Dhabi in October 1969. The summit failed because the rulers of Dubai and Qatar conspired to force Bahrain to withdraw from the Union 'without themselves incurring the odium of blackballing her'. However, Sheikh Isa's conciliatory tactics thwarted them. Sheikhs Ahmed and

Rashid, the rulers of Dubai and Qatar, also tried to exploit the enmity Sheikh Zayed had for Sheikh Saqr, ruler of Ras Al Khaimah, to impede progress. The two rulers adopted these tactics in order to placate the Shah, although there is no evidence that the Iranians encouraged them to do so. Sheikhs Ahmed and Rashid had other motives to stall the Union, which included their mutual suspicions of the Bahraini and Qatari ruling families.[117] By the end of 1969, there was little hope that the rulers would succeed in establishing a union. The rulers of Dubai and Qatar were concerned that their interests would be damaged by a more populous and educated Bahrain. The Union had given the rulers the excuse for not taking the necessary steps to prepare for independence.[118] Bullard argued:

> But after three years of standing mostly on the sidelines, on top of many decades during which we controlled the Trucial States in a negative rather than a positive sense, it seems to me too late to contemplate the sort of firm reshaping of the political structure which might be possible in a colony or protectorate. It comes down to this: we have spent the last 150 years sustaining the shaikhly system, but until recently not trying to equip it to survive our departure. Now the moment of departure is at hand, and we have not the time, the resources or the freedom of action that we had once but did not think to use.[119]

In February 1970, Antony Acland toured the Gulf and reported that unless the rulers had confidence in the formation of a union that could defend them, they would 'reinsure elsewhere'. He acknowledged that the Foreign Office could not impose a political framework on the protected states because it would not last. Nonetheless, the British Government had an obligation to encourage the rulers to reach an agreement. If a union of the nine sheikhdoms proved unworkable, then a grouping of the Trucial States should be established, with the Trucial States Development Office forming its nucleus and with the TOS as their defence force possibly with the ADDF.[120] British influence remained strong because 'this is largely a matter of confidence, and of self-confidence on our part'.[121] The Foreign Office despaired of these disputes, which led to a lively correspondence about whether the 'anachronistic regimes' in the Gulf had 'had it'. The conclusion was that the sheikhly regimes would not last for very long after they had achieved independence.[122]

By April 1970, it was clear that the Iranian claim to Bahrain would be settled, and when Evan Luard, the Foreign Office Parliamentary Under-Secretary, visited the Gulf at the end of April the Foreign Office incorrectly believed that union could be achieved without the rulers being pressurised.[123] The sheikhs claimed that they were working towards a Union of Nine, but there was no coherent definition about what a federation might entail.[124] However, the Iranian claim to the islands of Abu Musa and the Tunbs remained a major stumbling block. The Joint Intelligence Committee commented that the Shah's policy in the Gulf was governed by the conviction that he should take over Britain's military predominance, and that he was determined to acquire the islands.[125] The distinction between the Bahrain question and the islands was that with the former, the Shah wished only to save face, while with the latter, he insisted on acquiring the islands. The Foreign Office was very concerned about becoming caught up in the Arab–Iranian conflict, which is why it could not press the rulers too hard.[126]

A second impediment to the establishment of a union of nine states resulted from Sheikh Zayed's decision to visit Riyadh, against British advice, in May 1970.[127] The Saudis had discovered that oil exploration had occurred in Zarara oil field, which had been assigned to Saudi Arabia in the standstill agreement of 1952. King Faisal demanded the cessation of oil exploration and threatened to use force if his demands were not met.[128] King Faisal was surprised that Sheikh Zayed did not come to discuss territorial questions, and came up with a scheme of his own for solving the Buraimi Oasis question.[129] Sheikh Zayed's meeting with King Faisal was regarded as a failure because it led to the resumption of the Saudi claim to Buraimi. Prior to Zayed's excursion to Riyadh, the long-running dispute between the British and the Saudis over the Buraimi Oasis had been frozen for years,[130] and the Political Resident argued that there was no prospect for progress.[131] The boundary dispute was King Faisal's pre-eminent concern in the Gulf.[132] The State Department believed that the British had not put Sheikh Zayed under any serious pressure to resolve the boundary dispute, and that they were complacent in believing that the problem would not prevent the formation of the UAE.[133]

The Conservative Government and the formation of the UAE

In June 1970, the Conservative Party came to power, and Edward Heath, the new Prime Minister, was resoundingly critical of the Labour's Government's decision to withdraw.[134] Heath visited the region in April 1969,[135] and claimed that the rulers of Bahrain, Dubai and Sharjah were in favour of the retention of British forces in the Gulf, and that the ruler of Qatar wanted a defence treaty.[136] Glen Balfour-Paul argues that as a result of Heath's tour of the Gulf, 'the impetus for union ... dropped conspicuously for a year'.[137] Heath's actions led the rulers to believe that if the Conservatives returned to power, it might lead to the continuation of the British presence in the Gulf.[138] Foreign Office officials in the protected states unequivocally rejected Heath's perspective. Edward Henderson commented that the policy of reversing the decision to withdraw was dangerous because it would lead to disorder.[139] Sir Stewart Crawford, the Political Resident, reported from Bahrain that the reversal of the decision to withdraw would not help to maintain order or strengthen the position of the rulers. The presence of British troops in Bahrain and Sharjah had never attracted local hostility, and it made sense to leave before this occurred.[140] The Foreign Office was therefore totally opposed to reversing the decision to withdraw.[141]

Gause notes that the Conservatives 'never pledged outright to reverse Labour's decision, only to consult with the UK's "friends" in the Gulf'. Moreover, the Conservative policy was identical to Labour's because the new government was determined to rescind the treaties and withdraw.[142] Heath's policy was summarised as follows to members of the Cabinet on 22 July 1970: 'the establishment of a situation in which British interests would be safeguarded should be understood in the context of our long-term objective, which was to reduce our commitments and our expenditure in the area, and to bring about a state of affairs in which Gulf rulers, within the framework of an effective federation, which could fend for itself'.[143] Petersen is undoubtedly correct in arguing that Heath's criticism of Labour's withdrawal 'was largely a play to the gallery' of the Conservative Party.[144]

By July 1970, the Iranians had rescinded their claim to Bahrain, following a UN investigation of popular attitudes on the island. This was an important development since it allowed Sheikh Isa to opt for independence rather than membership of a union. The Iraqis also had a claim to the Gulf, which had never been extinguished following the threat to invade Kuwait in 1961.[145] The Iraqi challenge to the sheikhdoms and Iran was important because it was a manifestation of the Baathist or revolutionary Arab socialist threat. Glen Balfour-Paul, the British Ambassador at Baghdad, argued that the Iraqis were ideologically opposed to the archaic regimes in the Trucial States, and resented Iranian influence in the Gulf.[146] Iraqi influence in the Trucial States was limited, and any attempt to undermine the rulers would have entailed a vigorous Saudi response.[147]

Sir Alec Douglas-Home, the Foreign Secretary, stated in the House of Commons on 20 July 1970 that the Heath Government would consult the rulers and support the formation of new states.[148] As Roger Louis notes, Douglas-Home sympathised with Heath's perspective but realised it was unrealistic. He adopted the Foreign Office argument, that they had inherited a situation not of their choosing, and 'he wanted neither to pursue Labour's aim, as he saw of it, of cutting loose, nor the reverse course and become, in his own phrase, a permanent nanny'.[149] Douglas-Home argued that the rulers must be the architects of a new system of government. Not only must they have a vested interest, but the Shah and King Faisal must be reconciled to the UAE.[150]

Douglas-Home rigorously controlled the Foreign Office's policy on the future of the protected states. The Cabinet decided that the Foreign Office should play a more direct role in encouraging the rulers to shoulder the burden of their responsibilities. The objective was to safeguard British interests in the context of reducing commitments and expenditure in the Gulf, and to bring about a situation whereby the rulers could fend for themselves.[151]

At the end of July 1970, the Foreign Secretary appointed Sir William Luce as his personal representative. After retiring in 1966, Luce wrote several articles about the Gulf, in which he expressed his views on the future of the region. In 1967, he argued that if the Gulf remained a secure and stable region, there would be no requirement for the prolongation of the British military and political presence. However, he characterised the region as an 'inherently unstable power vacuum which has only been kept peaceful and secure hitherto by the British presence', and that if the imperial power withdrew its forces too fast, 'others will try to fill the vacuum by force'. Luce argued that the British would not be able to retain their special position indefinitely, but that they should be in a position to 'terminate honourably our special relationship' with the Trucial States. This objective could be achieved by an understanding between Iran and Saudi Arabia about the territorial inviolability of the Trucial States. He believed that a closer relationship between the Trucial States and Saudi Arabia was needed to ensure their sovereignty, while acknowledging Saudi leadership in foreign policy and defence. His experience of the Trucial States led him to argue that the rulers had to forgo 'the old and now pointless feuds which bedevil' their relations. According to Luce, a final requirement was that the rulers of the Trucial States had to adapt the system of sheikhly rule to new circumstances caused by oil wealth.

Luce believed that if the rulers failed to meet the needs of their people, they 'will commit political suicide', but observed that: 'we can advise and exhort them to this end, but our agreements with them give us no power to impose our views'.[152] He expressed similar views in a lecture at the Royal United Services Institute in November 1968, where he challenged the timing and method of the decision to withdraw. He did not believe that withdrawing before the mid-1970s 'was the way best calculated to bring about the conditions which give the best hope of a peaceful and honourable transition from the *Pax Britannica*'.[153] Luce was critical of the decision to depart, which was taken 'for reasons irrelevant to our interests and their interests in that area, and can only be regarded as morally wrong, unwise and unnecessary'. Nonetheless, he argued that it was unrealistic to reverse the decision. Luce also doubted whether it would be possible for British forces to remain in the protected states after the withdrawal because they would become 'the target of the young generation of nationalists'. Instead, it should be possible to the give the rulers an assurance of support, similar to the agreement with Kuwait in 1961, and the best way to achieve this objective was the presence of a naval force. The advantages of a naval presence in the Gulf were that it would be a 'credible deterrent' against aggression, and it would avoid the dangers of basing land forces in the region.[154]

Luce's articles are important because they provide some insight into his role as the Foreign Secretary's advisor on the future of the protected states. Luce believed that a federation could only succeed if Bahrain was a member, and he thought that it would be desirable for Saudi Arabia's claims to Abu Dhabi to be delayed until after independence.[155] He identified three main problems in the Gulf, which included Iran's claim to islands, the Saudi claim to Buraimi and the federation of the smaller sheikhdoms.[156] Over the following eighteen months, Luce played a central role in the complex diplomacy that eventually led to Bahrain and Qatar becoming sovereign states, and to the formation of the United Arab Emirates in December 1971.[157]

The Foreign Office was wary of imposing unity on the Gulf States, and the failure to establish a federation in South Arabia influenced the official mind.[158] Crawford observed in his valedictory:

> Britain is not in the Gulf an imperial power; the Protected States are not dependencies and as they have for long had their own systems of government, however imperfect, there is no question of our having, as in Aden and other colonies, to create them. Our role has been one of partnership in which with the rulers' agreement, albeit sometimes reluctantly given, we have done our best to prepare the states for the modern world and to push them into the world at a pace, which they could stand. There has been no feeling on the rulers' part, or that of the great majority of their people, that our presence is unwanted, and there have been none of the stresses associated with military occupation.[159]

Sir William Luce toured the region in August and September 1970. He reported that the states surrounding the Gulf wanted the British withdrawal to be carried out by the end of 1971. His tour made a significant impression on the rulers of the Trucial States, who were left in no doubt that it was their responsibility to make decisions about their future. However, after decades during which the British controlled the Trucial States 'in a negative rather than positive sense', it was too late to reshape the political structure, which might have been possible in a colony or protectorate.[160] The rulers of the protected states, with the exception of Qatar, wanted the British to retain a military presence after the withdrawal because they feared the implications of independence. Nonetheless, Luce made it clear to the rulers of the Trucial States that the British would not enter into any new treaty relationships. The union of the nine protected states remained the preferred solution, and the rulers expected the British to help them bring it about.[161] American diplomats shared his pessimism about the likelihood of establishing a union. In October 1970, American officials, who routinely toured the sheikhdoms, were reporting that a federation of nine was 'already dead', and that Luce's ability to influence the rulers was limited.[162]

In November 1970, Luce produced two reports about the future of the protected states. The first report was based on the supposition that there would be a union that would be sufficiently cohesive to obtain international recognition. He argued that the main threat to stability in the Gulf was subversion and revolution by Arab nationalist and 'left-wing elements against the remaining traditional regimes'. The only way of countering this threat was by 'wise government and efficient intelligence and security services'. Luce also argued that the presence of a British infantry battalion in the Trucial States would not deter this threat, and it might risk involvement in a 'fruitless internal security role'. Heath annotated this sentence and penned his disagreement with Luce's argument about the presence of British troops.[163]

Luce was opposed to any formal British military presence in the protected states after 1971, and he argued that no new defence agreements should be signed with Bahrain and the Trucial States. However, he did recognise that it was important to meet the rulers' demand for continuing British support, including the continuation of Royal Navy patrols in the Indian Ocean. He furthermore argued that Royal Navy and RAF units should be stationed at Bahrain and Sharjah to service visiting warships and aircraft. It was also possible for British forces to conduct exercises in the Trucial States.

Defence interests, including the arms sales, were therefore crucial requirements. Similarly, the future of the Trucial Oman Scouts was an important consideration, and Luce argued that the Scouts should be handed over to the

Union and form the basis of its land forces. British influence in the Trucial States could be maintained by the provision of officers to advise and command the armed forces of the Union. It was preferable to keep British officers in place rather than an infantry battalion because they could act as a safeguard against a 'military revolt'. He, in addition, advised that it was important to maintain support for police and intelligence services because of their ability to maintain stability.

Luce's second report was influenced by the failure of the rulers to agree on a future union, and it was based on the assumption that Bahrain and Qatar would become independent states. The worst-case scenario was that no political entity would be established amongst the seven sheikhdoms, of which Abu Dhabi and Dubai could be considered 'marginally viable'. He addressed the question of whether withdrawing military forces and terminating protection and the exclusive agreements at the end of 1971 would serve British interests, or whether protection of the Trucial States should continue for an additional period. Luce discussed this problem in great detail and reached the conclusion that it was a fallacy to argue that the continuation of protection would bring about a viable union. Under no circumstances should protection of the five smaller sheikhdoms be continued beyond the end of 1971, nor should any new agreement be made with them. He believed that the threat of abandonment would frighten the rulers of the five smaller sheikhdoms into a union with Abu Dhabi and/ or Dubai. This policy had the advantage of encouraging the neighbouring states, such as the Saudis, to adopt a more active policy in the Trucial States.[164] Luce was therefore determined to use all available means to show the rulers of the five sheikhdoms that British protection would be terminated in December 1971.

Sir Burke Trend, the Cabinet Secretary, advised Heath that Luce's key assumptions were acceptable, and that the government should not reverse the Labour Government's decision to withdraw by the end of 1971. Trend noted that Luce had made a convincing case for withdrawing forces because, if they remained in place, 'we should be in a position of responsibility without control. With Rhodesia and the Caribbean in mind this is an uninviting prospect'. Moreover, if the five 'non-viable' sheikhdoms failed to agree on the formation of a union, they should be left to fend for themselves.[165] The Cabinet's Defence and Oversea Policy Committee discussed Luce's reports on 11 December 1970.[166] The meeting reached the conclusion that more pressure should be placed on the rulers to unite, and that the British would not remain in the Gulf.

The Ministry of Defence (MOD) was instructed to examine the defence implications of Luce's reports. Lord Carrington, the Defence Secretary, emphasised the importance of maintaining the Trucial Oman Scouts at their current strength during and after the withdrawal. The Scouts still had a crucial role to play in maintaining the internal security of the Trucial States, and the rulers should be advised that they would have to rely on the TOS as a nucleus for their land forces. The MOD also argued that the provision of loan personnel and training teams should continue after independence. There was no interest in basing military personnel in the Gulf, but there was still a strategic requirement to maintain rights to staging facilities in the Trucial States, at Muharraq in Bahrain and in Qatar.[167] These findings showed that it might be possible to retain Britain's strategic interests in the Gulf after the withdrawal. Nonetheless, the MOD's proposals marked a significant reduction in the UK's interests in the Gulf because advisors would replace British forces.

By the end of 1970, the formation of a union had stood still for three years, and Julian Bullard argued that: 'the more we engage in discussion of the substance of the points at issue, the more difficult it becomes to cling to the position that the it is for the rulers to decide their own political future'.[168] This was a result of British support for the Trucial system, in which very little had been done to equip the rulers to persevere after the withdrawal. The Foreign Office lacked the resources and freedom of action that it once had, and the limitations of British influence were now fully exposed.

The final months of the *Pax Britannica* in the Gulf were characterised by a complex race to secure the agreement of the rulers for the union of the Trucial States. It was inevitable that if Bahrain became independent, so, too, would Qatar.[169] These objectives had to be achieved by the end of 1971, and Luce and British officials in the Trucial States played a central role in meeting this deadline. There was no question of any delay in the British departure from the Gulf. In March 1971, Douglas-Home was unequivocal in his views about British policy. He made it clear to the rulers that the British would offer a treaty of friendship and military assistance, and that regular exercises would be held in the sheikhdoms.[170] D. C. Watt argued that the government's policy 'marks a highly unsatisfactory end to a thoroughly bungled business'. The main weakness of Labour and Conservative policy towards the protected states was that they 'have based their policy on the establishment of the Union of Arab Emirates as a strong, viable political entity … the real truth is that the Union was always a shaky starter, to put it mildly'.[171] The government's decision to withdraw was deeply unpopular with Conservative MPs, but the *Financial Times* noted in

March 1971 that British troops were no longer needed to protect the rulers, sterling balances and access to oil.[172]

Sir Geoffrey Arthur argued that nearly all the rulers and their subjects behaved as if the Labour Government had never made its announcement to leave. The rulers did not expect the British to change their mind, but they could not imagine any relationship other than with the British.[173] The Political Agents at Abu Dhabi and Dubai played a key role in trying to persuade the rulers to cooperate, but they were hindered by the historic tendency of the sheikhs to avoid any action that would lead them to being blamed for disrupting unity.[174] The 'backstairs' influence of Foreign Office officials exemplifies how deeply embedded the British were in the sheikhdoms prior to the withdrawal.

Meanwhile, the rulers of Abu Dhabi and Dubai showed that they were willing to take steps to establish a union, regardless of the views of the five smaller sheikhdoms. Sato illustrates how the rulers reached a secret agreement prior to a meeting of the Trucial States Council on 12 July 1971.[175] As a result of this secret agreement, Abu Dhabi and Dubai were placed on an equal footing in the Union's constitution.[176] The rulers of the two sheikhdoms had to persuade the five other rulers to accept their inferior status in the union.[177] Arthur noted that the relationship between Sheikh Zayed and Sheikh Rashid was 'a strange friendship',[178] but the secret agreement 'unlocked the door' to the achievement of what was the best possible political structure, given the impossibility of reconciling Bahrain and Qatar.[179] On 18 July 1971, the rulers announced the formation of the United Arab Emirates, comprising six states: Abu Dhabi, Ajman, Dubai, Fujairah, Kalba and Umm Al Quwain. However, Ras Al Khaimah was unwilling to compromise on representation in the Union Council. As Frauke Heard-Bey notes, the July agreement was a milestone in the formation of the UAE because it provided the structure for government organisation.[180]

Saudi and Iranian attitudes towards the UAE

The perspective of the Saudis towards the Trucial States union and the Gulf was contradictory. King Faisal had a strong interest in supporting the sheikhly regimes in the Trucial States, Kuwait, Qatar and Bahrain because he feared that an Aden-type insurgency might arise following the termination of British protection.[181] However, Saudi diplomacy in the Gulf was characterised by the JIC as 'lethargic and hesitant' because very little had been done to promote Saudi interests.[182] Fear of subversion, rather than a belief in 'manifest destiny', determined Saudi policy towards the Trucial States and the Gulf, but King Faisal was anxious to achieve a compromise settlement before the British departure.[183] Although the Saudis and the Shah had a common interest in preventing the spread of Arab nationalism and communist influence, there was little indication of any attempt to cooperate. The main impediment to Saudi–Iranian cooperation in the Gulf was Arab and Iranian nationalism. The Iranians regarded Saudi Arabia as a buffer between them and Nasserism, whereas the Saudis were concerned about the Shah's relations with the Soviet Union, and their sense of pride made them resist the idea of cooperating with the Shah.[184]

The Saudis made an effort, in concert with the Kuwaitis, to encourage the rulers of the Trucial States to federate, but their mediation was counterproductive. King Faisal remained wedded to the formation of a union of the nine protected states despite all the evidence that it was unachievable.[185] The King maintained this position because he was opposed to the expansion of Sheikh Zayed's influence along the Trucial Coast if a union was established.[186] Antony Acland's[187] solution was simply to ignore King Faisal's demands.[188] Saudi policy on the Gulf was characterised by inertia because they were biding their time and waiting for the British to leave.[189]

One of the most significant challenges the Foreign Office faced during the final phase of the *Pax Britannica* was Iran's growing influence in the Gulf. The attitudes of the Trucial States rulers towards the Shah ranged from open admiration in Qatar and Bahrain to respectful wariness in Ras Al Khaimah.[190] The Shah was determined to assert Iran's economic, political and military independence. This meant holding a balance between the East and the West, which was aided by Iran's growing oil wealth. It was the Shah's conviction that once the British left the Gulf, Iran would be in a position to play a dominant role in the region. The Joint Intelligence Committee noted that the Shah was concerned about the likelihood of subversion on the Arab side of the Gulf.[191] However, the Shah created a dilemma in the Gulf. The establishment of a union was beneficial to the Iranians because it would ensure stability in the Gulf, but the Shah's determination to gain control of the Gulf islands was a significant impediment to the formation of the UAE.[192]

The Shah opposed any union until the Abu Musa and the Tunbs islands problem was settled, and Luce devoted a considerable amount of time to finding a solution. The planning of the withdrawal was contingent on an agreement with the Shah because if they failed, the Shah might have denied British aircraft access to Iranian airspace.[193] Iranian forces occupied the islands at the end of November 1971,[194] and no attempt was made by the British either to deter them[195] or to use warships deployed in the Gulf to defend the islands.[196] The CIA argued that the reaction in the Arab world would be restricted to propaganda, but the occupation of the islands became a major source of friction between Iran and its Arab neighbours.[197] A negotiated agreement between the Shah and the ruler of Sharjah in November 1971 about Abu Musa meant that it was possible for the UAE to be established shortly afterwards.[198] It was claimed that there was no evidence that the British colluded with the Iranians to occupy the islands but Simon Smith shows that Luce worked behind the scenes over the timing of an Iranian takeover.[199]

Implementing the withdrawal

Meanwhile, the preparations for the withdrawal and the establishment of the union continued unabated. The Bahrain Government belatedly requested in August 1971 that the treaty relationship be rescinded, and the Qataris immediately followed suit.[200] Bahrain, Qatar and Oman became members of the United Nations in October 1971. The withdrawal of British forces followed a clearly defined sequence. The military withdrawal from the Gulf was staggered between the autumn of 1970 and December 1971.[201] The first battalion left in the autumn of 1970 and the armoured car squadron left Sharjah in the spring 1971. The Hawker Hunter squadrons began to run down after the commitment to defend Kuwait lapsed in May 1971. The Royal Navy's minesweepers left in the autumn of 1971, the second battalion left Sharjah at the end of November, and the last transport, maritime reconnaissance aircraft and helicopters in December. By the middle of December, the Royal Navy's base in Bahrain, HMS *Jufair*, and the RAF stations at Muharraq in Bahrain and Sharjah had closed. The Headquarters of British Forces in the Gulf ceased to function on 16 December and the last British commander in the Gulf departed for the UK the following day. The withdrawal of British forces was uneventful and, on 19 December, all British forces had departed from the Gulf. Sir Geoffrey Arthur described the scene in his valedictory dispatch from Bahrain:

> At about half past two in the afternoon of 19 December 1971, HMS *Intrepid*, 12,000 tons, moved slowly through the tortuous channel that leads from Mina Sulman, the port of Bahrain, out to the open sea. There was no ceremony as the last British fighting unit withdrew from the Persian Gulf: a British merchant vessel in the opposite berth blew her siren, and *Intrepid's* lone piper, scarcely

audible above the bustle of the port, played what sounded like some Gaelic lament. That was all.[202]

The political relationship between the British and the Trucial States, Bahrain and Qatar also reached an orchestrated conclusion. On 1 December, Arthur exchanged notes with the rulers of the sheikhdoms, terminating the special treaty relationship. The following day, the rulers, with the exception of Ras Al Khaimah's, assembled at Dubai and the constitution of the United Arab Emirates was proclaimed. Arthur described Ras Al Khaimah as the 'odd man out' of the sheikhdoms, and noted that the regime was 'difficult' for geographic and historic reasons.[203] Ras Al Khaimah belatedly joined the Union in February 1972. The UAE was finally established against the odds, and Sheikh Zayed became president and portfolios in the government were quickly assigned.[204]

Economic and social development

Abu Dhabi and Dubai achieved significant economic growth between 1968 and 1971. This was despite the uncertainty caused by the British decision to leave by the end of 1971. The disputes that divided the rulers about the future political structure of the Trucial States had a minimal impact on their prosperity, but it did call into question the long-term viability of sheikhly rule. The sheikhdoms' rapidly increasing wealth meant that they needed to devise a complex system of government to manage the process of development. In the past, the rulers governed their sheikhdoms on a personal basis, and there had been a minimal necessity to develop a system of government. With the exception of Dubai, which was the most advanced economy in the Trucial States before oil, the economies of the other sheikhdoms were rudimentary. However, Abu Dhabi's exponential growth and a shortage of trained locals meant that Sheikh Zayed became increasingly reliant on foreign advisors and consultants.

The main requirements of developing the economy of the Trucial States in the late 1960s were striking a balance between a wide-ranging programme, including agriculture, education, health and water supplies, and avoiding the excessive growth of bureaucracy. The promotion of common services amongst the Trucial States was an urgent necessity in light of attempts to unify the sheikhdoms.[205] The most important economic development that occurred in the protected states in the late 1960s was the rapid growth of oil production. In 1969, the sheikhdoms (including Oman) represented 3 per cent of Free World oil production and

12 per cent of Middle Eastern oil production. Output in 1968 was 1,153,000 barrels a day, which increased to 1,379,000 in 1969. Proven oil reserves amounted to 22,250 billion barrels, or 4 per cent of the total world reserves. Abu Dhabi was the most important producer, and in 1969, the sheikhdom produced 601,000 barrels a day, compared to 15,000 barrels a day in 1962. Abu Dhabi's proven oil reserves in 1969 were 15 billion barrels. The combined oil income of the sheikhdoms in 1969 was $350 million.[206]

The startling expansion of the oil industry in the late 1960s had significant ramifications in the Trucial States. The development of the Trucial States rapidly increased between 1968 and 1971. In March 1965, the Trucial States Council decided to follow British advice and establish a development fund, with the objective of facilitating the joint planning and financing of development in the sheikhdoms. Between 1965 and 1968, the Trucial States Development Fund spent money on successful development projects, including electricity and water supplies, agricultural and hydrological surveys and health services. The five Northern Trucial States were the focus of the development effort because they remained markedly less developed than Abu Dhabi and Dubai.[207]

One of the most significant challenges was the increase in education, which was arguably the most important aspect of the development programme because of the shortage of indigenous trained labour. In 1968, the British Council's representative in the Gulf reported that significant advances had been made in the expansion of education in Abu Dhabi. It was recognised that progress would be slow but the foundations had been laid of an educational system. In Dubai and Sharjah, trade schools had grown, and there were plans to open a similar school in Ras Al Khaimah. The British Council's ability to widen the scope of teaching English was limited because the Kuwait State Office, which dominated education in Dubai and Sharjah, would not accept British teachers.[208] Heard-Bey argues that the Trucial States were not typical developing states because of their growing oil income, and that more could have been done in the late 1960s to provide the sheikhdoms with trained administrators, capable of running the state after independence. Nonetheless, the oil companies, Petroleum Development (Trucial Coast) and Abu Dhabi Marine Areas (ADMA), played an important role in the development of the sheikhdoms at the time.[209] The oil companies offered unprecedented job opportunities and training in the Trucial States and contributed towards the construction of infrastructure.[210]

Abu Dhabi and Dubai were growing increasingly wealthy but they lacked the skilled manpower to plan and initiate a long-term development programme. The CIA observed that one of the unusual characteristics of the Trucial States was the high percentage of foreigners employed in the area. Between 25 and 30 per cent of the total population were now expatriates, who worked as merchants and in the oil industry. The reliance on foreign labour reflected the indigenous population's lack of education and skills, and a traditional aversion towards wage employment that characterised the Bedouin.[211]

The fragmentation and inequality of resources of the Trucial States were serious obstacles to the coordinated development of the region. In 1968, Abu Dhabi had a population of 46,500 and an income of £65 million, derived almost entirely from oil. Sheikh Zayed faced huge challenges because there were no ministers advised by competent officials and supported by an efficient civil service. Chairmen, who were mainly members of the ruling family, headed departments and the government system relied heavily on foreign advisors. Julian Bullard summed up Sheikh Zayed's role:

> In all this land there is but a single policy maker – the ruler: autocrat and man of the people, an illiterate who possesses abundant native wit, wise councillor and intriguer and favoured with a personality and charm with which it is the fortune of few men to be blessed. If, at the end of this surprising year, Abu Dhabi has emerged with honour, the credit is due in large measure to Shaikh Zaid. He must be nominated Abu Dhabi Man of the Year and, barring accidents, he will carry the award for some years to come.[212]

Sheikhly rule characterised how the Trucial States were governed, but it was open to question whether it was suitable for a rapidly developing oil economy. Abu Dhabi adopted the Bahraini dinar (BD) in June 1966,[213] and in March 1968, Sheikh Zayed produced a five-year development plan, with a budget of BD250 million.[214] The development scheme envisaged spending BD196 million on infrastructural development, including on roads, airports, ports and the oil industry. BD12.4 million was spent on primary and secondary education, with an additional BD2.8 million being allocated to industrial training units with the long-term objective of reducing Abu Dhabi's reliance on foreign experts. The 1968 budget allocated BD6.5 million, to be spent on a network of hospitals, and BD13.4 million was provided for agricultural development. Most of this money was spent on the water supply system, to take into account increasing demand in Abu Dhabi and Buraimi. Sheikh Zayed also encouraged the development of central markets in the beginning of 1969, which were meant to aid safe food distribution.[215]

The objective of this programme was to develop the sheikhdom according to a planned strategy, but there were significant impediments. In October 1969, the

Financial Times reported that Abu Dhabi's development was being hindered by rapid growth and the overestimation of oil income, which amounted to £80 million–£85 million, rather than the anticipated £100 million.[216] The situation was worsened by a variety of problems, which included maladministration and significant expenditure on the Abu Dhabi Defence Force. The Foreign Office believed that Sheikh Zayed was allocating 25 per cent of the state's income to the Privy Purse, which was not unusual in the sheikhdoms.[217] As a result of this expenditure, in 1969, government debt amounted to £30 million and future prosperity depended on Sheikh Zayed cooperating with his newly appointed director of finance and imposing financial reform on the administration.[218] However, the financial problems were addressed in 1970, following the appointment of a new financial advisor, who attempted to impose some control over Abu Dhabi's rapid growth.[219] All the same, Luce commented in September 1970 that Abu Dhabi's system of government was chaotic and led to inefficiency and squandered funds.[220]

In November 1968, the Treasury provided a grant of £1 million for capital projects over a period of three to four years, as well as an annual contribution of £200,000 towards 'technical cooperation' in the Trucial States. The Foreign Office hoped that British aid would act as a catalyst for other states to make a contribution. However, Bahrain and Qatar provided £250,000 and £40,000, while the Saudi government funded a new road between Sharjah and Ras Al Khaimah. The Foreign Office hoped that Abu Dhabi would contribute significant sums to the development programme. By March 1969, the British had contributed £1,800,000 to the Fund,[221] but Abu Dhabi's rapid development called into question the continuation of British development expenditure in the Trucial States.

In March 1969, the Middle East Development Division of the Foreign Office produced a detailed analysis of British aid to the Trucial States. In 1968, the per capita income of the seven Trucial States, including Abu Dhabi, was approximately $1,800 per annum, and it was probable that the per capita income of Abu Dhabi was about $6,000, which compared to $1,600 in the UK in 1967, prior to the devaluation of the pound in November. These figures suggested that there was no case for any aid contribution to the richest sheikhdoms, according to the criteria of 'aid worthiness'. There was a wide variation in state income between Abu Dhabi, whose oil income in 1968 was £68 million, and the combined income of the five poorer states, which did not exceed £300,000.[222]

The main justification for continued British support was the importance of preserving influence in shaping the development policies of the rulers. The

Foreign Office had an ongoing interest in promoting economic stability and protecting capital investments in the oil industry. The expansion of British trade in the Trucial States was also regarded as a significant economic interest.[223] However, the Trucial States Development Fund was considered a British institution. A further criticism of the British aid contribution was the declining control over how the money was allocated. Between 1965 and 1972, the Development Office distributed over £13 million in aid. Abu Dhabi contributed over 70 per cent of this figure, and the British government, the remainder.[224] The growing disparity between the British aid contribution and Abu Dhabi's ability to fund development across the Trucial States called into question the relevance of British support.

Development varied in the other sheikhdoms. Dubai remained the most prosperous sheikhdom, apart from Abu Dhabi. Dubai's wealth was the result of limited restrictions on trade rather than oil, and it is often attributed to the role played by Sheikh Rashid, who became ruler in 1958. Sheikh Rashid was described as 'astute, charming, unspoilt, energetic, practical, expeditious in business, contemptuous of eyewash and nearly always sound in judgement'.[225] Between 1966 and 1968, imports grew from £22 million to over £66 million, although this figure did not include the traffic in illicit gold to India and Pakistan, which was estimated to be worth over £40 million a year. In 1969, Dubai started to export oil, which helped to fund the expansion of the sheikhdom's port and hospital, along with an airport and sewage system. In contrast with Abu Dhabi, Dubai benefited from a more efficient government that was characterised by Sheikh Rashid's personal rule. By the late 1960s, Dubai was regarded as the capital of the Northern Trucial States, with a population of 59,000 and an increasing number of expatriates. Julian Bullard noted that the rapid changes in Dubai were already having social consequences as the gap between rich and poor expanded. As a result of rapid growth, Dubai was 'fast losing the simplicity and harmony which used to be one of its main attractions'.[226]

The five smaller sheikhdoms were the focus of the British development programme because they lacked oil.[227] Between 1968 and 1970, Sharjah gradually became more prosperous.[228] Sharjah's main income was derived from the RAF base on its territory, and in 1968, Sheikh Khalid signed an oil concession with Shell. The sheikhdom's growing wealth was attributed to the efforts of Sheikh Khalid, who ran Sharjah like a family business. The four other smaller sheikhdoms of Ajman, Fujairah, Kalba and Umm Al Quwain, were consistently portrayed as economically inconsequential in British reports in the late 1960s.

Conclusion

The retreat from the Gulf at the end of 1971 was a diplomatic achievement because of the limited amount of time that was available, and the complexity of the issues that had to be resolved. The successful outcome can be attributed to Foreign Secretary Sir Alec Douglas Home taking control of government policy in the summer of 1970. Between January 1968 and the election of the Conservative Government in June 1970, British policy lost momentum as a result of Edward Heath's assertion that the Conservatives would reverse the decision to withdraw. This led the rulers of the Trucial States to reach the conclusion that the British would not leave. The indecisive message that emanated from Whitehall reinforced the sheikhs' long-standing tendency to disagree about the future of the sheikhdoms. Antony Acland, the Head of the Arabian Department at the Foreign Office, who played an important role in the development of policy, aided the impetus in his department. Furthermore, Douglas-Home's appointment of Sir William Luce as his personal representative sent a clear message to the rulers that they would have to reach an agreement about the formation of a union. In the Gulf, Sir Geoffrey Arthur, the Political Resident, and the Political Agents played a key role in cajoling the rulers to reach a conclusion about their collective future. The Foreign Office's influence in the Trucial States was pervasive, and it is open to question what would have transpired without British intervention.

The process of withdrawing British forces from Bahrain and Sharjah was straightforward because there was no discernable opposition to the British in the protected states. The relatively small number of British forces located in Bahrain and Sharjah meant that planning the withdrawal was not complex. The retreat from the Gulf heavily depended on the role of the rulers, and the ability of Foreign Office officials to persuade them to cooperate about the future political structure of the Trucial States. The imminent prospect of the British retreat from the protected states belatedly forced the rulers to cooperate. Although the rulers succeeded in forming the UAE in February 1968, they remained deeply divided. The federation of the Trucial States in 1971 was the most plausible solution because they shared many common features, including a sheikhly system of rule and the Trucial Oman Scouts who defended them.

The most important rulers in the Trucial States were Sheikh Zayed and Sheikh Rashid, the rulers of Abu Dhabi and Dubai, respectively, on account of their rapidly increasing prosperity. It was inevitable that Abu Dhabi would become the dominant sheikhdom after independence, whereas the rulers of the five smaller sheikhdoms were of limited importance. It was inconceivable that

Bahrain or Qatar would join a federation on account of the competing differences between the ruling families. Moreover, it made little sense for Bahrain to join a union with the other sheikhdoms on account of its larger population and greater economic development. There was a great deal of uncertainty about the future political arrangements of the protected states, almost until the end of the British era.

The Foreign Office had to contend with external influences in devising a successful withdrawal. The Shah had a growing interest in the future of the Gulf, and Iran's strategic importance to the Western powers placed him in a strong position. There was little the Foreign Office could do to prevent the Shah from taking control of the disputed Gulf islands of Abu Musa and the Tunbs in November 1971. The British had no interest or will in using force to prevent the Iranians from forcibly occupying the islands. In contrast, King Faisal and the Saudi government showed limited interest in the future of the Trucial States, apart from Saudi Arabia's long-standing claim to the Buraimi Oasis. The Foreign Office failed to achieve a diplomatic solution prior to the withdrawal, and it is doubtful whether British intervention would have succeeded. All previous attempts by the Foreign Office to negotiate a solution had failed.

One of the most significant British contributions towards the Trucial States was the development of their armed forces. The TOS played a central role in maintaining the internal security of the Trucial States and in protecting their external frontiers in the period leading to withdrawal in December 1971. However, the establishment of rival security forces, especially the ADDF, called into question the role of the TOS, which was supposed to be the army of the Trucial States. The TOS was, in reality, an instrument of British policy in the sheikhdoms, but the Foreign Office's attempts to establish a unified armed force failed because some of the rulers wanted to establish their own armed forces. There was little the Foreign Office could do to hinder the proliferation of armed forces in the Trucial States. Nevertheless, their establishment provided the British with an unrivalled opportunity to train and equip them.

The British played a key role in establishing the police forces in the Trucial States and in the development of a local intelligence capability. These forces were important on account of the growing potential threat of subversion in the Trucial States that were no longer immune from regional trends. The gradual expansion of these forces played an important role in maintaining internal security in the protected states. However, the extent of the internal security threat in the Trucial States was limited, which eased the role of the nascent security and intelligence forces.

The British contribution towards the economic and social development of the Trucial States had been significant since its inception in 1955. Despite this, the case for ongoing British assistance was weakened by the late 1960s as a result of Abu Dhabi's rapidly expanding oil economy. Sheikh Zayed was now in a strong position to fund the development of the five smaller Trucial States as well. The Trucial States benefited considerably from Abu Dhabi's rapidly expanding oil wealth, which called into question the continuation of British aid. Nonetheless, the sheikhdoms relied heavily on foreign advisors because the indigenous population lacked the requisite skills to run government departments. The provision of experts, such as a financial advisor to Abu Dhabi, was an important way in which the British could influence the development of the Trucial States after they became independent.

6

Epilogue

The British legacy in the Gulf

This chapter examines the British legacy during the first decade of the UAE's existence. The UK's influence in the Gulf region did not end when the British departed in December 1971. The British withdrawal from the Gulf was peaceful, and the termination of the treaties with the protected states inevitably meant that the nature of relations changed. Both the Foreign Office and the Labour Government adopted a hands-off policy in the UAE and Gulf region between 1974 and 1979. Relations with the rulers were also transformed in the post-independence era, and the Foreign Office was concerned about the stability of the UAE. Shortly after independence, coups occurred in Sharjah and Qatar, but British officials were no longer in a position to intervene. Nonetheless, the British had perennial interests in the UAE after independence, including in their access to oil, which was a legacy of expenditure on the development of the petroleum industry. The expansion of commercial relations with Abu Dhabi and Dubai became a key interest from the mid-1970s onwards. British companies obtained a significant share of the UAE's trade but they faced competition from rivals such as the French, who entered the region on an unprecedented scale.

One of the notable characteristics of the British legacy in the UAE was the extent of informal influence that prevailed after independence. British expatriates advised the rulers, and a wide range of corporate interests, alongside the oil companies, contributed to the economic development of the Emirates. However, there was little indication of any cultural impact in the Gulf, apart from English being the second language in the region.

A significant legacy of the British role in the UAE, and the other protected states, was an ongoing military relationship. Following independence, the British assisted in the development of the armed forces of the UAE, and British personnel remained, either on loan or acting on a personal basis. Gradually, the defence relationship was transformed from British officers commanding units to acting as advisors. Inevitably the rulers, especially in Abu Dhabi, wanted to assert their sovereignty, and the armed forces of the UAE established military relations with other Islamic states, most notably Jordan and Pakistan.

Another significant British legacy in the UAE was the failure to address certain aspects of the UAE's foreign policy prior to independence. A notable example was the long-standing Buraimi Oasis dispute, which was not resolved prior to the British withdrawal. In 1974, Sheikh Zayed and King Faisal signed an opaque agreement. The Jeddah Agreement was important because it led to the establishment of diplomatic relations between the UAE and Saudi Arabia, but did not resolve the frontier dispute. The British also departed from the Gulf, without establishing a regional security system, which meant that the UAE and the other newly independent states in the region were vulnerable to their more powerful neighbours. The British left a power vacuum in the Gulf, and the UAE became increasingly influenced by regional events. The Iranian Revolution in 1978–9 had a fundamental impact on British interests in the Gulf region. The revolution led to the Labour Government becoming more concerned with the UAE, which was marked by Queen Elizabeth II's landmark tour of the region in early 1979. The Queen's unprecedented tour, which included a visit to the UAE, was an unequivocal symbol of the British commitment to the region. The Conservative Government that came to power in June 1979 adopted a proactive policy in the Gulf region. The Foreign Office was able to take advantage of historical ties with the rulers, which contributed towards a positive legacy in the UAE and the Gulf region. These events showed that, although the British departed in 1971, they were determined to preserve long-standing economic and political interests, which endure to this day.

Political relations

The British withdrawal from the Gulf at the end of 1971 was a notable example of decolonisation. In contrast with other cases of retreat from Empire in the Middle East, the departure from the Gulf was achieved peacefully, with the consent of the rulers and the population. Robin Winks makes a useful observation about decolonisation in the informal empire: 'the process must seem less clearly defined than in the case of evolutionary independence from a formal condition of "tutelage"'. Since none of the preparatory stages could be applied consciously, consistently or fully within an informal sphere of influence, it is difficult to say when they ceased to be applied, if at all'.[1] Winks' argument is apposite in the Gulf, where Britain's interests did not disappear after 1971. In reality, they underwent a fundamental but subtle transformation.

The Foreign Office's changing role in the UAE was characterised by the significant decline in the scale of reporting from the former Trucial States. British diplomats were no longer as closely involved in the internal affairs of the UAE, and as a result of independence, they were engaged in traditional diplomatic functions. After independence, the Foreign Office unusually established embassies at both Abu Dhabi and Dubai, which raised questions about the division of labour between the two missions.[2] The Ambassador at Abu Dhabi was responsible for relations with the federal government, whereas the Consul General at Dubai handled contacts with Sheikh Rashid, the ruler of Dubai, and the five smaller sheikhdoms. The decision to retain two embassies in the UAE was intended to 'flatter' Sheikh Rashid, and it marked the continuation of the Political Agencies that had handled relations with the rulers prior to independence.[3]

During the 1970s, the number of British diplomats serving in the Gulf, from Kuwait to Muscat, increased from 60 in 1971 to 67 in 1980.[4] Jim Treadwell, the first British Ambassador to Abu Dhabi (1971–3), was instructed by the Foreign Office to assist in the UAE's political and economic development. Treadwell was also assigned the long-standing task of protecting the flow of oil and encouraging the UAE to become a good neighbour. The Foreign Office also urged that he take steps to prevent reductions in the sterling holdings of the UAE. The major British interest in the UAE after independence was the security of oil supplies and the expansion of trade.[5]

After independence, the Foreign Office deliberately adopted a low profile in the UAE, which suggests that the Emirates were not important to the British. The political significance of the UAE to the 'UK was secondary, as one senior official noted: 'stability in the region is what our political and economic interests require. The UAE is a means and not an end.'[6] The Foreign Office was careful not to chaperone the rulers, but Rosemary Hollis argues that during the 1970s, the UK's diplomatic relations with the UAE could be characterised as an 'era of benign neglect', but this book suggests otherwise.[7] Saul Kelly believes that the British 'simply abandoned their former subjects and protégés to their respective fates, and did not really care what followed or made adequate provision for it'.[8] Donal McCarthy in Abu Dhabi and St John Armitage in Dubai were highly experienced Arabists, with many years of experience in the Arab world. They had the confidence of Sheikh Zayed, Sheikh Rashid and the rulers of the five smaller sheikhdoms, and frequently discussed regional politics with them.[9] Nonetheless, the rapid withdrawal at the end of 1971 meant that there were significant limitations about what could have been achieved.

Anthony Parsons, who was the Superintending Under-Secretary responsible for the Middle East (1971–4), commented in May 1972 that: 'we have not cut and run from the Gulf and have no intention of doing so. We still regard ourselves as having considerable influence in the area and will use it to the best of our ability to protect our and Western interests there.'[10] The Foreign Office wanted to avoid the appearance of interfering in the internal affairs of the newly established federation. The Labour Government under Harold Wilson and James Callaghan (1974–9) avoided overplaying its hand with the UAE. Alan Munro notes that the Labour Government ignored the Gulf and 'certain of our Labour ministers show a measure of antipathy towards the Gulf minnows, seeing their traditional autocratic ways of governance as anachronisms that are unlikely to survive, and perhaps do not deserve to do so'. Ministers met the Foreign Office's proposals to re-engage with the UAE with little enthusiasm.[11]

The expansion of trade with the UAE, Iran and Saudi Arabia became a major characteristic of British policy in the Gulf region during the 1970s. Parsons, who was Ambassador to Iran during 1974–9, commented that the embassy at Tehran emphasised defence sales and trade promotion, whereas political reporting became a secondary consideration.[12] The significance of trade was emphasised when David Ennals, a Minister of State in the Foreign Office, toured the Gulf in February 1975. Ennals was advised by the Foreign Office that the Gulf was a vital economic interest to the UK because it represented, excluding Saudi Arabia, 26 per cent of Britain's oil supplies. Moreover, British exports to the Gulf amounted to £250 million in 1975, an increase from £151 million in 1973.

Abu Dhabi and Dubai became growing markets for British goods and services after independence, and between 1974 and 1977, the value of exports to the UAE grew from £96.9 million to £455 million.[13] These exports were vital for the British economy, which was known as the 'Sick Man of Europe'. Briefing papers given to Ennals exemplify the extent to which oil and trade dominated British interests in the UAE.[14] Ennals reported that the UK's political relations with the UAE were 'on a sound basis' but the rulers and British expatriates believed that more could have been done to counter the efforts being made by the Americans, French and Japanese.[15] Donal McCarthy, Treadwell's successor as the British Ambassador at Abu Dhabi (1973–7), pointedly wrote that: 'I doubt, first, whether Mr Ennals did much to improve the Labour Party's image – it is still regarded as the anti-European and pro-Zionist party, however over simplified the former view in particular may be. What he did undoubtedly to was put the

Labour Administration's attitude in perspective and reassure people on that. And, of course, that is what matters.'[16]

The decline in Whitehall's interest in the UAE contrasted with the residual British influence in the Gulf region after 1971. In Dubai, there was 'a remarkable continuum' after the withdrawal because British expatriates 'constituted much of the sinews of this state'. In June 1974, British experts held the same key positions in the government, and Jack Briggs, the Commander of the Police, was responsible for establishing the most capable police force in the UAE. Likewise, the head of the Dubai Special Branch was also British. British firms such as Sir William Halcrow and Partners remained the dominant consultants, and construction companies, including the Costain Group and Taylor Woodrow, played a key role in the building boom in Dubai.[17] McCarthy noted that the situation was more than just Sheikh Rashid's Anglophilia, but because he trusted long-serving British experts. Nonetheless, McCarthy argued that Sheikh Rashid's reliance on British expatriates was behind the times because there were Arabs who were capable of filling these roles. It seemed inevitable that they would replace Sheikh Rashid's British advisors, which is what happened in Abu Dhabi.[18] Sheikh Zayed employed numerous Algerian and Iraqi advisors in Abu Dhabi's oil industry, which gave French companies, such as the arms manufacturer Dassault, an entrée into the UAE.

British influence was pervasive from Kuwait to Muscat, and British diplomats reported on how their 'soft power' was utilised after 1971. Edward Henderson, the first British Ambassador to Qatar and one of the Foreign Office's most experienced envoys in the Gulf, commented on Britain's residual influence. Henderson observed in his valedictory letter that:

> At a personal level at all points in the Government and in the business community I think we have even better relations after independence than we had before. The Qataris welcome British experts and engineers in the Government and armed forces and seem to want more of them.

Henderson also commented that it was 'Britain's presence alone which enabled her (Qatar) to achieve independence in 1971', and that there was significant demand for British experts and engineers in the Qatar government.[19] By the late 1970s, the British maintained a dominant position, and as one of Henderson's successors noted: 'we have three trump cards in our hands, all mutually reinforcing our commercial advantage here'. These included Britain's historical relationship with Qatar, which made the Qataris accustomed to doing business with the British. These ties were reinforced by the British Council, which encouraged English teaching that fostered commercial relations. The presence of a British expatriate community in Qatar played a central role in 'guiding and advising the inexperienced Qataris in every field ... often going for long periods without being paid by the government for doing so'. The final strength of the residual British presence was that:

> the combination of history and experience seems to have induced the Qataris a feeling of affinity with Britain and the British which defies analysis. They flock to London in droves – to spend the summer, to buy houses, to have their children educated part-time there and worship devotedly at the twin shrines of 'shopping' and 'check up'. They feel at home in Britain as nowhere else in Europe, or the Arab world – an affinity that brings material rewards in the shape of orders for British goods and services'.[20]

A similar situation prevailed in Kuwait and Bahrain after the British withdrawal. Kuwait had succeeded in countering revolutionary movements by a generous system of social welfare, high wages and the deportation of dissidents. The CIA believed that the Kuwaiti government's attempts to increase its security by buying friends aboard through loans and development had not secured the backing of the Arab states against the long-standing Iraqi threat. The CIA concluded that Bahrain was potentially unstable but its more educated population meant that it had the best chance amongst the smaller states to develop economic and political institutions. However, Bahrain faced the long-term problems of declining oil production and perennial schisms between its Shia and Sunni population.[21]

The UK's diplomatic relations with the Emirates were positive following the withdrawal, in spite of the precipitous decision to retreat, which the rulers lamented until the early 1980s.[22] David Roberts, who became Ambassador to the UAE in the autumn of 1977 and had previously served as Political Agent at Dubai in 1966–8, commented on Britain's relations with the UAE in various dispatches to the Foreign Office. Roberts argued that contacts were good because the rulers had been accustomed to the advice and friendship of British businessmen, experts and officials. Roberts believed that the British could preserve their position in Abu Dhabi and Dubai, and even survive the dissolution of the union. He observed that 'it is one of the joys of this Post that it is one of the few places, it seems to me, where one can and indeed must practice the old diplomacy of personal relations to a considerable degree. This is the result partly of sheikhly rule and partly of our long association with the area. We have a strong position here but we shall have to strain every nerve to keep it.'[23] A similar situation prevailed in Bahrain, which feared losing British protection, but continued engagement was bound to reap dividends in the future.[24] Relations remained cordial partly as a result of habit, and because 'there is genuine friendliness and readiness to listen to us'.[25]

Immediately after the British withdrawal, political insecurity occurred in the former protected states. On 24 January 1972, Sheikh Saqr bin Sultan, who had been deposed as ruler of Sharjah in 1965, attempted to overthrow his cousin, Sheikh Khalid.[26] The British-commanded Union Defence Force prevented Sheikh Khalid's violent overthrow,[27] but he was assassinated during the course of these events. On 22 February 1972, a non-violent coup also occurred in Qatar, when Sheikh Ahmed bin Ali Al Thani was replaced by Khalifa bin Hamad Al Thani because he failed to perform his constitutional duties by establishing an advisory council and remaining engaged in foreign policy.[28] These coups were examples of the long-standing tradition of disputes within the ruling families that continued after independence. There is little indication that they weakened the stability of the states, and the Foreign Office had no direct role in these events.

The instability that characterised the UAE after independence was a legacy of Britain's long association with the protected states. The British did very little to prevent these schisms within the sheikhly families. The rulers had limited experience working together, let alone running a system of government that was free of British interference. Furthermore, Britain's rapid departure from the Trucial States meant that not enough time was available to prepare them for independence. Immediately after independence, Sheikh Zayed took responsibility for the UAE's foreign policy and was determined to establish the Emirates' international standing. As one former Foreign Office diplomat who served in the Gulf during the 1970s noted: 'as far as domestic politics were concerned we would not have wanted to teach granny to suck eggs!'[29] The absence of an educated indigenous population in the Trucial States was also a significant impediment that prevented the establishment of a stable political system. The rulers had no choice but to rely on British and other expatriates to act as their advisors. Not all the states experienced coups following the British withdrawal, and in 1974, the first peaceful succession within the Emirates occurred when the ruler of Fujairah died and his son, Sheikh Ahmed, who continues to rule the sheikhdom, replaced him.

The Foreign Office was surprised that the UAE managed to survive its first years of existence. One of the significant themes in the reports from the Gulf in the years after independence was whether the UAE was a viable entity. The weaknesses of the UAE were a consequence of the rapid British departure. The British might have established a government for the UAE and trained personnel to administer it. Instead, the Foreign Office allowed the UAE federal government in Abu Dhabi to acquire sixteen ministries, each with a bureaucracy of Egyptian, Iraqi and Palestinian advisors. As Roberts noted in 1978, a secretariat should have been established, staffed by a small number of officials who could have been trained in British universities. If this had been done, there might have been less of a decline in British influence in Abu Dhabi and the federal government. Federal structures in the UAE were rudimentary because Dubai never wanted to be part of them.[30] Roberts argued that it was no surprise that there were significant limitations with the UAE because experience of federations and Arab unions such as the United Arab Republic had been unsuccessful.[31] Previous British attempts to unify states, such as the West Indies Federation (1958–62), had failed due to internal disputes and were an ominous sign for the Emirates.

The federal structure of the Emirates was based on the equality of the states and the rulers' continuing prerogatives. The federal constitution arrogated power to the centre, and ministries reflected the states' relative importance.[32] The new state faced several challenges that included Sheikh Zayed's inevitable domination of the UAE on account of Abu Dhabi's oil wealth. The rulers of the smaller sheikhdoms resented Sheikh Zayed's domineering attitude towards them, which led to fears that they might reject the Union and look to the Saudis for protection.[33] There were early signs of serious political differences between the different rulers, which were a continuation of long-running disputes between the seven Emirates. Sheikh Zayed attempted to become the father of the UAE; however, he was described as well-meaning but with a vainglorious approach to the presidency.[34] This meant that attempts to achieve closer integration of the UAE were hindered by the mutual mistrust of the individual states' rulers, and, in particular, continued misgivings about Abu Dhabi's use of its dominant position.[35]

Sheikh Zayed made great efforts to develop the UAE, but the system of sheikhly rule underwent a subtle transformation in the post-independence era. The development of a complex society in a short period had inevitable consequences on the system of rule, which was suitable for a pre-modern society. As the administration became more complex, it was harder for the rulers to maintain contact with their subjects. Sheikh Zayed appointed numerous foreign Arabs to work in the government, but they were described as venal.[36] The regime was also criticised for spending large amounts of the oil bonanza on the UAE's burgeoning foreign policy and development interests. It was estimated in 1975 that at least $1 billion, over a third of the total oil revenue, had been spent on the armed forces, investment in other states and on multilateral aid.[37]

The British account of the UAE in the post-independence era was overwhelmingly pessimistic about the future. However, it was hardly surprising that after over a century of British tutelage, the process of state formation was incremental. In October 1975, McCarthy wrote a detailed account of the internal problems facing the UAE. He gave the UAE another decade to improve significantly or face a point at which the combination of ageing rulers and internal pressures would combine to put its political and social norms in acute question.[38] The Foreign Office had to strike a balance between relations with the federal government and the maintenance of amicable bonds with each Emirate, and, as one official noted in 1978, 'we must walk a tight-rope stretched between Federal affairs and the Federal government which is striving to assert itself and the eternal rivalry of the Arab rulers. It is a frustrating and fascinating exercise.'[39]

Edward Henderson, who had considerable experience of serving in the sheikhdoms prior to independence, wrote that the UAE was weak and might break up. Writing from Qatar, he argued that there was also the possibility that the UAE might fall under the influence of a foreign power. The Iranian and Saudi regimes, which were supposed to be at the centre of the Nixon Administration's 'twin-pillars' policy that was premised on their role as the Gulf policeman, were not providing a lead.[40] The greatest danger to the stability of the Emirates were traditional divisions between the rulers rather than the threat of subversion.[41] Sheikh Zayed and Sheikh Rashid were the cornerstones of the Emirates, but they were described in temperament 'as different as chalk and cheese'. Although there were signs that ministries were beginning to form, the rulers had little comprehension of 'modern political government'. A further impediment was that the UAE was partly a British federation and Treadwell noted in February 1972 that without 'our guidance, coaxing, encouragement and plain interference, it would have come to nothing'. Treadwell also commented on how Abu Dhabi underwent a fundamental transformation between 1968 and 1973, whereas Dubai was already flourishing, 'thanks mainly to the shrewdness and flair' of Sheikh Rashid.[42]

Developments elsewhere in the Middle East had significant economic and political implications in the UAE. The Arab–Israeli War in 1973 and the oil boom led to a significant increase in Abu Dhabi's income, which, in 1974, was valued at between £600 million and £700 million. By 1976, the figure had increased to $7 billion.[43] The 'oil shock' that was caused by the 1973 war and the Arab oil embargo had significant consequences for Sheikh Zayed, who used his significant increase in wealth to maintain the loyalty of the poorer sheikhdoms. Abu Dhabi's affluence helped to smooth the transition to independence and reduced the ability of Iran and Saudi Arabia to interfere in the domestic affairs of the UAE.[44] The Emirates were still characterised by significant variations in development. By the early 1980s, Abu Dhabi had become an 'Arabian Klondyke', which funded infrastructure projects on an unprecedented scale. Dubai became a thriving entrepôt, whereas Fujairah on the Indian Ocean 'has shepherds and fishermen, palm-trees and pounding surf'.[45] Expenditure on large-scale projects, such as Jebel Ali Port in Dubai which was opened in 1979, was also important for strategic reasons. If the Emirates had not installed modern infrastructure, they could not have defended themselves against their neighbours, nor could they have invited their allies in to do so.[46]

The huge increase in oil wealth had considerable implications for the traditional way of life in the Emirates, something that Sheikh Shakhbut had feared in the early 1960s. The Bedouin, who had historically populated the desert periphery of the UAE, were becoming sedentarised, and attracted by service in the armed forces and police in order to secure a guaranteed income. In the towns, large sums were spent on education and development schemes, but this placed significant pressure on the government to meet the interests of a population that was already far outnumbered by expatriates. Notwithstanding the divisions between the rulers, J. B. Kelly argues that: 'it is only selfish interest and the need for mutual security that unites them, and in the last resort holds the federation together'.[47] The predictions that were made during the 1970s were wayward, and the UAE achieved staggering growth since independence.

Military and security relations after independence

One of the most important British legacies in the UAE was the establishment of the armed forces and security institutions of the new state. As we have seen in previous chapters, the British created the security forces in the UAE, and after independence the Emirates became an important market for British arms. The British were also heavily involved in the insurgency in Oman during the 1970s, and in September 1973, there were 1,129 British military personal based in the country.[48]

The Foreign Office failed to establish a unified military organisation prior to independence, and inadvertently this led to the proliferation of security forces in the UAE. Another explanation for the growth of these forces was the uncertain political situation that prevailed in the Emirates after independence. In January 1973, Colonel John Agar, the Defence Attaché in Abu Dhabi, wrote a detailed report about the armed forces of the UAE. Agar argued that 'the military picture in the Union, as it stands, is potentially harmful, defying logic and almost all the precepts of sound military planning'. He reached this conclusion because there were two ministries of defence and five armed forces in the Emirates. It was hard to determine whether the UAE had a defence policy since it was surrounded by larger powers that made the defence of the UAE 'more a slogan than a reality'. Defence policy appeared to be little more than the prevention of internal disorder and the settlement of interstate and intertribal disputes.[49]

There was a considerable disparity in the defence budgets of the Emirates. The Abu Dhabi Defence Force (ADDF) was the largest and best-equipped unit, and in 1973 it numbered 9,565 personnel, with a budget of £50 million. The ADDF transcended the other defence forces within the Emirates. It was doubtful whether it could have been effective against any aggressor, and, in practice, it was only capable of coercing dissenting members of the UAE. The Union Defence Force (UDF), which was the successor of the Trucial Oman Scouts, numbered 2,060 men in 1973, with a budget of £11 million. The UDF was responsible for the suppression of intertribal and interstate disputes, but its future was bleak because it was unlikely that Sheikh Zayed would continue to fund it. The other military forces, including the Dubai Defence Force, Sharjah National Guard and Ras Al Khaimah Mobile Force, had no military role and were responsible for protecting their rulers.

Agar argued that in order for these forces to be effective, they had to have an organisation that was able to coordinate their operations. They also needed an intelligence machine that was capable of collating and disseminating information.[50] In 1973, neither of these existed, and the Special Branch organisations that the Foreign Office had established during the 1960s were disbanded after independence. Each state also had its own police force but there was no clear division between the operational responsibilities of the armies and the police. The UAE faced a variety of security threats during its first decade of existence, and it was open to question whether they were capable of mitigating these challenges. However, the UAE's economic prosperity and the absence of political consciousness made it difficult for subversive groups to have any impact. Tribal loyalties remained strong and the main subversive threat was the large number of Omanis in the ADDF and the police.[51]

The withdrawal from the Gulf left a security vacuum in the region. Richard Helms, the American Ambassador at Tehran and the former Director of the CIA, noted in March 1973 that the UAE was trying to be too progressive, too soon. Although the UAE was tolerant towards political activity and dissent, it was 'not sophisticated enough to handle it. Thus, ideologies find fertile ground in the UAE, particularly among the educated, while there is no counter effort by the government.' Helms added that discussing the stability of the UAE and Saudi Arabia was a complex matter, and Western observers were 'too ready to write off family, tribe, local nationalism and pride'.[52] In June 1973, the CIA argued that the Gulf States had weathered the withdrawal of British forces better than had been expected. The durability of the sheikhly regimes was less assured. According to the CIA perspective of the Gulf, the UAE was still challenged by traditional tribal factionalism, instead of dissidents who were seeking to overthrow the sheikhs. Although the rulers were slowly learning to work together, it would take a long time before they spoke with one voice. The CIA reached the conclusion that the UAE, and the neighbouring Gulf monarchies, were fragile and could have been suddenly overthrown.[53]

The Foreign Office and the Ministry of Defence (MOD) agreed that the provision of British loan service personnel was the most important contribution to Britain's aims in the UAE. In July 1973, the MOD noted that British influence was already declining in the ADDF. This was the result of a growing number of non-British expatriates, especially from Jordan and Pakistan, who were recruited by Sheikh Zayed. In July 1973, there were 21 loan service personnel and 110 contract officers in Abu Dhabi, whereas the number of Jordanians and Pakistanis had increased from 49 in 1972 to 136 in 1973.[54] Similarly, the British Military Advisory Team (MAT) that was sent to the UAE in December 1971 had a limited impact.[55] The MAT was supposed to facilitate British military exercises, engage in civil engineering projects and assist local forces. The rulers were reluctant to request the MAT's assistance because the MOD demanded that they pay for its help. The MAT was withdrawn from the UAE in June 1975, having completed its advisory role.

McCarthy argued that Britain's influence in the ADDF was on a 'downward curve' by the end of 1973. He believed that this was an inevitable result of independence and of Sheikh Zayed's replacement of British officers with soldiers recruited from Jordan and Pakistan. McCarthy characterised the ADDF as 'Frankenstein's monster', on account of its rapid expansion. In 1973, Sheikh Zayed purchased advanced weapons, including Mirage fighters and Panhard armoured cars, and spent large sums on military infrastructure.[56] Sheikh Zayed's decision to purchase these arms from the French was an alarming prospect for the Foreign Office and the MOD because it symbolised the UK's declining influence in Abu Dhabi.[57] In the past, the UK had monopolised arms sales in the region, but after independence, rulers such as Sheikh Zayed were able to exploit the international arms market.

The sale of arms to the UAE was a key requirement for the UK after independence. In January 1973, Jim Treadwell, writing from Abu Dhabi, commented that: 'we ourselves cannot afford to stand back in the race to provide Abu Dhabi with bigger and better weapons, for as the Minister of Defence said to me: "if you don't sell us missiles, the French will".[58] Between 1972 and the spring of 1974, the British supplied the UAE armed forces with a variety of weapons, including twelve Hawker Hunter jets, fast patrol boats, armoured vehicles, Swingfire anti-tank missiles and the Rapier surface-to-air missile system. Between 1972 and 1974, the French secured from Abu Dhabi arms contracts worth over £100 million, whereas British export totals were only valued at £49.9 million.[59]

The UAE's expenditure on arms was insignificant compared with the Saudis, who were by far the most important purchaser of British arms in the Arabian Peninsula. In 1973, the Saudis signed a deal worth £290 million for training and supporting their air force. In May 1974, James Callaghan, the Labour Foreign Secretary, outlined the government's policy on arms to the Middle East states not in conflict with the Israelis. Callaghan argued that the government should be ready to accept orders from the UAE and the Gulf States because the Americans and French were competing for this lucrative market.[60]

In the post-independence era, an arms race occurred in the Gulf region. The CIA estimated that arms sales increased from $330 million annually during 1954–71 to $4.8 billion annually over the 1972–4 period. Arms purchases grew again during 1975–7 to an annual average of $11.8 billion, nearly half of the total arms sold to the developing world. These arms purchases were funded by a significant increase in oil income, following the 1973 Arab–Israeli War. However, Kuwait and the former protected states accounted for no more than 5 per cent of the total, which was dominated by Iran, Iraq and Saudi Arabia.[61] The Gulf States purchased large quantities of arms to ensure their sovereignty, acquire status and compete with regional rivals for political influence.

In the UAE, the British and the French fuelled the arms race. British officials regarded Abu Dhabi's arms build-up as a danger to itself because Sheikh Zayed might have been inclined to use them against his less well-equipped neighbours. Nevertheless, it was estimated that it would be a long time before Abu Dhabi would be capable of sustained military operations.[62] In 1976, the Dubai Defence Force, Ras Al Khaimah Mobile Force and the Sharjah National Guard were turned into military districts, and the Union Defence Force, formerly the Trucial Oman Scouts, became an independent brigade group. Colonel Nigel Bromage, the British Military Attaché at Abu Dhabi, who had considerable experience of serving in Arab armies, including the Jordanian Arab Legion and the Saudi National Guard, noted that this radical reorganisation was based on the desire for unity and the 'absolute determination on the part of the UAE to run their own show'. The number of British loaned officers had significantly decreased during the year, and Bromage argued that the decision not to appoint a new British chief of staff was a wise one. He observed that the British should:

> not look upon our departure with regret but with pride in a job well done; we have after all, managed to disengage without recriminations and without becoming the focus for discontent, a feat rarely achieved in the Middle East since the war. That we have reduced our presence at the right time, and that it will continue in the staff, technical and training field for a few years to come, I am convinced.[63]

Bromage's reports provide clear evidence of how the UK's defence relationship with the UAE changed during the first decade of independence.

Abu Dhabi's growing armed forces, which totalled 18,000 men in 1978, outnumbered the neighbouring states'. In January 1978, Sheikh Zayed issued a decree abolishing the separate armed forces of the UAE and placing them under the direct control of the Federal Military Command in Abu Dhabi.[64] Sheikh Zayed also appointed his son, Sheikh Sultan, as Commander-in-Chief of the Armed Forces.[65] Sheikh Rashid, the ruler of Dubai, and Sheikh Saqr of Ras Al Khaimah refused to recognise these decrees, complaining that they had been issued without consultation. Sheikh Zayed's attempt to dominate the armed forces of the UAE reignited traditional antipathy between the rulers. Sheikh Rashid made it clear to the British Ambassador that he was contemplating withdrawing from the UAE. The British and the Saudis persuaded Sheikh Rashid not to leave the Union because it was against his interests, and would threaten the stability of the Gulf.[66] The Foreign Office was concerned that if the UAE broke up, 'all the dangers which threatened when British forces were withdrawn from the Gulf and our special treaty relationships with the Emirates terminated in 1971 would arise again, perhaps in more acute form'.[67]

The dispute between Abu Dhabi and Dubai highlighted the extent to which British officials were able to influence the rulers of the UAE. The threat to the cohesion of the UAE led the Foreign Office to contemplate whether it should continue to arm Abu Dhabi and Dubai. The suggestion that the British and French should impose a 'self-denying ordinance' in the provision of weapons was ruled out because of the economic value of defence contracts. Furthermore, the imposition of a ban on arms exports would achieve little since the rulers would have had little difficulty in finding alternative supplies.[68] Bromage wrote in his valedictory report from Abu Dhabi that the 'sheikhs seem to have an insatiable appetite for buying arms', but he had no doubt that if the UK was reluctant to sell arms, 'the resulting political damage would affect our normal trade in what is a considerable export market'.[69] Roberts concurred with this impression that the disinclination to sell arms would be bitterly resented by the rulers.[70]

The UAE–Saudi boundary dispute

One of the significant legacies of the British role in the Trucial States was the demarcation of the internal frontiers of the protected states. British officials such as Julian Walker were responsible for this complex process,[71] and by the late 1960s, significant progress had been made.[72] However, the Foreign Office failed to reach an agreement between Abu Dhabi and Saudi Arabia about the boundaries of the Buraimi Oasis.[73] The Foreign Office had been responsible for negotiating a solution to the Buraimi issue because the treaty relationship with Abu Dhabi meant that the British were responsible for its foreign relations. The Buraimi Oasis had bedevilled Anglo-Saudi relations since the removal of Saudi forces from the area in 1955, and there appeared to be little prospect of a diplomatic solution.

Richard Schofield argues that the British and Saudi governments would have been prepared to reach an agreement by the end of 1970. This could have been based on the Saudi abandonment of their claim to the Buraimi Oasis, in return for Abu Dhabi agreeing to renounce its claim to the Khor Al Udeid inlet. The British were unable to compel Sheikh Zayed to negotiate a solution with King Faisal because of the discovery of the Zarrara oil field in 1970.[74] This meant that Sheikh Zayed had no interest in reaching an agreement.[75] The Foreign Office had made significant attempts to persuade Sheikh Zayed to settle his boundary dispute with King Faisal prior to independence but to no avail. In June 1972, British officials made it clear to their American counterparts that the chances of an agreement 'were almost nil'.[76] The Foreign Office dispelled the notion that it was responsible for any initiative that emanated from Abu Dhabi, and it was determined to antagonise neither the Saudis nor the UAE. In February 1973, Anthony Parsons, the Foreign Office Middle East Under-Secretary, wrote that: 'we are no longer acting as Abu Dhabi's lawyer. We had no intention of reinvolving ourselves in the dispute'.[77] The Foreign Office's ability to persuade Sheikh Zayed to reach a negotiated settlement was limited because he was determined to establish the UAE's foreign policy.

Saudi attempts to persuade the British to re-engage with the border dispute in 1973 were equally forlorn. The Foreign Office observed that: 'our long association with this problem has convinced us that there is no profit to be gained from playing the role of honest broker. The gap between the two sides is as great as ever.' The Foreign Office had no interest in acting as an intermediary because it doubted whether Sheikh Zayed really wanted a settlement. The evidence suggested that Sheikh Zayed 'probably calculated that the Saudis would not implement their claim by force', and in the circumstances, any further involvement in the dispute 'would achieve nothing accept further recriminations'.[78]

However, on 23 July 1974, the UAE and the Saudi Government signed the so-called Jeddah Agreement.[79] The negotiations that led to the agreement took place in great secrecy, and British and American diplomats were unaware of what transpired.[80] Even Sheikh Zayed's family learned about the agreement after it was signed. Prince Fahd, who played a key role in the negotiations that led to the agreement, acknowledged that Ibn Saud had made a serious error in using force over the Buraimi Oasis in the autumn of 1952. Prince Fahd adopted a more conciliatory approach and appealed to Sheikh Zayed on the basis of their personal friendship and made it clear that the Saudis would not use force to press their claim.[81] Sheikh Zayed and King Faisal signed the agreement in secret and its details were unknown at the time. James Akins, the American Ambassador at Jeddah, observed that King Faisal was happy with the agreement because the Saudis had achieved their key objective, which focused on a corridor to the Gulf between Qatar and the UAE.[82] Indeed, Michael Sterner, the American Ambassador to the UAE, reported that the Saudis had been given a corridor to the Gulf between Qatar and Abu Dhabi. In return for these territorial concessions, the Saudis agreed to waive their claim to the Buraimi Oasis.[83] J. B. Kelly argues that Sheikh Zayed 'gave the Saudis nearly everything they wanted – a corridor to the sea, west of the Sabkhat Matti, separating Qatar from Abu Dhabi and affording Saudi Arabia an outlet to the lower Gulf; a goodly slice of the western part of his sheikhdom; and, in the south, the bulk of the Zarrara oilfield'.[84] In return, the Saudis recognised the UAE and diplomatic relations were established, thereby strengthening the Emirates because its legitimacy was reinforced.

The Jeddah Agreement was only published in English in June 1995,[85] and it remains to this day a source of contention between the UAE and Saudi Arabia. Schofield characterises the agreement as 'perhaps the most bizarre international boundary agreement ever signed between two states' because 'even the signatories were in the dark as to what, precisely, had been introduced by the agreement'.[86] The ambiguous terms of the Jeddah Agreement led the American ambassadors to Riyadh and Abu Dhabi in September 2005 to examine its terms in light of a 'rising volume of private and public sniping between the UAE and Saudi Arabia'.[87] As one Foreign Office official noted, 'the Saudi–UAE boundary kept coming back like a bad penny'.[88]

The British re-engage in the UAE

One of the notable characteristics of the *Pax Britannica* in the Gulf was the way in which the region was largely kept out of regional developments, including the spread of Arab nationalism. The British left a legacy of detachment from trends that had affected the Arab world in the post-war era, but by the late 1970s, the Gulf States were no longer isolated. The rulers were now responsible for the conduct of their foreign relations, and they had to contend with upheavals that could not be ignored. The Camp David agreements in the autumn of 1978, which led to Egypt signing a peace treaty with Israel, and the Iranian Revolution in 1978–9 shook the region. The Iranian Revolution, which led to the fall of the Pahlavi monarchy, had profound implications for the Gulf monarchies because Ayatollah Khomeini promised to 'export the revolution' across the Middle East.[89] The revolution had significant consequences for British interests in the UAE and Saudi Arabia, and the Foreign Office understood that it had to take steps to enhance Britain's standing, from Kuwait to Muscat. In early 1978, the Foreign Office started to plan a Royal visit to the Gulf region that was originally meant to include a visit to Iran, which was cancelled after the revolution. The Shah's deposition and the legacy of the withdrawal in 1971 reinforced the importance of re-engagement with the Gulf States. Queen Elizabeth II made a very successful tour of the Gulf States in February–March 1979. The tour was also a show of force because the Royal yacht *Britannia* was escorted by a Royal Navy destroyer.[90]

The Queen's excursion was the first visit by a British sovereign of any kind since the British entered the region in the early nineteenth century. The Queen's tour was regarded in the UAE as a 'welcome, if belated, mark of our interest in their destiny'. The initial objective of the Queen's tour was to generate goodwill and encourage trade in the Gulf States, but the Iranian Revolution added urgent political goals.[91] These included the requirement to reassure the rulers of Britain's continued support, and to encourage the rulers, 'without preaching', to respond to domestic criticism and satisfy the aspirations of the people. The Foreign Office also wanted to use the Queen's visit to encourage the rulers to cooperate with one another in facing common external threats.[92] Dr David Owen, the Foreign Secretary, reported that the timing of the Queen's visit had been opportune because it allowed the Foreign Office to demonstrate its support for the Gulf States. Owen found few signs of concern amongst the rulers following the Iranian Revolution, and commented that the maintenance of internal stability depended on progressive social and economic policies.[93] The Queen's tour of the Gulf calls into question the argument that the Labour Government ignored the region because the visit 'has brilliantly established our presence once more in the region'.[94]

In February 1979, the Middle East Department of the Foreign Office produced a detailed memorandum on UK policy in Saudi Arabia and the Gulf.[95] Alan Munro, the author of this report, acknowledged that Britain's relations with the Gulf States were less exclusive than in the past but the Foreign Office was closer to the rulers than any other Western state. This meant that it was difficult for British diplomats to achieve an 'arms-length' approach in the area, and that any 'sharp measure of disengagement would be likely to cause further instability'. Munro also argued that the continued relations with the rulers were not inimical 'to our longer term interests' because they remained accessible to their subjects compared with the presidents of the 'progressive republics'. There was no question of the Foreign Office backing off from the rulers because it would 'risk exposing us to suspicion by the regimes we have traditionally supported (and often brought into independent existence) without gaining compensating credit elsewhere'. The paper outlined three policy options, the first of which entailed a closer relationship with the Gulf States. Munro noted that the resumption of a tutelary or policing role, backed up by a military intervention capacity, would have no appeal for the rulers of the Gulf States. Greater intervention might escalate Cold War tensions, exacerbate local nationalism and encourage 'immobilisme' among the them. The second option depended on a 'balanced relationship', and the Foreign Office could also encourage regional cooperation so as to reinforce security and political stability without excessive Western interference. The third option rested on the accelerated disengagement, but was rejected because it would undermine British interests.

The report recommended a relationship that aimed at 'striking a balance between over-involvement in internal affairs and security and withdrawal from a demonstration of interest in the political stability of the area'. The objective of this policy was to encourage the rulers 'to stand on their own feet, and prepare for non-violent change (pious though this hope may be a judicious blend of help and self-help may serve to serve our essential interest without aggravating the strains which regional turbulence and change will impose on stability)'. Munro argued that advice on political development 'should be proffered where sought, but not dictated, lest this bring us into the kind of dependency relationship we have abjured'. The main difficulty was over defence relations and was caused by the failure to achieve international cooperation on arms sales. However, the West's military interests could be achieved by occasional visits by warships and military training exercises. The Royal Navy made regular calls to the UAE after independence, but these operations became more important as a result of the Iranian Revolution. Naval stopovers were also valuable for promoting trade and displaying defence equipment to dignitaries.[96]

David Roberts, the British Ambassador at Abu Dhabi, challenged some of Munro's assumptions. Roberts argued that the British faced a dilemma in the UAE concerning what could be done to help. He argued that: 'if we do not intervene enough we shall be ineffective. If we intervene too much it will be counter-productive.' Roberts also doubted whether it should be Foreign Office policy to 'pursue a course of steady political disengagement in the UAE. In military terms we have already disengaged. Political disengagement has in my view gone far enough, if not too far'.[97] Notwithstanding these criticisms, Labour ministers supported a 'balanced relationship with the traditionalist states'.[98]

In May 1979, the Conservative Party came to power and adopted a more proactive policy in the Gulf. Anthony Parsons toured Iran, Saudi Arabia, the UAE and Oman in June 1979. He wrote a trenchant appraisal of the UAE and observed that 20 per cent of the population who were indigenous to the UAE continued their traditional way of life, 'prosperous and possibly even proud of these modern Egyptian pyramids'. The UAE's rapid development 'does, thanks largely to our historical ties with the area, continue to produce substantial business for British firms and skilled labour'.[99] Parsons reported in June 1979 that the rulers did not think that the Iranian Revolution was likely to have any imminent destabilising effects on their regimes. However, they regarded the Camp David Accords as a greater threat than the revolution because it had divided the Arab world.[100] As Munro noted, 'this is no time to be cold-shouldering old friends' in the Gulf. The Iranian Revolution and the Camp David process led Lord Carrington, the Foreign Secretary, to authorise a detailed evaluation of British policy in the Gulf.[101]

The Soviet invasion of Afghanistan in December 1979 and the outbreak of the Iran–Iraq War the following year provided added impetus for an increase in British involvement in the UAE and the Persian Gulf. In August 1980, the Chiefs of Staff Committee proposed a range of defence options in the Gulf that included joint service exercises that would contribute towards deterrence and stability. The provision of 300 loan service personnel from Kuwait to Muscat was a low-profile and inexpensive mechanism for offering help. Furthermore, training local armed forces in modern weapons systems was a useful spinoff of extensive defence sales. These mechanisms allowed the British to demonstrate their continued interest in the region.[102] The clearest sign of the British commitment to the Gulf occurred in 1980, when the Royal Navy started to conduct the 'Armilla patrol', which was intended to protect British shipping. The Royal Navy's presence in the Gulf is ongoing.

Conclusion

The British left a political vacuum in the Gulf because no attempt was made to establish a regional security system. Although they did abandon the Emirates after independence, the legacy in the UAE and the Gulf States was overwhelmingly positive. Inevitably, the level of formal influence declined after independence, but relations remained cordial because the British departure from the Gulf was carefully orchestrated and peaceful. The Labour Government has been criticised for ignoring the UAE after independence but it had to show that the rulers were responsible for their own affairs. Nonetheless, in Dubai and other former protected states, British influence was pervasive because the rulers trusted their advisors and consultants. British expatriates played an important role in running Dubai's Police Force, port and water supply, and a wide range of companies were involved in the development of the newly formed UAE.

A further important legacy of British imperialism in the Gulf was the maintenance of the local system of sheikhly rule that characterised all the states. British protection meant that the rulers were shielded from external threats, and internally their power was consolidated. Sheikhly rule continued after independence, although the ability of the rulers to conduct their affairs along traditional lines was open to question as their governments became more complex. Some of the rulers, such as Sheikh Zayed, did employ large numbers of non-British expatriates. One of the criticisms that can be levelled against the Foreign Office is that more could have been done to provide the Emirates with a cadre of trained bureaucrats to administer the new state. Inevitably, the UAE faced a variety of problems in its first decade of existence, and the rulers needed expatriates to assist in state formation.

The Foreign Office also played an important role in the demarcation of the internal frontiers of the UAE. It had no interest in unifying the protected states, and a legacy of the British presence is the territorial patchwork that still characterises the Emirates. One of the characteristics of British imperialism in the protected states was that the Foreign Office was responsible for the external relations of the rulers, which meant that they had limited experience of dealing with the outside world. The Foreign Office had been responsible for attempts to negotiate a solution to the long-running Buraimi Oasis dispute but it failed to reach an agreement with the Saudis prior to independence. The Buraimi Oasis was a fundamental Saudi interest, and it was now Sheikh Zayed's responsibility to reach an agreement, which was achieved in controversial circumstances in 1974.

One of the most significant legacies of the British role in the former Trucial States was the establishment of the Emirates armed forces. British officers continued to command the armed forces of the UAE after independence, but their contribution rapidly declined. This was particularly the case in Abu Dhabi, where Sheikh Zayed replaced British officers with recruits from Jordan and Pakistan. The defence relationship with the UAE was transformed to an advisory role but the sale of large quantities of arms became a notable characteristic of Britain's enduring relationship with the Emirates. The British, along with the United States and France, were responsible for the development of a regional arms race. Vast sums have been spent on advanced weapons systems but it is open to question whether these states are capable of defending themselves. By the late 1970s, regional developments led the Foreign Office to become much more engaged politically and militarily in the UAE and in Gulf region. The defence relationship remains an enduring characteristic of Anglo-UAE relations.

Conclusion

The British imperial project in the Trucial States was an uncharacteristic success
story. With the exception of Jordan, the Trucial States, Bahrain, Qatar, Kuwait
and Oman, the other examples of British imperialism in the Middle East were
failures. The successful outcome in the Trucial States was not preordained due
to the Government of India's policy of indirect rule in the sheikhdoms. The
Government of India's stance in the Trucial States, and along the Arab littoral of
the Persian Gulf, had significant long-term implications. The Indian Government
made no attempt to improve the economic and social conditions of the Trucial
States for financial reasons. This was one of the main failings of the Government
of India's policy because the population had little to show for its neglectful
presence. The maritime truces and treaties that the Government of India signed
with the rulers of the sheikhdoms of Eastern Arabia were of great significance
since they enforced peace at sea. This was one of the most enduring implications
of the Government of India's policy in the Gulf because it led to maritime
security, which allowed the development of trading networks across the Persian
Gulf region and further afield to India. The *Pax Britannica* meant that the Gulf
became a British imperial lake, in which no other foreign power was able to
challenge its maritime supremacy.

However, on land, the situation was very different. The Government of India
had no interest in becoming involved in the internal affairs of the Trucial States
or any of the protected states as long as their interests were not impinged. Britain's
hands-off approach had long-term consequences in the Trucial States because
the 'veiled protectorate' in the Gulf was premised on a working relationship with
the ruling families of the region. The sheikhs accepted British protection and a
mutually beneficial relationship was established. British officials made little
attempt to interfere with the system of sheikhly rule that characterised the
Trucial States. British protection solidified the position of the ruling families,
who became the hereditary rulers of the United Arab Emirates (UAE). The
political geography of the UAE, which resembles a patchwork quilt where some
of the states are divided into separate enclaves, was caused by the Government of
India's determination not to rationalise these frontiers on account of the rulers'
inevitable opposition. The Foreign Office reinforced the geographic status quo

by drawing the boundaries of the Trucial States during the later years of the British presence in the region.

It is debateable whether the Foreign Office should have taken over control of the protected states following the demise of the Raj. The states were unique entities, and the Foreign Office had very limited knowledge of, or interest in, the Trucial States. The Foreign Office might have continued a modified form of the Government of India's non-interventionist policy in the Trucial States, but instead it gradually became more concerned with the internal affairs of the sheikhdoms. This was the result of changing regional circumstances, and the requirement to enhance British prestige in the Trucial States. After the Foreign Office took control of the protected states, Indian methods of indirect rule continued.

The Political Resident was the most powerful personality in the Gulf, and was unique on account of his pro-consular powers. Political Residents played a key role in the development of British policy in the Trucial States because the Government of India and Whitehall regarded the Gulf region as an imperial backwater. The British Political Agents in Abu Dhabi and Dubai were also influential in the development of British policy in the protected states. The Trucial States were an unparalleled posting for British diplomats, some of whom had previously served in the Sudan Political Service, which meant that they had experience of development issues. By the 1950s, the Foreign Office was sending Arabist diplomats to the Trucial States who performed a multitude of tasks, some of which had little to do with traditional diplomacy. British policy in the Trucial States remained the preserve of the Foreign Office and ministers rarely intervened in, or visited, the region. The most important role of the Political Resident and the Political Agents in Abu Dhabi and Dubai was to establish close relations with the rulers. Foreign Office officials were also responsible for 'flying the flag', and played a crucial role in the sheikhdoms of Eastern Arabia in the last two decades of the *Pax Britannica* in the Gulf.

Until the 1950s, the sheikhdoms had been scarcely affected by regional developments, but the Foreign Office understood that it had to take steps to defend the Trucial States and instigate a limited development programme. The objectives of these policies were to enhance British prestige in the sheikhdoms, and demonstrate to the rulers and their subjects that the Foreign Office was belatedly looking after their needs. The Foreign Office's policy can be characterised as enlightened self-interest because it showed the rulers and international critics of British policy in the sheikhdoms that something beneficial was being done.

The defence of the Trucial States against the possibility of Saudi incursions, and belatedly against subversion, were fundamental interests, alongside oil. The protection of the burgeoning oil industry and sterling balances held by the rulers from Kuwait to Abu Dhabi was of great significance. One of the most far-reaching initiatives that the Foreign Office adopted was the establishment of the Trucial Oman Levies in 1951 (Trucial Oman Scouts after 1956). The British typically established indigenous armed forces across the Empire, and the Trucial States were no exception. British officers commanded the TOS and the soldiers were recruited from a variety of locations. The Saudi occupation of the Buraimi Oasis in the autumn of 1952 provided added impetus for the development of the Scouts because the Foreign Office had to take decisive steps to defend the Trucial States. The Saudis had intermittently attempted to take control of the sheikhdoms, which they regarded as part of their territory, since the early nineteenth century. There were also significant financial and political imperatives that led to the expansion of the TOS after the Saudi occupation of Buraimi in 1952. Without British intervention, the Trucial States would have been vulnerable to Saudi force majeure, and it was essential to show the rulers that the Foreign Office was willing to take all necessary steps to prevent this occurrence. Furthermore, it was much cheaper to gradually expand the TOS than base British forces in the sheikhdoms. The Foreign Office had learned the lesson from bitter experience in Egypt that British forces were a primary cause of nationalist opposition.

The establishment of the TOS was also significant because it played an unprecedented role in patrolling and maintaining the peace in the desert hinterland of the Trucial States. The tribes of the region had been raiding for millennia, and one of the most enduring legacies of British imperialism in the protected states was the peaceful pacification of the region. The Foreign Office's decision to establish the TOS marked the equivocal reversal of the long-standing policy of non-intervention in the internal affairs of the Trucial States. The TOS dominated British expenditure during the last two decades of the Foreign Office's primacy in the protected states. There can be little doubt that these funds were well spent because the TOS's impact was well beyond its annual cost.

The Foreign Office's attempts to improve the economic and social conditions of the Trucial States during the 1950s had less impact. This was the result of a variety of circumstances that included the Treasury's refusal to adequately fund the development scheme that was initiated in 1955. A further impediment was the remarkably low level of development that characterised the Trucial States, with the exception of Dubai, which became the region's entrepôt. Increasingly, the British presence in the Trucial States appeared to be anachronistic. In contrast with the retreat from Empire elsewhere in the Middle East, the Foreign Office became more and more committed in the Trucial States and the Gulf.

The Foreign Office continued the Government of India's policy of excluding the sheikhdoms of Eastern Arabia from regional trends. During the 1950s, political and technological developments made it increasingly difficult for the Foreign Office to treat the protected states as an imperial backwater. The Trucial States, and Bahrain in particular, were no longer marginalised in the Arab world. The Suez Crisis in 1956 had far-reaching implications because it showed that the Trucial States were no longer immune to the tide of Arab nationalism that was sweeping the Middle East. Arab nationalist sentiment disseminated by Egyptian radio propaganda was highly influential across the protected states.

The main impediments the Foreign Office faced in the Trucial States were limitations on its ability to enforce meaningful economic, political and social change. The rulers had no interest in sharing power, and sheikhly rule was pervasive. The Trucial States were unusual because the Foreign Office was in a position of responsibility without having the power to introduce administrative and political reforms. This was a long-term consequence of the treaties that had been signed in the nineteenth and early twentieth centuries that confirmed the rulers' supremacy. The Foreign Office's attempts to persuade the rulers to cooperate in the Trucial States Council had very limited impact. They were divided by long-standing animosities and their desire to preserve their independence. The continuation of sheikhly rule in the Trucial States was a significant legacy of British imperialism in the Trucial States and the Gulf because the Foreign Office could see no viable alternative.

The Foreign Office recognised as early as 1961, which is much earlier than is commonly assumed, that the British presence in the Trucial States, Bahrain and Qatar would be terminated by 1975. The question the Foreign Office had to address was how to manage its relations with the protected states. The Kuwait crisis in 1961 forced the Foreign Office to consolidate its position in the region, but it had little discernable impact in the Trucial States. The rulers were concerned about the Iraqi threat to the Lower Gulf but they did nothing at the time to counter this problem. The Foreign Office recognised that it had to gradually prepare the rulers for independence, which led to the introduction of 'retrocession' or the gradual handing-over of domestic powers to the rulers. Progress was glacial because the rulers were recalcitrant, and by 1968, only limited progress had been made.

The Foreign Office continued to have limited success with the development scheme in the Trucial States. Progress proved to be incremental at best, on account of the shortage of money and the problem of finding suitable projects. The Treasury was increasingly sceptical about funding a limited development programme in the Trucial States for the valid reason that Abu Dhabi's oil bonanza undercut the case for the British taxpayer underwriting this initiative. The Treasury had always questioned the Foreign Office's ability to spend money effectively on the Trucial States' development, and the main reason for its continuation was the maintenance of British prestige. The Treasury correctly argued that the rulers of Abu Dhabi and Dubai should be forced to make a significant contribution to their own development. The Trucial States were very different from other examples of development because their sudden wealth discredited the case for financial aid.

The Treasury's objections to British money being spent in the Trucial States were challenged by regional events. Nasser remained the most powerful force in the Arab world at the time, and the nationalist propaganda that emanated from Cairo was very influential. Egyptian radio propaganda consistently attacked the British presence in the Trucial States and the rulers. The most significant threat to the *Pax Britannica*, and to sheikhly rule, occurred in 1965, when the Arab League attempted to penetrate the sheikhdoms. The policy that was initiated by Sir William Luce, the Political Resident at Bahrain, and was fully supported by the Foreign Office, showed that the British were willing to take extreme measures to preserve their predominant position. Luce argued with great conviction that if the Foreign Office failed to prevent the Arab League from establishing a presence in the Trucial States, the implications for Britain's standing with the rulers would be severe. The Foreign Office had to show the rulers that it would protect them in accordance with the treaties, or Britain's credibility with the rulers would be fatally undermined. The level of British interference was marked by the overthrow in 1965 of Sheikh Saqr, the ruler of Sharjah, because he was determined to accept the Arab League's assistance. The Foreign Office regarded Sheikh Saqr's conduct as a clear contravention of the treaties his forefathers had signed, and an unambiguous message was sent to the other rulers that flagrant violations of the treaties would not be tolerated.

The exercise in British power reached its apotheosis in August 1966, when the Foreign Office took steps to depose Sheikh Shakhbut, the ruler of Abu Dhabi. In contrast with Sheikh Saqr, Shakhbut did not contravene his treaty relations with the British. However, his long-standing resistance to economic and political change was a source of great frustration for Foreign Office officials. Sheikh Shakhbut was a notable example of an old-fashioned ruler who had succeeded in controlling Abu Dhabi since 1928. However, his opposition to developing his sheikhdom made his position untenable, and the expansion of Abu Dhabi's oil industry meant that the Foreign Office was determined to appoint Sheikh Zayed in Shakhbut's place. These events marked the pinnacle of British interference in the internal affairs of the Trucial States.

The Foreign Office took other steps to enhance its position in the Trucial States, including the development of the police and intelligence services in the sheikhdoms. The extent of the subversive threat in the Trucial States was minimal, even during the peak of the Arab League's efforts to penetrate the region. Although the sheikhdoms were developing and large numbers of migrants were arriving to work in the oil fields, they were less vulnerable to the nationalist sentiment that characterised the other Gulf States, such as Bahrain. The Trucial States lacked the usual mechanisms for the growth of indigenous opposition to the ruling sheikhs, who still relied on traditional methods to guarantee their predominance. A further impediment to nationalist pressure in the Trucial States was the absence of an educated population and print media that might have generated opposition to the British and the rulers.

The Trucial States were clearly anomalous, and the Foreign Office continued to invest heavily in the Trucial Oman Scouts. Ostensibly, the Scouts were meant to be the army of the Trucial States, but their role in Shakhbut's overthrow in August 1966 called into question the validity of this assumption. The TOS remained the private army of the Political Resident and they were still the most important factor in the maintenance of internal security in the sheikhdoms. Nevertheless, the TOS's omnipotence was called into question by the gradual development of sheikhly armies, such as the Abu Dhabi Defence Force (ADDF). There was nothing the Foreign Office could do to prevent the raising of the ADDF or any other local security force, but it was possible for them to command and guide the expansion of these forces.

These developments suggest that British influence in the Trucial States was inconsistent and limited in its scope. The Foreign Office intervened in certain circumstances, but there were inherent limitations on British power that were caused by the Trucial system. The Foreign Office's efforts to retain control of its position in the Trucial States, and in the other protected states, were undermined when the Labour Government decided that the withdrawal would take place by the end of the 1971. The causes of this decision are hotly debated but this book supports the contention that domestic political considerations led the government to adopt a policy that had no strategic or political rationale. There was no regional demand for the British to leave, and the Wilson Government badly handled its policy with its allies in the Trucial States and Washington. The decision to leave was an example of ministers directing policy, although they had scant knowledge of the protected states.

Between January 1968 and June 1970, the Foreign Office adopted a hands-off policy in the protected states. Somehow, the rulers were expected to reach an agreement about their future political organisation despite all the evidence to the contrary. The Foreign Office's efforts to persuade the rulers to cooperate in the past had failed, and there was little indication that they would succeed without British assistance. Edward Heath's intervention in 1969, and his assertion that the Conservative Party would reverse the decision to leave, was implausible, and weakened any prospect of an agreement between the protected states. The situation was complicated by the growing influence of the Shah, who was determined to replace British power in the Persian Gulf. In contrast, the Saudis appeared to be disinterested in these developments. King Faisal's main preoccupation was the long-running Buraimi Oasis dispute, though there was no likelihood of an agreement before the British departed for good. The King strongly supported the union of nine protected states despite all the evidence that it was unworkable.

The time allocated to orchestrate the future of the protected states was derisory, and British influence declined as a result of the Labour Government's abrupt reversal of policy. The change in government in London in June 1970 led to the Foreign Office becoming much more engaged in the future of the protected states. Sir Alec Douglas-Home, the Conservative Foreign Secretary, instigated a policy that led to the UK's withdrawal from the protected states, the independence of Bahrain and Qatar, and the formation of the UAE. British officials in the Gulf played a central role in this process, and the rulers of Abu Dhabi and Dubai realised that they had to take decisive steps to cooperate. Douglas-Home's appointment of Sir William Luce as his personal representative was pivotal. Luce, as a result of his tenure as Political Resident, had unrivalled knowledge of the protected states, and his 'shuttle diplomacy' was decisive in showing the rulers that the British would not amend the timetable of their departure. The differences that characterised relations between the rulers, some of whom were concerned about Abu Dhabi's domination of the Emirates, meant that the political structure of the UAE was open to question almost until the British departed. The status of the five smaller sheikhdoms was especially unclear, on account of their perennially inconsequential influence in the Trucial system. It was hardly surprising that such a situation prevailed in a federation that was rapidly developing and had little experience of direct rule.

The withdrawal of British forces from Bahrain and Sharjah was straightforward in comparison with other withdrawals, such as from Aden or Mandatory

Palestine. Regardless of the intelligence apparatus that had been established in the Trucial States, no meaningful opposition had ever emerged to challenge the British. This allowed the Foreign Office and the Ministry of Defence to devise a carefully orchestrated plan to leave by December 1971, regardless of political developments. British forces departed from Bahrain and Sharjah gradually and without a shot being fired, which was a rare occurrence in British decolonisation in the Middle East. Nonetheless, the Foreign Office left a security vacuum in the Persian Gulf after 1971, which appeared to contradict one of the fundamental tenets of British policy in the area. The United States had no interest in replacing British supremacy, and, instead, London and Washington were content for Iran and Saudi Arabia to act as the policemen of the Gulf.

One of the most significant consequences of Britain's long association with the rulers of the protected states was that they relied on the British to conduct their foreign relations. The British departure was an unprecedented challenge for the rulers. In spite of long-standing schisms that divided them, Abu Dhabi and Dubai were buoyed by rapid economic growth, and Sheikh Zayed's rapidly increasing oil income was hugely significant. In contrast with most developing states, the UAE had vast financial resources that were used to develop the Emirates in a remarkable fashion. Although the protected states relied heavily on foreign labour, their indigenous population remained politically quiescent, which allowed the British to leave peacefully. The Foreign Office might have done more to establish an effective bureaucracy for the UAE, and as a result of this omission, some of the rulers chose to turn to other foreign advisors for assistance.

The formal British presence in the protected states was quietly terminated in December 1971, but Britain's military and political role in Oman significantly expanded during the 1970s in response to the insurgency that affected the Sultanate. British forces left the Trucial States and the nomenclature of British imperialism in the region was transformed into a formal diplomatic relationship. There can be little doubt that the Foreign Office abandoned the rulers in December 1971 and deliberately adopted a hands-off policy for most of the 1970s. The Foreign Office's representatives in the UAE, Bahrain and Qatar were still influential after independence, but British interests were transformed as trade became increasingly important. British advisors and consultants were still employed by the rulers and the contractors played an important role in assisting them in the development of the Emirates, but their influence in the UAE's armed forces declined during the decade. The Foreign Office and defence contractors were able to exploit significant regional demand for advanced weapons systems.

The supply of arms to the UAE armed forces was very lucrative for British companies, but this led to an unprecedented arms race in the region. The significant increase in oil income following the 1973 Arab–Israeli War meant that the rulers could afford an arms bonanza. Although large sums were spent on arms acquisitions during the first decade of independence, it was debatable whether the Emirates could have defended themselves. The Iranian Revolution and the outbreak of the Iran–Iraq War showed that the UAE and the other Gulf States relied on British and American support. Defence relations continue to be a significant facet of Anglo-UAE relations.

Although the British left a power vacuum in the Trucial States and the Gulf region after they left in 1971, the imperial legacy was overwhelmingly positive. The British succeeded in the Trucial States, and in the other protected states, because their footprint was minimal, in contrast to other examples of imperialism in the Middle East. The British achieved their economic, political and strategic objectives in the Trucial States, and they also benefited from close relations with rulers such as Sheikh Zayed and Sheikh Rashid, who were forward-looking.

Notes

Introduction

1   Referred to as 'the Gulf' in British records.
2   Peter Sluglett, 'Formal and informal empire in the Middle East', in *The Oxford History of the British Empire*, Vol. 5, *Historiography*, ed. by R. Winks (Oxford, 1999), p. 422.
3   J. G. Lorimer, *Gazetteer of the Persian Gulf, Oman and Central Arabia*, Vol. 1: *Historical* (Calcutta: Superintendent Government Printing, 1915), p. 695. Committee of Imperial Defence, Persian Gulf Sub-Committee, PG 4, 28 June 1928, TNA: CAB 16/94.
4   C. U. Aitchison, *A Collection of Treaties, Engagements and Sanads Relating to India and Neighbouring Countries*, Vol. 11 (Delhi: Manager of Publications, 1933), pp. 190–239, 258–60.
5   'Historical summary of events in territories of the Ottoman Empire, Persia and Arabia affecting the British position in the Persian Gulf, 1907–1828', PG 13, TNA: CAB 16/94, p. 87.
6   Minute by Rendel of a talk with the Persian Ambassador, 30 May 1936, TNA: FO 371/19977/E3146.
7   Minute by Given, 11 January 1962, TNA: FO 371/162792/B1052/3.
8   Briefs for the Minister of State's visit to Washington, November 1967. Steering Brief No. 1: The Protected States, TNA: FCO 8/142.
9   Examples include the Aden Protectorate Levies. For a detailed account of colonial armies, see James Lunt, *Imperial Sunset: Frontier Soldiering in the 20th Century* (London: Macdonald, 1981).
10 For a discussion of these developments, see, J. B. Kelly, *Eastern Arabian Frontiers* (New York: Frederick A. Praeger, 1964).
11 Helene von Bismarck, *British Policy in the Persian Gulf, 1961–1968: Conceptions of Informal Empire* (London: Palgrave Macmillan, 2013).
12 Simon Smith, *Britain's Revival and Fall in the Gulf: Kuwait, Bahrain, Qatar and the Trucial States, 1950–1971* (London: Routledge, 2004).
13 Shohei Sato, *Britain and the Formation of the Gulf States: Embers of Empire* (Manchester: Manchester University Press, 2016).
14 Tore T. Petersen, *The Decline of the Anglo-American Middle East, 1961–1969: A Willing Retreat* (Brighton: Sussex Academic Press, 2006).

15 Saif Mohammad Obaid Bin-Abood had access to documents in the UAE – see 'Britain's withdrawal from the Gulf: With particular reference to the Emirates', PhD thesis, Durham University (1992), pp. xxi–xxii, 402–10.

16 Penelope Tuson, *The Records of the British Residency and Agencies in the Persian Gulf* (London: India Office Library and Records, 1978).

17 See: https://www.qdl.qa/en (accessed 3 June 2018).

18 Paul Rich, *Creating the Arabian Gulf: The British Raj and the Invasions of the Gulf* (Lanham, MD: Lexington Books, 2009), pp. 280–3.

19 Lorimer, *Gazetteer*, Vol. 1; ibid., *Gazetteer of the Persian Gulf, Oman and Central Arabia*, Vol. 2: *Geographical and Statistical* (Calcutta: Superintendent Government Printing, 1915).

20 R. Thomas Hughes, Arabian Gulf Intelligence, *Selections from the Records of the Bombay Government*, New Series, No. 24, 1856: *Concerning Arabia, Bahrain, Kuwait, Muscat and Oman, Qatar United Arab Emirates and the Islands of the Gulf*, referred to as *Bombay Selections* (Cambridge: Oleander Press, 1985).

21 For example, J. A. Saldanha, *Précis of Correspondence Regarding the Affairs of the Persian Gulf, 1854–1905* (Calcutta: Office of the Superintendent of Government Printing, 1906), p. 319, British Library, India Office Records (IOR): L/P&S/20/C248/C; ibid., *Précis of Nejd Affairs, 1804–1904* (Simla: Office of the Superintendent of Government Printing, 1904), IOR: L/P&S/20/C240; ibid., *Précis of Correspondence Regarding the Trucial Chiefs, 1801–1853* (Calcutta: Office of the Superintendent of Government Printing, 1906), IOR: L/P&S/20/C248/D.

22 See, for example, 'Historical summary of events in territories of the Ottoman Empire, Persia and Arabia affecting the British position in the Persian Gulf, 1907–1828', PG 13, October 1928, TNA: CAB 16/94; and 'Historical memorandum on the relations of the Wahabi Amirs and Ibn Saud with Eastern Arabia and the British Government, 1800–1934', September 1934, IOR: L/P&S/18/B437.

23 https://www.gov.uk/guidance/fco-non-standard-files (accessed 10 June 2018).

24 https://www.cia.gov/library/readingroom (accessed 10 June 2018).

1. Benign neglect

1 J. E. Peterson, 'Britain and the Gulf: At the periphery of Empire', in Lawrence G. Potter (ed.), *The Persian Gulf in History* (New York: Palgrave, 2009), pp. 277–93.

2 Malcolm Yapp, 'British policy in the Persian Gulf', in Alvin J. Cottrell (ed.), *The Persian Gulf States: A General Survey* (Baltimore, MD, and London: Johns Hopkins University Press, 1980), pp. 72–4.

3 Salil-ibn-Razik, *The History of the Imams and Seyyids of Oman: From AD 661–1856* (Cambridge: Cambridge University Press, 1871), pp. lxxix–lxxx;

Saldanha, *Précis of Correspondence Regarding the Trucial Chiefs, 1801–1853*, pp. 93–9, 103–5, 107–17.

4   Charles Rathbone Low, *History of the Indian Navy*. Vol. I (London: Richard Bentley & Son, 1877), pp. 310–66.

5   Aitchison, *A Collection of Treaties*, pp. 245–9.

6   Saldanha, *Précis of Correspondence Regarding the Trucial Chiefs*, p. 319.

7   Aitchison, *A Collection of Treaties*, pp. 250, 253.

8   Ibid., pp. 256–7.

9   Ibid., p. 257.

10 Ibid., p. 261.

11 'Historical summary of events in the Persian Gulf Shaikhdoms and the Sultanate of Muscat and Oman, 1928–1953', TNA: FO 371/174700, PG 53, pp. 163–5.

12 Aitchison, *A Collection of Treaties*, pp. 24–236.

13 Rosemary Hollis, 'From force to finance: Britain's adaptation to decline: Transforming relations with selected Arab Gulf States, 1965–1985', George Washington University, Washington, DC, PhD thesis (1988), p. 36.

14 Aitchison, *A Collection of Treaties*, p. 238.

15 Ibid., pp. 238–9.

16 Ibid., pp. 258–60.

17 Lorimer, *Gazetteer*, Vol. 1, p. 1030.

18 Aitchison, *A Collection of Treaties*, pp. 265–6.

19 Smith, *Britain's Revival*, pp. 37–8.

20 Husain M. Al-Baharna, 'The consequences of Britain's Excusive Treaties: A Gulf View', in B. R. Pridham (ed.), *The Arab Gulf and the West* (Beckenham: Croom Helm, 1985), p. 19.

21 Francis Owtram, *A Modern History of Oman: Formation of the State since 1920* (London: I.B. Tauris, 2004), p. 39.

22 Aitchison, *A Collection of Treaties*, pp. 317–19.

23 For a discussion of the difference between the de jure and de facto role of British influence see J. A. Saldanha, *Précis of Correspondence on International Rivalry and British Policy in the Persian Gulf, 1872–1905* (1906), IOR: L/P&S/20/C247, pp. 34–5.

24 Newton to Viscount Halifax, 31 March 1940, TNA: FO 371/24545/E1637/1637/91.

25 Michael H. Fisher, *Indirect Rule in India: Residents and the Residency System, 1764–1858* (New Delhi: Oxford University Press, 1991), p. 6.

26 Ibid., pp. 24, 29, 458–77; Gifford, Prosser, 'Indirect rule: Touchstone or tombstone for colonial policy?', in Prosser Gifford and William Roger Louis (eds), *Britain and Germany in Africa: Imperial Rivalry and Colonial Rule* (New Haven, CT: Yale University Press, 1967), pp. 351–91.

27 Ronald Robinson, 'Non-European foundations of European imperialism: Sketch for a theory of collaboration', in R. Owen and B. Sutcliffe (eds), *Studies in the Theory of*

Imperialism (London: Longman, 1972), pp. 117–42; Robinson, 'The excentric idea of imperialism, with or without empire', in W. J. Mommsen and J. Osterhammel (eds), *Imperialism and After: Continuities and Discontinuities* (London: Allen & Unwin, 1986).

28 Robinson, 'Non-European foundations', p. 120.

29 Ibid., p. 121.

30 George Nathaniel Curzon, *Persia and the Persian Question*, Vol. 2 (London: Longmans, Green & Co., 1892), p. 451.

31 Anthony Kirk-Greene, *Britain's Imperial Administrators, 1858–1966* (Basingstoke: Macmillan, 2000), pp. 71–7.

32 Fisher, *Indirect Rule in India*, p. 463.

33 Lorimer, *Gazetteer of the Persian Gulf*, Vol. 1, p. 678.

34 James Onley, 'India's native agents in Arabia and Persia in the nineteenth century', *Comparative Studies of South Asia, Africa and the Middle East*, Vol. 24, No. 2 (2004), pp. 129–37.

35 Janes Onley, *The Arabian Frontier of the British Raj: Merchants, Rulers and the British in the Nineteenth Century Gulf* (Oxford: Oxford University Press, 2007), pp. 66–71, 93–6.

36 Craig to the Bahrain Residency, 27 September 1964, TNA: FO 371/174742/BT1891/1.

37 India Office memo, 'Political control in the Persian Gulf', 5 October 1928, IOR: L/P&S/18/B393; Draft instructions for Burrows, 17 July 1953, TNA: FO 371/104270/EA1053/8.

38 Hay to Churchill, 25 June 1953, TNA: FO 371/104270/EA1053/7.

39 Middleton to Lloyd, 23 February 1959, TNA: FO 371/140110/BA1053/3; Rupert Hay, *The Persian Gulf States* (Washington, DC: Middle East Institute, 1959), pp. 19–27.

40 Onley, *The Arabian Frontier*, p. 102.

41 Donald Hawley, *Trucial States* (London: Michael Russell, 1970), pp. 167–8.

42 *The Persian Gulf Gazette*, Vol. 1, No. 1, 1 October 1953; and ibid., Vol. 8, No. 1, 1 October 1960; *The Persian Gulf Gazette and Supplements*, 1953–1972, Vol. 1 (Gerrards Cross: Archive Editions, 1987).

43 'Historical summary of events in the Persian Gulf Shaikhdoms and the Sultanate of Muscat and Oman 1953–64', Vol. 1, PG 64, 19 January 1967, TNA: FO 464/51.

44 Horner to DOS, 26 December 1961, National Archives and Records Administration (NARA), College Park, MD: RG 59, CFPF 1963, Box 4070.

45 Donald Hawley, 'A political agent's life: The Trucial States, 1958–1961', Palace Green Library, Durham University (DUL): HAW 10/7/1–8, f. 6.

46 For an entertaining account, see, Glencairn Balfour-Paul, *Bagpipes in Babylon: A Lifetime in the World and Beyond* (London: I.B. Tauris, 2006), pp. 190–200.

47 Hay to Furlonge, 13 May 1950, TNA: FO 371/82033/EA1053/2.

48 Craig to the Acting Political Resident, 27 September 1964, TNA: FO 371/117474/BT1891/1.

49 Private information provided to the author.

50 Balfour-Paul, *The End of Empire in the Middle East: Britain's Relinquishment of Power in Her Last Three Arab Dependencies* (Cambridge: Cambridge University Press, 1991), p. 104.

51 Fowle to Metcalfe, 17 March 1939, TNA: FO 371/23180/E3179.

52 Minute by Crawford, 1 November 1964, TNA: FO 371/174489/B1052/31.

53 John F. Standish, 'British maritime policy in the Persian Gulf', *Middle Eastern Studies*, Vol. 3, No. 4 (1967), pp. 324–54.

54 For a discussion of the distinction between a protected state and protectorate, see Onley, 'The Raj reconsidered: British India's Informal Empire and spheres of influence in Asia and Africa', *Asian Affairs*, Vol. 11, No. 1 (2009), pp. 51–3.

55 Balfour-Paul, *End of Empire*, pp. 101–2.

56 Uzi Rabi, 'Britain's "special position" in the Gulf: Its origins, dynamics and legacy', *Middle Eastern Studies*, Vol. 42, No. 6 (2006), p. 354.

57 Minute by Stevens, 9 February 1959, TNA: FO 371/141878/V1892/4/G.

58 Wilfred Thesiger, *Arabian Sands* (London: Longmans, 1959), p. 241.

59 Kelly, *Eastern Arabian Frontiers*, p. 25.

60 *Arbitration Concerning Buraimi and the Common Frontier between Abu Dhabi and Saudi Arabia: Memorial Submitted by the Government of the United Kingdom of Great Britain and Northern Ireland*, Vol. 1 (London: 1955), p. 10.

61 Report by J. F. Walker on the Trucial Coast frontiers settlement, March 1955, TNA: FCO 164/35.

62 Personal information provided to the author.

63 'Tribes of the Trucial States', August 1958, National Army Museum (NAM), Chelsea, London: 2018-06-12-19-22.

64 'Historical summary of events in territories of the Ottoman Empire, Persian and Arabia affecting the British position in the Persian Gulf, 1907–1828', PG 13, TNA: CAB 16/94, p. 87.

65 For a discussion of the meaning of 'segmentary', see Dale F. Eickelman, *The Middle East and Central Asia: An Anthropological Approach*, 4th edn (Upper Saddle River, NJ: Prentice Hall, 2002), pp. 120–6.

66 Peter Lienhardt, 'Shaikhdoms of Eastern Arabia', DPhil thesis, Oxford University (1957), p. 49.

67 Michael Herb, *All in the Family: Absolutism, Revolution, and Democracy in the Middle Eastern Monarchies* (Albany, NY: State University of New York Press, 1999), pp. 23–5.

68 Frauke Heard-Bey, *From Trucial States to United Arab Emirates: A Society in Transition* (London: Longman, 1997), p. 81.

69 Ibid., pp. 124–5.

70 'History of topographical, geophysical surveys of Trucial Coast States, and Qatar, 1937–1950', BP Archive: 62746, d. 24.

71 Emirates Centre for Strategic Studies and Research, *With United Strength: H.H. Shaikh Zayed bin Sultan Al Nahyan: The Leader and the Nation* (Abu Dhabi, 2005), pp. 32–3.

72 J. P. Bannerman, 'The impact of the oil industry on society in the Arabian Peninsula', in R. I. Lawless (ed.), *The Gulf in the Early 20th Century: Foreign Institutions and Local Resources*, Working Paper, Centre for Middle Eastern and Islamic Studies, University of Durham (1986), pp. 76–7.

73 Heard-Bey, *Trucial States*, p. 112.

74 For a discussion of the role of the *majlis*, see, Fuad I. Khuri, *Tribe and State in Bahrain: The Transformation of Social and Political Authority in an Arab State* (Chicago, IL: University of Chicago Press, 1980), pp. 35–6; Peter Lienhardt, *Shaikhdoms of Eastern Arabia*, ed. by Ahmed Al-Shahi (Basingstoke: Palgrave, 2001), pp. 197–9.

75 Uzi Rabi, 'Oil, politics and tribal rulers in Eastern Arabia: The reign of Shakhbut (1928–1966)', *British Journal of Middle Eastern Studies*, Vol. 33, No. 1 (2006), p. 41.

76 'Constitutional development in the Trucial States', 19 February 1968, TNA: FCO 51/45.

77 Ibid.

78 Andrea B. Rugh, *The Political Culture of Leadership in the United Arab Emirates* (New York: Palgrave Macmillan, 2007), pp. 10–11.

79 Allen J. Fromherz, *Qatar: A Modern History* (London: I.B. Tauris, 2012), p. 66.

80 Philip S. Khoury and Joseph Kostiner (eds), *Tribes and State Formation in the Middle East* (Berkeley, CA: University of California Press, 1990), pp. 8–9.

81 Yoav Alon, 'From Abdullah (I) to Abdullah (II): The monarchy, the tribes and shaykhly families in Jordan, 1920–2012', in Uzi Rabi (ed.), *Tribes and States in a Changing Middle East* (London: Hurst and Company, 2016), p. 14.

82 Peter Lienhardt, 'The authority of shaykhs in the Gulf: An essay in nineteenth-century history', in R. B. Serjeant and R. L. Bidwell (eds), *Arabian Studies*, Vol. 2 (London: C. Hurst & Company, 1975), pp. 63–5.

83 Hawley to Middleton, 30 December 1958, TNA: FO 371/140087/BA10110/1.

84 Rosemarie Said Zahlan, *The Origins of the United Arab Emirates: A Political and Social History of the Trucial States* (New York: St. Martin's Press, 1978), pp. 34–8, 57–9; Lienhardt, *Shaikhdoms*, pp. 175–81.

85   Hay to Churchill, 25 June 1953, TNA: FO 371/104270/EA1053/7.

86   J. E. Peterson, 'Tribes and politics in Eastern Arabia', *Middle East Journal*, Vol. 21, No. 3 (1977), pp. 297–8.

87   James Onley and Sulayman Khalaf, 'Shaikhly authority in the pre-oil Gulf: An historical-anthropological study', *History and Anthropology*, Vol. 17, No. 3 (2006), pp. 189–208.

88   H. R. P. Dickson, *The Arab of the Desert: A Glimpse into Badawin Life in Kuwait and Saudi Arabia* (London: George Allen & Unwin, 1951), pp. 53, 117.

89   J. E. Peterson, 'The nature of succession in the Gulf', *Middle East Journal*, Vol. 55, No. 4 (2001), p. 600.

90   Lienhardt, *Shaikhdoms*, pp. 184–6, 212–15.

91   Lienhardt, 'Shaikhdoms', (DPhil), p. 56.

92   Jill Crystal, *Oil and Politics in the Gulf: Rulers and the Merchants in Kuwait and Qatar* (Cambridge: Cambridge University Press, 1990), p. 3.

93   Herb, *All in the Family*, p. 57.

94   Heard-Bey, *Trucial States*, pp. 112–19.

95   Fatma Al-Sayegh, 'Merchants' role in a changing society: The case of Dubai, 1900–90', *Middle Eastern Studies*, Vol. 34, No. 1 (1998), pp. 94–5.

96   Crystal, *Oil and Politics*, pp. 9–10.

97   Lienhardt, 'Shaikhdoms', (DPhil), p. 25.

98   Lorimer, *Gazetteer*, Vol. 2, p. 1437.

99   Military Report and Route Book: The Arabian States of the Persian Gulf, 1939, IOR: L/P&S/20/C252.

100   Said Zahlan, *Origins*, p. 3.

101   For a detailed account, see Lienhardt, 'Shaikhdoms', pp. 13–48.

102   Nelida Fuccaro, *Histories of City and State in the Persian Gulf: Manama since 1800* (Cambridge: Cambridge University Press, 2009), pp. 50–1.

103   Mark Hayman, 'Economic protectorate in Britain's Informal Empire: The Trucial Coast during the Second World War', *Journal of Imperial and Commonwealth History*, Vol. 46, No. 2 (2018), pp. 261–78; Heard-Bey, *Trucial States*, pp. 219–21, 243–4.

104   James Onley, 'The politics of protection in the Gulf: The Arab Rulers and the British Resident in the nineteenth century', *New Arabian Studies*, Vol. 6 (2004), pp. 32–3.

105   Peterson, 'Tribes and politics in Eastern Arabia', p. 302.

106   Lienhardt, 'Shaikhdoms', (DPhil), p. 15.

107   Hughes, *Selections*, p. 69.

108   J. B. Kelly, *Britain and the Persian Gulf, 1795–1880* (Oxford: Oxford University Press, 1968), pp. 368–9; Hughes, *Selections*, p. 74.

109   Onley, 'The politics of protection', pp. 71–6.

110 Paul Dresch, *Tribes, Government and History in Yemen* (Oxford: Oxford University Press, 1989), pp. 59–65.

111 Gregory F. Gause III, *Oil Monarchies: Domestic and Security Challenges in the Arab Gulf States* (New York: Council on Foreign Relations Press, 1994), p. 22.

112 For an alternative perspective, see Abdullah Omran Taryam, *The Establishment of the United Arab Emirates 1950–85* (Beckenham: Croom Helm, 1987), pp. 9–11.

113 Onley and Khalaf, 'Shaikhly authority', p. 204.

114 Louise E. Sweet, 'Camel raiding of North Arabian bedouin: A mechanism of ecological adaption', *American Anthropologist*, Vol. 67, No. 5 (1965), pp. 1132–50.

115 Tancred Bradshaw, 'The hand of Glubb: The origins of the Trucial Oman Scouts, 1948–1956', *Middle Eastern Studies*, Vol. 53, No. 4 (2017), pp. 656–72.

116 Jordan was a notable success story. See Yoav Alon, *The Making of Jordan: Tribes, Colonialism and the Modern State* (London: I.B. Tauris, 2007), pp. 84–109.

117 Gause, *Oil Monarchies*, pp. 24–5.

118 Ibid., p. 22.

119 Minute by McCarthy, 18 December 1969, TNA: FCO 8/1331, f. 18.

120 Balfour-Paul, *End of Empire*, p. 103.

121 TNA: FO 371/174700, PG 53, pp. 145, 163.

122 Peel (India Office) to the Under-Secretary of State (Foreign Office), 3 August 1938, TNA: FO 371/21825/E4579.

123 Rosemarie Said Zahlan, *The Making of the Modern Gulf States: Kuwait, Bahrain, Qatar, the United Arab Emirates and Oman*, Foreword by Roger Owen, revised and updated edn (Reading: Garnett Publishing, 1998), pp. 109–10.

124 See Gause, *Oil Monarchies*, pp. 42–77.

125 Herb, *All in the Family*, p. 259.

126 Mary Ann Tetreault, *Stories of Democracy: Politics and Society in Contemporary Kuwait* (New York: Columbia University Press, 2000), pp. 50–3.

127 Falle to Stewart, 1 December 1969, TNA: FCO 8/1028.

128 For a breakdown of roles in the Trucial States, see the 'Trucial Oman Scouts: handbook', c. 1967, NAM: 2016-03-12-1 to 14.

129 Tetreault, *Stories of Democracy*, pp. 8, 236.

130 Fromherz, *Qatar*, p. 131.

131 Crystal, *Oil and Politics*, pp. 11–13.

132 Burrows to Lloyd, 25 October 1958, TNA: FO 371/132533/BA1018/11.

133 Herb, *All in the Family*, p. 113.

134 Ibid., p. 136; Lamb to Crawford, 2 January 1967, Abu Dhabi annual review for 1966, TNA: FCO 8/827.

135 For a detailed account of the ruling families of the UAE Government after independence, see, 'UAE Government, leading personalities and organisations in Abu Dhabi', April 1974, BP Archive: 5317.

2. The neo-Raj

1   Joint Intelligence Committee memo, 'The political, economic and strategic importance of Buraimi', 23 December 1957, TNA: DEFE 11/271.

2   Fuccaro, *Histories of City and State*, pp. 170–2, 180–6.

3   Uzi Rabi, *The Emergence of States in a Tribal Society: Oman under Sa'id bin Taymur, 1932–1970* (Eastbourne: Sussex Academic Press, 2006), pp. 102–4.

4   Memo by Burrows, 27 May 1957, TNA: FO 371/126916/EA1051/16.

5   'The Arab States of the Gulf since 1947: Their evolution and development with particular reference to their neighbours, Arab nationalism and the British presence', 1 September 1966, TNA: FO 371/185217/B1672/6.

6   Minute by Riches, 10 November 1958, TNA: FO: 371/132533/BA1018/11.

7   'Middle East Policy', CP (45) 174, 17 September 1945, TNA: CAB 129/2.

8   'The Arab States of the Gulf since 1947', TNA: FO 371/185217/B1672/6.

9   J. B. Kelly, *Arabia, the Gulf and the West: A Critical View of the Arabs and Their Oil Policy* (New York: Basic Books, 1980), pp. 97–8.

10 Report by Gore-Booth, 28 May 1957, TNA: FO 371/127749/V1051/82.

11 Foreign Relations of the United States (FRUS), 1947, Vol. 5: *The Near East and Africa* (Washington, DC: Government Printing Office, 1971), pp. 535, 579; 1955–57, Vol. 13: *The Near East: Jordan–Yemen* (Washington, DC: Government Printing Office, 1988), pp. 314–16.

12 Pelham to Bowker, 5 July 1953, TNA: FO 371/104258/ES10345/40; Peterson, 'Britain and the Gulf', pp. 283–5.

13 See Annex III in JP (48) 61 (Final), 12 October 1948, TNA: DEFE 6/6. Defence of oil interests remained the defining aspect of British interests; see COS (57) 20, 16 January 1957, TNA: DEFE 5/73.

14 'Jurisdiction in Dubai in the 1950s and 1960s', 26 October 1991, DUL: Hawley Papers, HAW 9/7/29–30.

15 'The British Protectorates, Protected States and Protected Persons Orders in Council, 1949 to 1953', Clive Parry, *Nationality and Citizenship Laws of the Commonwealth and of the Republic of Ireland* (London: Stevens & Sons Limited, 1957), pp. 356–62.

16 Draft memorandum Persian Gulf: The Trucial States, 1 July 1948, TNA: FO 371/68343/E8863/605/91/G.

17 Hay to Pyman, 19 July 1948, ibid., E10151/605/91/G.

18 'The Arab Sheikhdoms of the Persian Gulf', 8 June 1949, TNA: FO 464/3/E7129/1056/91.

19 The Marquess of Salisbury to Burrows, 24 July 1953, TNA: FO 371/104270/EA1053/8.

20 Ibid.

21 Ibid.

22 Minute by Ross, 17 July 1953, ibid.

23 James Bamberg, *The History of the British Petroleum Company*, Vol. 2: *The Anglo-Iranian Years, 1928–1954* (Cambridge: Cambridge University Press, 1994), pp. 410–58.

24 Wm. Roger Louis, 'Musaddiq and the dilemmas of British imperialism', in James A. Bill and Wm. Roger Louis (eds), *Musaddiq, Iranian Nationalism and Oil* (London: I.B. Tauris, 1988), pp. 229–30.

25 For a discussion of the scale and value of Abadan, see, Wm. Roger Louis, *The British Empire in the Middle East 1945–1951: Arab Nationalism, the United States, and Postwar Imperialism* (Oxford: Clarendon Press, 1984), pp. 9 and 761.

26 Hay to Eden, 31 October 1952, TNA: FO 371/98378/EA1084/292.

27 Hawley to Middleton, 30 December 1958, TNA: FO 1016/624, No. 21.

28 Hawley to Middleton, 31 March 1959, TNA: FO 371/140087/BA10110/4.

29 Tripp to Burrows, 15 February 1957, enclosed in Burrows to Lloyd, 2 April 1957, TNA: FO 371/126900/EA1019/3.

30 Hay to Churchill, 16 March 1953, TNA: FO 371/104270/EA1053/7.

31 Burrows to Lloyd, 6 June 1958, TNA: FO 371/132760/EA10110/2.

32 Man to Beaumont, 7 March 1961, TNA: FO 371/157019/BT1015/3.

33 The following pages are based on my article, 'The hand of Glubb'.

34 Minute by Greenhill, 6 November 1952, TNA: FO 371/98828/ES1015/17. Jeffrey R. Macris, *The Politics and Security of the Gulf: Anglo-American Hegemony and the Shaping of the Region* (London: Routledge, 2010), pp. 85–8.

35 Military Report and Route Book, The Arabian States of the Persian Gulf, 1939. IOR: L/P&S/20/C252, ff. 36–7, 73–4, 118–19, 150.

36 Dawson to Rogers, 3 April 1950, TNA: FO 371/82075/EA1196/1.

37 JIC (47) 80 (O) Final, 6 January 1948, TNA: CAB 158/2. A US Army military intelligence (G2) estimate in December 1950 argued that the Saudi Army numbered 18,000 men, NARA: RG 59 780.5/12–1.

38 Arbuthnott to the War Office, TNA: FO 141/1265/126/2/48/G; Trevelyan to Bevin, 6 March 1950, TNA: FO 371/82450/EQ12101/1. For details of the problems faced by the military mission to Saudi Arabia, see Calvert to Hankey, 26 April 1950, TNA: FO 371/82673/ES1201/6/G.

39 Stephanie Cronin, *Armies and State-Building in the Modern Middle East: Politics, Nationalism and Military Reform* (London: I.B. Tauris, 2014), p. 10.

40 P. J. Vatikiotis, *Politics and the Military in Jordan: A Study of the Arab Legion, 1921–1957* (London: Frank Cass, 1967), pp. 17–30.

41 Tancred Bradshaw, *The Glubb Reports: Glubb Pasha and Britain's Empire Project in the Middle East, 1920–1956* (London: Palgrave Macmillan, 2016). Yoav Alon, 'British colonialism and orientalism in Arabia: Glubb Pasha in Transjordan, 1930–1946', *British Scholar*, Vol. 3, No. 1 (2010), pp. 105–26.

42 Report on the Arab Legion, 28 May 1945, No. 166729, NARA: RG 319, Army Intelligence document file, entry 85, Box 1076; Cairo to Washington, 6 April 1948, No. 255072, NARA: RG 319, entry 85, Box 1705.

43 Burrows to the Ministry of Defence, 16 August 1948, TNA: FO 371/68344/E10151/G; Hay to Burrows, 7 December 1948, ibid., E16004/G.

44 Burrows to the Ministry of Defence, 16 August 1948, ibid., E1015/G.

45 Hay to Burrows, 20 May 1949, FO 371/75019/E6758/G; FO to the British Middle East Office (BMEO), 20 September 1949, TNA: FO 371/75020/E11470/G.

46 COS (49) 70, 23 February 1949, TNA: DEFE 5/13.

47 Memo by Burrows, 8 June 1949, TNA: FO 371/74960/E7129.

48 'The Aden Protectorate Levies', undated, NAM: 9204–165; Lunt, *Imperial Sunset*, pp. 129–49; J. E. Peterson, *Oman's Insurgencies: The Sultanate's Struggle for Supremacy* (London: Saqi Books, 2007), pp. 48–51.

49 FO minute of 6 May 1949, TNA: FO 371/75018/E5875/G. Details of Glubb's proposals can be found in Pirie-Gordon to FO, 26 July 1949, TNA: FO 371/75019/E9490/G.

50 'Middle East policy', CP (49) 183, 25 August 1949, TNA: CAB 129/36. British Diplomatic Oral History Programme (BDOHP), interview with Sir Clive Rose, 20 August 2003, pp. 7–9, available at: www.chu.cam.ac.uk/archives/collections/BDOHP/#R (accessed 2 August 2018).

51 Minute by Rose, 26 July 1950, TNA: FO 371/82174/EA2181/41.

52 For a description of this process, see minute by Rose, 5 February 1972, TNA: FCO 8/1940.

53 Burrows to Butler-Bowden, 6 September 1949, TNA: FO 371/75018/E2829/G.

54 Clough to Burrows, 24 January 1950, TNA: FO 371/82172/EA2181/1.

55 Burrows to FO, 19 November 1953, No. 965, TNA: FO 1016/307.

56 COS (56) 38, 27 January 1956, TNA: DEFE 5/64.

57 Memorandum of a conversation at the Department of State, 16 April 1951, NARA: RG 59 780.022/4–1651.

58 Memo by Ryan, 13 February 1932, TNA: FO 371/16013/E1000; Trott to Bevin, 4 December 1947, TNA: FO 371/62112/E11752.

59 Wadsworth to the Department of State, 5 July 1947, NARA: RG 59, 890F.00/7–547; Childs to the Department of State, 26 February 1948, NARA: RG 59, 790F.90I/2–2648. FRUS, 1949, Vol. 6: *The Near East, South Asia and Africa* (Washington, DC: Government Printing Office, 1977), pp. 88–9, 1624; 1951, Vol. 5: *The Near East and Africa* (Washington, DC: Government Printing Office, 1982), p. 1039.

60 Scott-Fox to FO, 22 June 1949, TNA: FO 371/75019/E7718/G; Pirie-Gordon to FO, 30 June 1949, ibid., E9490/G.

61 Minute by Greenhill, 11 December 1952, TNA: FO 371/98385/EA1084/446; Hay to Churchill, 25 June 1953, TNA: FO 371/104270/EA1053/7.

62 Trott to FO, 19 December 1950, TNA: FO 371/82175/EA2181/79/G.

63 Pelham to Eden, 19 November 1952, TNA: FO 371/98822/ES1013/2.

64 Minute by Furlonge, 22 February 1951, TNA: FO 371/91310/EA1201/10/G.

65 Pelham to Eden, 17 December 1952, TNA: FO 371/98828/ES1015/18.

66 Hay to FO, 14 April 1951, TNA: FO 371/91311/EA1201/30.

67 Le Quesne to Rose, 6 November 1951, TNA: FO 371/91313/EA1201/95; Burrows to
    FO, 19 November 1953, No. 965, TNA: FO 1016/307.

68 Lunt, *Imperial Sunset*, pp. 92–3.

69 Hay to Eden, 17 May 1951, TNA: FO 371/98323/EA1011/1.

70 Bahrain to FO, TNA: FO 371/104364/EA1203/69.

71 COS (52) 501, 9 September 1952, TNA: DEFE 5/41.

72 Burrows to Bowker, 8 September 1953, TNA: FO 371/104270/EA1053/10.

73 Memo by Makins, 20 March 1953, TNA: FO 371/98343/EA1051/53. Lienhardt,
    Shaikhdoms, pp. 12–13.

74 Michael Mann, *The Trucial Oman Scouts: The Story of a Bedouin Force* (Norwich:
    Michael Russell, 1994), pp. 28–9.

75 Burrows to Macmillan, 31 May 1955, TNA: FO 371/114589/EA1018/9.

76 Memo by Makins, 20 March 1952, TNA: FO 371/98343/EA1051/33.

77 Robertson to Brownjohn, 18 March 1952, TNA: WO 216/516.

78 The following section is based on my article, 'The dead hand of the Treasury: The
    economic and social development of the Trucial States, 1948–60', *Middle Eastern
    Studies*, Vol. 50, No. 2 (2014), pp. 329–31.

79 CP (49) 183, 25 August 1949, TNA: CAB 129/36

80 ME (O) (49) 35, 19 December 1949, TNA: CAB 134/501.

81 Hawley, *Trucial States*, pp. 195–7.

82 Hay to Churchill, 25 June 1953, TNA: FO 371/104270/EA1053/7; Heard-Bey,
    Trucial States, p. 206.

83 Pelly to FO, 26 June 1950, TNA: FO 371/82047/EA1101/3.

84 Julian Walker, *Tyro on the Trucial Coast* (Durham: Memoir Club, 1999), pp. 58–80.

85 Crystal, *Oil and Politics*, p. 74.

86 Kuwait economic report for 1950, NARA: RG 59 886D.00/1-2951.

87 US Consulate at Kuwait to DOS, 20 March 1953, NARA: RG 59 886D.00/2-2053.

88 Hay to FO, 2 May 1952, TNA: FO 371/98325/EA1015/1; FO memo, 30 August 1952,
    ibid., EA1055/69.

89 US Consulate at Kuwait to DOS, 4 September 1954, NARA: RG 59 886D.00/9-454;
    Crystal, *Oil and politics*, pp. 75–8.

90 Kuwait economic review for 1953, NARA: RG 59 886D.00/1-454.

91 Hay to FO, 25 November 1950, TNA: FO 371/82032/EA1057/12.

92 Hay to FO, 29 January 1951, TNA: FO 371/91326/EA1511/1.

93 Burrows to Bowker, 8 September 1953, TNA: FO 371/104270/EA1053/10.

94 Burrows to Eden, 7 December 1953, ibid., EA1053/13.

95 FO memo, 20 October 1952, TNA: FO 371/98358/EA1059/3.

96 Hay to Furlonge, 13 May 1950, TNA: FO 371/82151/EA1741/3.

97 Memo by Makins, 20 March 1952, TNA: FO 371/98343/EA1051/33.

98 Minutes by Greenhill and Rose, 20 March 1953, TNA: FO 371/104270/EA/1053/3.

99 There is a significant literature on the Buraimi crisis and the demarcation of frontiers in Eastern Arabia. See: Foreign Office Research Department memo, 'The claims of Ibn Saud against His Majesty's Government', 21 November 1950, TNA: FO 371/82656/ES1082/1; Liebsney and Starr to Hart, 'The problem of boundaries in Eastern Arabia', 2 January 1953, NARA: RG 59 780.022/1–253; Bernard Burrows, *Footnotes in the Sand: The Gulf in Transition, 1953–1958* (Salisbury: Michael Russell, 1990), pp. 92–111; Nathan J. Citino, *From Arab Nationalism to OPEC: Eisenhower, King Saud, and the Making of US–Saudi Relations*, 2nd edn (Bloomington, IN: Indiana University Press, 2010), pp. 19–37; Kelly, *Arabia*, pp. 61–73; Tore T. Petersen, 'Anglo-American rivalry in the Middle East: The struggle for the Buraimi Oasis, 1952–1957', *International History Review*, Vol. 14, No. 1 (1992), pp. 71–91.

100 Alexei Vassiliev, *The History of Saudi Arabia* (London: Saqi Books, 1998), pp. 112–14.

101 Anthony B. Toth, 'Control and allegiance at the dawn of the Oil Age: Bedouin, *zakat* and struggles for sovereignty in Arabia, 1916–1955', *Middle East Critique*, Vol. 21, No. 1 (2012), pp. 60–2.

102 'Historical Memorandum on the Relations of the Wahabi Amirs and Ibn Saud with Eastern Arabia and the British Government, 1800–1934', 26 September 1934, IOR: L/P&S/18/B437.

103 'The southern frontiers of Arabia', 30 June 1940, TNA: FO 371/40266/E6545.

104 C. M. Le Quesne, 'The boundary between Saudi Arabia and the shaikhdoms of Qatar and Abu Dhabi and the Sultanate of Muscat and Oman: A summary of the history of the dispute together with a statement of the evidence in support of the claims of Qatar, Abu Dhabi and Muscat', *c.* 1954. TNA: FO 371/109837/EA1081/398.

105 For a discussion of Ibn Saud's motives for occupying Buraimi, see Hay to Eden, 31 October 1952, TNA: FO 371/98378/EA1084/292. Citino, *From Arab Nationalism to OPEC*, pp. 25–6.

106 The Saudi claim to Buraimi is detailed in a report written by ARAMCO researchers: *Arbitration for the Settlement of the Territorial Dispute between Muscat and Abu Dhabi on the One Side and Saudi Arabia on the Other: Memorial of the Government of Saudi Arabia* (Cairo, 1955).

107 Minute by Sarell, 20 September 1952, TNA: FO 371/98373/EA1084/147; minute by Blackham, 15 October 1952, TNA: FO 371/98381/EA1084/346/G.

108 Minute by Rose, 29 September 1952, TNA: FO 371/98373/EA1084/139. The Foreign Office perspective was outlined in Eden's Cabinet memorandum C. (52) 450, 19 December 1952, TNA: CAB 129/57.

109   Burrows to Ross, 26 April 1952, TNA: FO 371/98828/ES1051/2; Pelham to Eden,
      17 December 1952, ibid., ES1051/18.

110   Memo on specific problems with the United Kingdom, White House Memoranda
      Series, General Foreign Policy, Box 8, folder 4, Seeley Mudd Library, Princeton
      University, NJ: Dulles Papers; minute by Riches, 9 April 1957, TNA: FO 371/
      127756/V1075/18.

111   Citino, *From Arab Nationalism*, pp. 21–2.

112   Balfour-Paul, *End of Empire*, p. 115.

113   Burrows to FO, 16 September 1953, No. 745, TNA: FO 1016/234.

114   Minute by Brownjohn, 7 April 1953, TNA: DEFE 13/413.

115   Galt to FO, 11 July 1955, TNA: FO 371/114860/EA1204/3.

116   Details of this correspondence can be found in TNA: T 220/1281.

117   Minute by Greenhill, 7 October 1952, TNA: FO 371/98375/EA1084/208.

118   Minute by Ross, 16 October 1952, TNA: FO 371/98377/EA1084/259; minutes by
      Blackham and Bowker, TNA: FO 371/98384/EA1084/409.

119   CC. (52) 107th meeting, 22 December 1952, TNA: CAB 128/25; COS (52) 175th
      meeting, 23 December 1953, TNA: DEFE 4/58.

120   GHQ MELF to MOD, 18 December 1952, TNA: FO 371/98388/EA1084/502.

121   GHQ MELF to SAOPG and SRAFOPG, 14 January 1953, TNA: PREM 11/698.
      Peter Clayton, *Two Alpha Lima: The First Ten Years of the Trucial Oman Levies and
      Trucial Oman Scouts (1950–1960)* (London: Janus Publishing, 1994), pp. 29–31.

122   Weir to Le Quesne, 18 February 1953, TNA: FO 1016/226; Note by Brownjohn,
      21 July 1953, TNA: DEFE 13/413.

123   Minute by Brownjohn, 7 April 1953, ibid.

124   Martin to Pirie-Gordon, 7 November 1953, TNA: FO 1016/307.

125   Pirie-Gordon to Le Quesne, 11 November 1953, TNA: FO 1016/307, COS (52) 665,
      8 December 1952, TNA: DEFE 5/43.

126   P. S. Allfree, *Warlords of Oman* (New York: Barnes & Co, 1967), pp. 22–4.

127   Galt to FO, 11 July 1955, TNA: FO 371/114860/EA1204/3.

128   Note for Churchill, 15 February 1954, TNA: PREM 11/944.

129   Burrows to FO, 16 September 1953, No. 745, TNA: FO 1016/234.

130   'The possibility of increasing the strength of Arab forces in the Persian Gulf',
      12 December 1954, Toronto: Baird Papers.

131   Bailey to Samuel, 30 May 1955, TNA: FO 371/114892/ES1192/2; minute by Fry,
      4 June 1955, ibid. ES1192/3.

132   COS (55) 253, 5 October 1955, TNA: DEFE 5/61; Central Intelligence Agency,
      Special National Intelligence Estimate 30-3-55, 12 October 1955, 'Probable
      consequences of the Egyptian Arms deal with the Soviet bloc', CIA: FOIA.

133   Minute by Blackham, 14 January 1954, TNA: FO 371/110112/ES1193/1/G; Allen
      to Dulles, 26 April 1956, NARA: RG 59 786.56/4–2656.

134 Stephens to Millard, 27 February 1956, TNA: WO 32/16264.

135 JP (54) 67 (Final), 5 August 1954, TNA: DEFE 6/26.

136 COS (56) 3, 3 January 1956, TNA: DEFE 5/64.

137 JP (55), 127 (Final), 28 February 1955, TNA: DEFE 6/32.

138 Operation Bonaparte operational diary, TNA: FO 1016/451; Clayton, *Two Alpha Lima*, pp. 71–8.

139 The competing British and Saudi claims can be found in the *Arbitration Concerning Buraimi*; J. C. Wilkinson, *Arabia's Frontiers: The Story of Britain's Boundary Drawing in the Desert* (London: I.B. Tauris, 1991), pp. 323–4.

140 Minute by Samuel, 22 September 1955, TNA: FO 371/114625/EA1081/392; Evelyn Shuckburgh, *Descent to Suez: Diaries 1951–56* (London: Weidenfeld and Nicolson, 1986), p. 278.

141 Mann, *Trucial Oman Scouts*, pp. 57–61.

142 These differences were manifested in numerous documents, including TNA: FO 371/120581/EA1081/107; Shuckburgh to Lloyd, 28 January 1956, TNA: FO 371/120582/EA1081/146; and Allen to Dulles, 17 January 1956, NARA: RG 59 780.022/1–1756. See also Dulles to Dulles, autumn 1955, White House Memoranda Series: General Foreign Policy, Box 8, folder 4, Seeley Mudd Library, Princeton University: Dulles Papers.

143 Residency Bahrain to Riches, 21 November 1955, TNA: FO 371/114630/EA1081/542/G; COS (55) 95th meeting, 21 November 1955, Confidential Annex, TNA: DEFE 4/80.

144 JP (55) 129 (Final), 19 January 1956, TNA: DEFE 6/32.

145 COS (56) 3, 3 January 1956, TNA: DEFE 5/64.

146 JP (55) 129, 19 January 1956, TNA: DEFE 6/32; minute by Russell Edmunds, 6 February 1956, TNA: T 220/1281.

147 Mann, *Trucial Oman Scouts*, p. 62.

148 Richards to Samuel, 18 August 1955, TNA: FO 371/114680/EA1204/4.

149 Burrows to FO, 21 March 1956, TNA: FO 371/120626/EA1204/18; Clayton, *Two Alpha Lima*, p. 90.

150 Minute by Riches of a meeting with Brigadier Baird, 20 July 1956, TNA: FO 371/120628/EA1205/3.

151 Operations in Muscat and Oman, 1952–1959, Prepared by the Historical Section Army Department Library, July 1964, TNA: WO 337/9; Mann, *Trucial Oman Scouts*, pp. 88–97, 99–105.

152 Bahrain Residency to the Ministry of Defence, LIC 8757, 13 August 1957, TNA: DEFE 11/178.

153 Butts to Crawford, 25 January 1967, TNA: FCO 8/883. See also Allen to the Department of State, 23 June 1965, NARA: RG 59 Central Foreign Policy File 1964–66, POL 2 Trucial St, Box 2745.

154 Tripp to Gault, 1 July 1957, TNA: FO 371/126984/EA1648/27.

155 Marshall to Wigmore, 5 February 1959, TNA: FO 371/140239/B1643/1.

156 Ash Rossiter, 'Britain and the development of professional security forces in the Gulf Arab States, 1921–1971: Local forces and Informal Empire', PhD thesis, University of Exeter (2014), pp. 146–8.

157 Burrows to FO, 21 February 1957, TNA: FO371/126983/EA1648/6/G.

158 OPD (67) 1, 2 January 1967, TNA: CAB 148/31.

159 Minute by Greenhill, 22 January 1953, TNA: FO 371/104332/EA1106/4; Hay to Ross, 15 April 1953, TNA: FO 371/104292/EA1081/485.

160 Minute by Greenhill, 3 November 1953, TNA: FO 371/104332/EA1106/11.

161 Eden to Butler, 12 November 1953, TNA: T 220/1284.

162 Minute by Lane, 27 January 1953, TNA: FO 371/104332/EA1106/1.

163 Minute by Greenhill, 22 January 1953, ibid., EA1106/4.

164 Laver to Samuel, 11 February 1954, TNA: FO/371/109859/EA1105/3.

165 Minute by Russell-Edmunds, 16 May 1955, TNA: T 220/1284.

166 Reilly to Peck, 12 December 1956, TNA: T 220/1285.

167 Tripp to Burrows, 25 October 1955, TNA: FO 1016/405.

168 See, for example, *BBC Summary of World Broadcasts*, Part 4: *The Arab World, Israel, Greece, Turkey, Persian* (Caversham Park: British Broadcasting Corporation, 1956; henceforth, *SWB*), 6 January 1956, pp. 33–5; ibid., 17 April 1956, p. 1; ibid., 1 June 1956, pp. 1–2.

169 Burrows to Macmillan, 8 November 1955, TNA: FO 371/114656/EA1108/33.

170 Russell-Edmunds to Denson, 8 August 1956, TNA: FO 371/120610/EA1108/7.

171 OME (57) 11 (First Revise), 11 March 1957, TNA: CAB 134/2339.

172 Foreign Office minute, 28 March 1957, TNA: FO 371/127755/V1075/8/G.

173 Trucial States annual review for 1956, TNA: FO/371/126869/EA1011/1.

174 Burrows to the Foreign Office, 2 April 1957, TNA: FO 371/126900/EA1019/3.

175 Burrows to Riches, 14 April 1956, TNA: FO 371/120561/EA10316/12.

176 Smith, *Britain's Revival*, pp. 12–14.

177 Kuwait to the Department of State, 13 November 1956, NARA: RG 59 786D.00/11-2756.

178 Burrows to Lloyd, 23 November 1956: TNA: FO 371/120558/EA10113/50.

179 Burrows, *Footnotes*, p. 84.

180 Baker to Musker, 17 January 1957, confidential letter 68/23, HSBC Group Archives: HQ BBME 0851.

181 Geoffrey Jones, *Banking and Oil: The History of the British Bank of the Middle East*, Vol. 2 (Cambridge: Cambridge University Press, 1986), pp. 134–5, 149–57.

182 JIC (56) 104, 18 October 1956, TNA: CAB 158/26.

183 'Prospects for the British position in the Middle East during the next decade: Causes and consequences of decline', INR 7313, 17 September 1956,

NARA: RG 59 Policy Planning Staff subject files, 1952–1962, entry 1272, Box 75.

184 National Intelligence Estimate 30–57, 'The British position in the Persian Gulf and the Arabian Peninsula', 19 February 1957, CIA: FOIA.

185 Stevens to Lloyd, 8 December 1956, TNA: FO 371/120571/EA1055/17.

186 Wright to Lloyd, 4 January 1957, TNA: FO 371/126923/EA1071/1.

187 Burrows to Lloyd, 24 January 1957, TNA: FO 371/126915/EA1051/1.

188 C. (57) 138, 'Persian Gulf', 5 June 1957, TNA: CAB 129/87.

189 W. Taylor Fain, *American Ascendance and British Retreat in the Persian Gulf Region* (New York: Palgrave Macmillan, 2008), p. 73.

190 ME (O) (56) 27, 6 May 1956, TNA: CAB 134/1298.

191 Committee on the Prime Minister's tour of the Commonwealth, Middle East memorandum, 12 December 1957, GEN 622/1/3, TNA: CAB 130/138.

192 C. (56) 122, 'Persian Gulf', 15 May 1956, TNA: CAB 129/81.

193 *The Times*, 26 February 1956, p. 11.

194 Trucial States annual report for 1956, TNA: FO 371/126869/EA1011/1.

195 Treasury minute, 9 January 1959, TNA: T 220/1286.

196 Middleton to Lloyd, 2 February 1959, TNA: FO 371/140064/BA1011/4; Hawley to Middleton, 23 January 1960, TNA: FO 371/148896/BA1101/5.

197 Burrows to Riches, 14 April 1956, TNA: FO 371/120561/EA10316/12.

198 Hay to Eden, 11 June 1952, TNA: FO 371/98333/EA1023/3.

199 British Council Persian Gulf. Representative's Annual Report, 1957–58, TNA: BW 114/6.

200 Lienhardt, *Shaikhdoms*, pp. 9–10.

201 Burrows to the Foreign Office, 2 April 1957, TNA: FO 371/126900/EA1019/3; Hawley to Middleton, 31 March 1960, TNA: FO 371/140087/EA10110/4.

202 See, for example, *SWB*, 6 January 1956, pp. 33–5; ibid., 17 April 1956, p. 1; ibid., 1 June 1956, pp. 1–2.

203 JIC (58) 63 (Final), 3 December 1958, enclosed in OME (58) 15, 19 June 1959, TNA: CAB 134/2342.

204 Elizabeth Monroe, 'Consequences of the Egyptian Revolution in the Persian Gulf area', Chatham House Special Course: Middle East, 1–3 October 1958, Chatham House Archive: 11/26.

205 Middle East diary, 6–7 January 1958, pp. 1931, 1935, MECA: John Slade-Baker Collection, Box 5/3.

206 Tripp to Burrows, 15 February 1957, enclosed in Burrows to Lloyd, 2 April 1957, TNA: FO 371/126900/EA1019/3.

207 Private information provided to the author.

208 JIC (59) 13 (Final), 10 February 1959, TNA: CAB 158/31.

209 JIC (59) 23 (Final), 11 June 1959, enclosed in OME (59) 15, 19 June 1959, TNA: CAB 134/2343.

210 JIC (58) 85 (Final), 21 August 1958, TNA: CAB 158/34.

211 Middleton to Lloyd, 27 January 1960, TNA: FO 371/148896/BA1101/4.

212 Ibid.

213 Burrows to the Foreign Office, 15 April 1957, TNA: FO 371/126869/EA1011/5.

214 Tripp to Burrows, 15 February 1957, TNA: FO 371/126900/EA1019/3.

215 Burrows to Lloyd, 2 April 1957, ibid.

216 Burrows to the Foreign Office, 3 September 1957, TNA: FO 371/120916/EA1051/22.

217 Hawley to Middleton, 30 December 1958, TNA: FO 371/140087/BA10110/1; Donald Hawley, *The Emirates: Witness to a Metamorphosis* (Norwich: Michael Russell, 2007), pp. 18, 38–41.

218 Hawley to Middleton, 30 December 1958, TNA: FO 371/140087/BA1011/1; Middleton to Lloyd, 2 February 1959, TNA: FO 371/140064/BA1011/4.

219 'The future of the United Kingdom in World affairs: The Middle East', 5 July 1956, GEN 540/2, TNA: CAB 130/119.

220 British Council Persian Gulf, Representative's Annual Reports, 1957–1959, TNA: BW 114/6.

221 Burrows to Lloyd, 25 October 1958, TNA: FO 371/132533/EA1018/58.

222 Middleton to Lloyd, 23 February 1959, TNA: FO 371/140110/BA1053/3.

223 C. (57) 138, 7 June 1957, TNA: CAB 129/97; minute by Hayter, 3 March 1958, TNA: PREM 11/2418.

224 Foreign Office minute, 16 October 1958, TNA: FO 371/132533/BA1892/5.

225 Charles Tripp, *A History of Iraq* (Cambridge: Cambridge University Press, 2007), pp. 139–42. For an account of the British position in Iraq, see, Wm. Roger Louis, 'The British and the origins of the Iraqi Revolution', in Robert A. Fernea and Wm. Rogers Louis (eds), *The Iraqi Revolution of 1958: The Old Social Classes Revisited* (London: I.B. Tauris, 1991), pp. 31–61.

226 Rashid, Khalidi, 'The impact of the Iraqi revolution on the Arab world', in ibid., pp. 106–17.

227 Minute by Trevelyan, 28 August 1957, TNA: FO 371/125924/EA1071/1; OME (58) 45, 15 October 1958, TNA: CAB 134/2342.

228 Minute by Middleton, 14 October 1958, TNA: FO 371/132621/BA1892/5.

229 Morris to the Department of State, 28 February 1958, NARA: RG 59 641.80/2–2858.

230 Minute by Riches, 9 April 1957, TNA: FO 371/127756/V1075/18; minute by Trevelyan, 6 June 1957, TNA: FO 371/127757/V1075/56.

231 Middleton to Lloyd, 17 February 1960, TNA: T 220/1287; Heard-Bey, *Trucial States*, pp. 321–2.

232 'The Arab States of the Gulf since 1947', TNA: FO 371/182521/B1672/6.

233 Minute by Riches, 9 January 1957, TNA: FO 371/126864/EA1632/1; minute by Stevens, 9 February 1959, TNA: FO 371/141878/V1892/4/G.

234 See, for example, Sir James Craig, *Shemlan: A History of the Middle East Centre for Arab Studies*, Foreword by Lord Hurd of Westwell (Basingstoke: Macmillan in association with St Antony's College, Oxford University, 1998).

3. The consolidation of British influence

1 Said Zahlan, *Making of the Modern Gulf States*, pp. 39–40.

2 Horner to DOS, 19 February 1964, NARA: RG 59, Central Foreign Policy Files (CFPF) 1964–1966, Pol 2 Trucial St, Box 2745.

3 C (60) 35, 29 February 1960, TNA: CAB 129/100.

4 Foreign Office Steering Committee, 'Future policy in the Persian Gulf', 3 November 1960, TNA: FO 371/152118/ZP15/45/G.

5 Steven G. Galpern, *Money, Oil and Empire in the Middle East: Sterling and Postwar Imperialism, 1944–1971* (Cambridge: Cambridge University Press, 2009), pp. 229–47.

6 See minutes by Lucas, 8 and 13 March 1963, TNA: T 317/42.

7 'The economic importance of Kuwait and the Persian Gulf to the United Kingdom: Background paper', 19 April 1963, NARA: RG 59, Records Relating to the Persian Gulf and Arabian Peninsula, 1952–1975, entry A1-5666, Box 2.

8 BNSP planning task number III-H: 'Oil and interdependence in the Middle East', August 1962, ibid.

9 Minute by Lamb, 'British oil interests in the context of HMG's policy in the Middle East', 10 July 1964, TNA: FO 371/174507/B1531/2.

10 'Future policy in the Persian Gulf', 3 November 1960, TNA: FO 371/152118/ZP15/45/G.

11 Middleton to the Earl of Home, 30 April 1961, TNA: FO 371/156673/B1052/18.

12 Minutes by Lucas, 8 and 12 March 1963, TNA: T 317/42.

13 Minute by Sir Burke Trend for the Prime Minister, 25 May 1965, TNA: PREM 13/3326.

14 'Winter in the Trucial States 1960–61', DUL: Hawley Papers, HAW 10/3/46.

15 Donald Hawley, *Desert Wind and Tropic Storm: An Autobiography* (Norwich: Michael Russell, 2000), p. 66.

16 Hawley to Man, 29 January 1961, TNA: FO 371/157022/BT1051/1.

17 Earl of Home to Luce, 25 May 1961, TNA: FO 371/156673/B1052/23.

18 Balfour-Paul, *Bagpipes in Babylon*, p. 199.

19 M. W. Daly, *The Last of the Great Proconsuls: The Biography of Sir William Luce* (San Diego, CA: Nathan Berg, 2014), p. 202.

20 Easa Saleh Al-Gurg, *The Wells of Memory: An Autobiography*, with an introduction by Sir James Craig GCMG (London: John Murray, 1998), pp. 87, 90–5.

21 Miriam Joyce, *Kuwait 1945–1996: An Anglo-American Perspective* (London: Frank Cass, 1998), pp. 93–105.

22 For an analysis of Qasim and his intentions, see 'Outlook for Iraq over the next twelve months', JIC (61) 10 (Final), 15 March 1961, TNA: CAB 158/42.

23 See 'Iraqi threat to Kuwait during the next twelve months', JIC (61) 58 (Final), 18 August 1961, TNA: CAB 158/44; FCO Research Department memorandum 'Kuwait-Iraq Relations', 6 February 1969, TNA: FCO 51/49.

24 There are several accounts of the Kuwait crisis in 1961, including: Nigel Ashton, 'Britain and the Kuwait crisis, 1961', *Diplomacy and Statecraft*, Vol. 9, No. 1 (1998), pp. 161–81; Helene von Bismarck, 'The Kuwait crisis and its consequences for Great Britain's Persian Gulf policy', *British Scholar*, Vol. 2, No. 1 (2009), pp. 75–96.

25 Fain, *American Ascendance*, p. 117.

26 Newsom to DOS, 10 May 1962, NARA: RG 59, Central Decimal Files (CDF) 1960–1963, 641.80/5-1062, Box 1333.

27 Interdepartmental Regional Group for the Near East and South Asia, record of IRG meeting, 1 February 1968, Lyndon Baines Johnson Library (LBJL): National Security File, files of Harold Saunders, Box 29.

28 See, for example, Horner to DOS, 26 December 1961, NARA: RG 59, CDF 1960–1963, 786G.00/12-2661, Box 2079.

29 Horner to DOS, 22 July 1964, NARA: RG 59, CFPF 1964–1966, POL 2 Saud, Box 2646.

30 Horner to DOS, 11 July 1962, NARA: RG 59, CDF 1960–63, 786G.00/7-1162, Box 2079.

31 Luce to the Earl of Home, 22 November 1961, TNA: FO 371/156670/B1019/2.

32 Ibid.

33 'The situation in Bahrain, Qatar and the Trucial States', 25 April 1966, NARA: RG 59, Records Relating to the Persian Gulf and Arabian Peninsula, 1952–1975, entry A1-5666, Box 3.

34 Minute by Walmsley, 1 May 1963, TNA: FO 371/168634/B1052/31.

35 'The Aden folly', 26 December 1963, enclosed in briefing papers for US–UK talks on the Middle East, 29 to 30 January 1964, NARA: RG 59, CFPF 1964–1966, Box 2785.

36 Rostow to Kitchen, 4 October 1965, NARA: RG 59, Policy Planning Council/Staff subject and country files 1965–69, Near and Middle East 1965–66, lot 72D139, Box 315.

37 'Oil and interdependence in the Middle East', August 1962, ibid., Box 2.

38 Speares to Walmsley, 4 December 1962, TNA: FO 371/162783/B103145/12. A copy of the US document is located in this file.

39 Luce to Stevens, 17 January 1963, TNA: FO 371/168632/B1052/5/G.

40 CIA Special Report, 'Persian Gulf: Western interests vs. Arab nationalism', 12 April 1963, CIA: FOIA.

41 National Intelligence Estimate (NIE) 36–64, 'Main trends in the Arab World', 8 April 1964, LBJL: National Security File, National Intelligence Estimates, Box 6.

42 Special National Intelligence Estimate (SNIE) 36.1-62, 'Prospects for Nasser', 28 March 1962, LBJL: National Security File, National Intelligence Estimates, Box 6.

43 Hilsman to Rusk, 'Arab radio propaganda', 23 January 1963, JFKL: National Security File, files of Robert W. Komer, Box 408. Personal information provided to the author.

44 Phillips to Jackson, 21 December 1964, TNA: FO 371/179928/BT1201/1.

45 Fitzgibbon to Elwell, 15 June 1967 and 16 May 1968, TNA: FCO 95/280.

46 'The threat to the Lower Persian Gulf', JIC (64) 27 (Final), 17 July 1964, TNA: CAB 158/52.

47 Ibid.

48 Luce to Stevens, 17 January 1963, TNA: FO 371/168632/B1052/5/G.

49 Luce to Harrison, 4 February 1964, TNA: FO 371/174481/B1016/1. See von Bismarck, *British Policy in the Persian Gulf*, pp. 196–8.

50 Minute by Crawford, 10 February 1964, TNA: FO 371/174481/B1016/1.

51 'The threat to the lower Persian Gulf', 17 July 1964, JIC (64) 27 (Final), TNA: CAB 158/52.

52 Akins to DOS, 28 February 1965, NARA: RG 59, CFPF 1964–1966, Pol Trucial St, Box 2745.

53 Arabian Department memorandum 'Iraqi interest in the Persian Gulf', 27 November 1964, TNA: FO 371/174486/B103193/20.

54 Arabian Department submission, 4 December 1964, TNA: FO 371/174515/B1903/6.

55 Joint Intelligence Bureau, Intelligence briefing memorandum: Trucial States, 24 November 1961, TNA: DEFE 11/369.

56 Persian Gulf annual review for 1964, 2 January 1965, TNA: FO 371/179738/B1011/1.

57 Allen to DOS, 10 February 1965, NARA: RG 59, CFPF 1964–66, Pol 2 Trucial St, Box 2745.

58 Minute by Brenchley, 24 November 1964, TNA: FO 371/174489/B1052/32.

59 Newsom to DOS, 10 May 1962, NARA: RG 59, CDF 1960–63, 641.80/5-1062, Box 1333.

60 Hawley to Middleton, 12 December 1960, TNA: FO 371/157017/BT1011/1.

61 Horner to DOS, 27 May 1964, No. 263, NARA: RG 59, CFPF 1964–66, Pol 19 Trucial St, Box 2745.

62 Said Zahlan, *Making of the Modern Gulf States*, pp. 40–9.

63 For a detailed account, see, Jackson to Stuart, 'The life and death of Shaikh Abdullah Salim, first constitutional Amir of Kuwait', 10 December 1965, TNA: FO 371/179854/BK1941/24. See also, the FCO Joint Research Department memo 'Constitutional development in the Persian Gulf States', 19 February 1968, TNA: FCO 51/45.

64 'The Arab States of the Gulf since 1947: Their evolution and development with particular Reference to their neighbours, Arab nationalism and the British presence', September 1966, TNA: FO 371/182521/B1672/6.

65 Crystal, *Oil and Politics*, pp. 18–26.

66 'Constitutional development in the Persian Gulf States', TNA: FCO 51/45.

67 Heard-Bey, *Trucial States*, pp. 258–68.

68 Joint Intelligence Bureau, Intelligence briefing memorandum: Trucial States, 24 November 1961, TNA: DEFE 11/369.

69 Craig to the Acting Political Resident, 20 September 1964, TNA: FO 371/174711/BT1101/7.

70 Schwinn to DOS, 1 February 1961, NARA: RG 59, CDF 1960–63, 786G.00/2-161, Box 2079.

71 Allen to DOS, 23 June 1965, No. A-217, NARA: RG 59, CFPF 1964–66, POL 1 Trucial St, Box 2745.

72 Allen to DOS, 10 February 1965, No. A-115, NARA: RG 59, CFPF 1964–66, POL 2 Trucial St, ibid.

73 Schwinn to DOS, 10 July 1961, NARA: RG 59, CDF 1960–63, 786F.00/7-1061, Box 2079.

74 Allen to DOS, 23 June 1965, No. A-217, NARA: RG 59, CFPF 1964–1966, POL 2 Trucial St, Box 2745.

75 Brenchley to Mark, 6 November 1964, TNA: T 317/801.

76 Henderson to Hawley, 29 December 1959, TNA: FO 1016/680.

77 Hawley, *Desert Wind*, p. 60.

78 Lienhardt, *Shaikhdoms*, pp. ix–xi.

79 Peter Lienhardt, *Letters from Kuwait (1953–1955)*, ed. by Ahmed Al-Shahi (Kuwait City: Centre for Research and Studies on Kuwait, 2017), p. 19.

80 Craig to Luce, 11 December 1961, Trucial States Annual Review for 1961, TNA: FO 371/157017/BT1011/2.

81 Minute by Brenchley summarising the experiences expatriate staff, 11 June 1964, TNA: FO 371/174703/BT1017/12.

82 Brown to the Earl of Home, 4 July 1962, TNA: FO 371/163036/BT1102/55.

83 Boustead to Crawford, 24 February 1964, TNA: FO 371/174714/BT1112/1.

84 Henderson to Middleton, 6 December 1960, TNA FO 371/148918/BA1019/35.

85 Luce to Home, 6 January 1962, enclosing a report by Tripp, 'First impressions of the Southern Persian Gulf', TNA: FO 371/162806/B1101/1.

86 Henderson to Hawley, 29 December 1959, TNA: FO 1016/680.

87 Sir Archie Lamb, *A Long Way from Swansea* (Pembroke: Starborn Books, 2003), pp. 106–7.

88 Musker to Baker, 9 August 1956, and Baker to Musker, 25 February 1957, confidential letter 68/31, HSBC Group Archives: HQ BBME 0851.

89 Lamb to Parkes, 16 April 1966, TNA: FO 371/185578/BT1941; Hawley, *Desert Wind*, p. 61.

90 McClelland to DOS, 10 July 1961, No. 10, NARA: RG 59, CDF 1960–63, 786F.00/7-1061, Box 2079.

91 Majid Khadduri, *Arab Personalities in Politics* (Washington, DC: Middle East Institute, 1981), p. 297.

92 Allen to DOS, 27 August 1966, NARA: RG 59, Records Relating to Arabian Peninsula Affairs, 1964–1966, Box 6.

93 CIA Special Report, 'Persian Gulf: Western interests vs. Arab nationalism', 12 April 1963, CIA: FOIA.

94 Rabi, 'Oil, politics', p. 44.

95 Lamb to Crawford, 2 January 1967, Abu Dhabi Annual Review for 1966, TNA: FCO 8/827.

96 Daly, *Last of the Great Proconsuls*, p. 230.

97 Schwin to DOS, 5 February 1960, No. 227, NARA: RG 59, CDF 1960–63, 786E.11/2-560, Box 2079.

98 Colonel Sir Hugh Boustead, *The Wind in the Morning: The Autobiography of Hugh Boustead* (London: Chatto & Windus, 1971), pp. 230–3.

99 Lamb, *A Long Way from Swansea*, p. 99.

100 These problems were summarised by Boustead in several manuscripts, MECA: Boustead Collection, Box 2, folder 2.

101 *The Times*, 'The Sheikh with oil millions to spend', 3 February 1964, p. 11; *The Guardian*, 'Frightened oil sheikh sits on his millions', 11 April 1964.

102 Boustead to Luce, 20 January 1964, Abu Dhabi Annual Review for 1963, TNA: FO 371/174697/BT1011/2.

103 Minute by Walmsley, 15 May 1962, TNA: FO 371/163025/BT1051/7/G.

104 Luce to Crawford, 17 April 1962, ibid., BT1015/5.

105 Khuri, *Tribe and State*, pp. 94–6.

106 Minute by Crawford, 15 May 1962, TNA: FO 371/163025/BT1015/7/G.

107 Luce wrote these comments on 29 October 1963 and they were enclosed in TNA: FO 371/168918/BT1015/68/G. This document has been withheld until 1 January 2026. However, they were repeated verbatim in Luce to Crawford, 27 May 1964, TNA: FO 371/174701/BT1016/14/G.

108 Minute by Brenchley, 10 June 1964, ibid., BT1016/15/G; Lamb to Luce, 4 June 1966, FO 1016/737.

109 Shakhbut signed the agreement in September 1965, Boustead to Brenchley, 1 January 1966, Abu Dhabi annual review for 1965, TNA: FO 371/185523/BT1011/1.

110 Luce to Crawford, 27 May 1964, TNA: FO 371/174701/BT1016/14/G.

111 Minute by Brenchley, 10 June 1964, TNA: ibid., BT1016/15/G.

112 Luce to Crawford, 28 October 1964, TNA: FO 371/174702/BT1016/26/G.

113 Minute by Gordon Walker, 27 November 1964, ibid, BT1016/32/G.

114 See minutes by Brenchley and Crawford, 25 and 27 November 1964, ibid., BT1016/35/G.

115 Minute by Brenchley, 9 December 1964, ibid., BT1016/32/G.

116 Luce to FO, 1 November 1964, TNA: FO 371/174489/B1052/28.

117 Memos by 'GGS', 22 January 1964 and 15 July 1964, BP Archive: 12185.

118 Stewart to Luce, 11 March 1965, TNA: FO 371/179749/B1051/9.

119 Foreign Office circular telegram, 18 February 1965, ibid., B1051/7.

120 'Jurisdiction in Dubai in the 1950s and 1960s', 26 October 1991, DUL: Hawley Papers, HAW 9/7/29–30.

121 Minute by Brenchley, 20 December 1963, TNA: FO 371/174509/B1641/2.

122 Sir John Whyatt (Judge of the Chief Court for the Persian Gulf) to Butler, 13 July 1964, TNA: FO 371/174509/B1641/10.

123 Butler to Luce, 14 January 1964, ibid., B1641/2.

124 Luce to FO, 21 January 1965, Persian Gulf annual review for 1965, TNA: FO 371/179738/B1011/1.

125 Horner to DOS, 8 January 1964, No. A-142, NARA: RG 59, CFPF 1964–1966, Pol 19 Trucial St, Box 2745.

126 Smith, *Britain's Revival*, pp. 49–54.

127 Middleton to the Earl of Home, 30 April 1961, TNA: FO 371/156673/B1052/8.

128 Persian Gulf annual review for 1960, 31 December 1960, TNA: FO 371/156668/B1011/1.

129 Man to Beaumont, 7 March 1961, TNA: FO 371/157019/BT1015/3.

130 Persian Gulf annual review for 1964, 21 January 1964, TNA: FO 371/179738/B1011/1.

131 Luce to Stewart, 19 July 1966, TNA: FO 371/185167/B1016/51.

132 Minute by Brenchley, 24 November 1964, TNA: FO 371/174489/B1052/32.

133 Schwinn to DOS, 1 February 1961, No. 201, NARA: RG 59, CDF 1960–1963, 786G.00/2-161, Box, 2079.

134 Middleton to Lloyd, 17 February 1960, TNA: FO 371/148974/BA1104/20.

135 Corkhill to Boustead, 28 March 1964, Interim Report on Health in Abu Dhabi, MECA: Corkhill Collection, File 7.

136 'Trucial States development programme, 1961–1966', enclosed in Middleton to Lloyd, 17 February 1960, TNA: FO 371/148974/BA1104/20.

137 Minute by Lawrence, 15 March 1960, TNA: T 220/1287, f. 89.

138 Russell-Edmunds to Walmsley, 24 July 1961, TNA: FO 371/157026/BT1102/33.

139 Memo by Tripp, 15 August 1961, ibid, BT1102/44.

140 Minute by Walmsley, 15 May 1962, TNA: FO 371/163036/BT1102/45.

141 Luce to Home, 28 December 1962, TNA: FO 371/163034/BT1102/62.

142 British Council annual reports for 1961–62 and 1962–63, TNA: BW 114/6.

143 Tripp to Lamb, 30 March 1962, TNA: FO 371/163035/BT1102/37.

144 Minute by Brenchley, 1 November 1963, TNA: FO 371/168929/BT1102/87 and 94.

145 Minute by Edwards, 22 May 1964, TNA: T 317/801.

146 Tripp to Lamb, 20 July 1962, TNA: FO 371/163037/BT1102/61.

147 Trucial States economic report for 1962, 19 January 1963, TNA: FO 371/168924/BT1101/3.

148 British Council annual report for 1964–65, TNA: BW 114/6.

149 BDOHP, interview with Sir Archie Lamb, 20 August 2003, pp. 7–9, available at: www.chu.cam.ac.uk/archives/collections/BDOHP/#R (accessed 4 August 2018).

150 Lamb to Luce, 12 October 1965, TNA: FO 371/179906/BT1016/25.

151 Walmsley to Brown, 16 January 1963, TNA: FO 371/168925/BT1102/3.

152 Boustead to Crawford, 24 February 1964, TNA: FO 371/174714/BT1112/1.

153 Craig to Crawford, 27 January 1964, TNA: FO 371/174712/BT1102/6.

154 Mark to Brenchley, 19 October 1964, TNA: T 317/801.

4. Responsibility without power

1 Said Zahlan, *Making of the Modern Gulf States*, pp. 39–40.

2 Tore T. Petersen, 'Crossing the Rubicon: Britain's withdrawal from the Middle East, 1964–1968: A bibliographical review', *International History Review*, Vol. 22, No. 2 (2000), pp. 318–40.

3 John Darwin, *Britain and Decolonisation: The Retreat from Empire in the Post-War World* (Basingstoke: Macmillan, 1988), pp. 290–1.

4 Saki Dockrill, *Britain's Retreat from East of Suez: The Choice between Europe and the World?* (Basingstoke: Palgrave Macmillan, 2002), p. 210.

5 Summarised in Petersen, *Decline of the Anglo-American Middle East*, p. 25.

6 F. Gregory Gause III, 'British and American policies in the Persian Gulf, 1968–1973', *Review of International Studies*, Vol. 11 (1985), p. 250.

7 Bureau of Intelligence and Research (INR), 'The foreign policy of the British Labour Government', 8 October 1964, NARA: RG 59, Policy Planning Council, Subject Files 1963–1973, entry A1 5041, Box 14.

8 Statement on the Defence Estimates, February 1965, p. 9.

9 Petersen, 'Crossing the Rubicon', pp. 114–15.

10 Middle East defence policy: Personal note by the Secretary of State for Defence, 28 June 1965, TNA: DEFE 25/196.

11 Defence review study, Middle East: Persian Gulf and South Arabia, Note by the Secretaries, OPD (O) (65) 66 (Final), 27 October 1965, TNA: CAB 148/45.

12 OPD (65) 52nd meeting, 24 November 1965, TNA: CAB 148/18.

13 OPD (O) (65) 24th meeting, 22 October 1965, TNA: CAB 148/41.

14 OPD (65) 52nd meeting, 24 November 1965, TNA: CAB 148/18.

15 'Forces and facilities in the Persian Gulf', 12 January 1966, COS 3/66, TNA: DEFE 5/165.

16 C. (66) 33, 11 February 1966, TNA: CAB 129/124.

17 Von Bismarck, *British Policy in the Persian Gulf*, pp. 186–7; Smith, *Britain's Revival*, pp. 25–7.

18 OPD (66) 22, 19 January 1966, TNA: CAB 148/27.

19 Balfour-Paul to Weir, 1 September 1967, TNA: FCO 8/41.

20 'Mediterranean and the Middle East. Annex F. The Persian Gulf', OPD (O) (65) 31, 5 May 1965, TNA: CAB 148/43.

21 Submission by Brenchley, 16 December 1965, TNA: FO 371/179750/B1051/81/G.

22 Persian Gulf annual review for 1964, 21 January 1965, TNA: FO 371/179738/ B1011/1.

23 Foreign Office guidance telegram to certain diplomatic missions, 1 July 1966, TNA: FO 371/185199/B1194/67.

24 'The effects in the Middle East and Africa of an announcement of a British withdrawal from South Arabia in 1967 or 1968', 23 December 1965, JIC (65) 92 (Final), TNA: CAB 158/60.

25 Counter-subversion in the Persian Gulf: Report by the Persian Gulf Working Group of the Counter-Subversion committee, July 1966, TNA: DEFE 28/150.

26 CIA Special Report, 'Britain East of Suez', 18 June 1965, CIA: FOIA.

27 'The foreign policy of the British Labor Government', 8 October 1964, NARA: RG 59, Policy Planning Council, subject files, 1963–1973, entry A1 5041, Box 14 (old box 253).

28 Memo for Johnson, 1 June 1965, LBJL: National Security File, Country File, box 215.

29 The Prime Minister's visit to the United States and Canada, December 1965, REF 1, TNA: CAB 130/465.

30 Briefing book for Wilson visit on 29 July 1966: UK defence commitments East of Suez, LBJL: National Security File, Country File, Box 215.

31 Brief for the PM's visit to Washington, 27 July 1966, TNA: FO 371/185177/B1051/21.

32 Ball to Johnson, 22 July 1966, LBJL: National Security File, Country File, Box 209 (two of two).

33 Briefing book for Brown's visit to Washington, 14 October 1966. Memo on UK policies in the Persian Gulf, LBJL: National Security File, Country File, Box 215.

34 Stewart to Wilson, 25 January 1966, PM/66/5, TNA: PREM 13/2209.

35 OPD (65) 174, 22 November 1965, TNA: CAB 148/23.

36 Crawford to FO, 20 January 1966, TNA: FCO 8/2; Balfour-Paul to Weir, 1 September 1967, TNA: FCO 8/41.

37 Wright to Harrison, 22 February 1964, TNA: FO 371/174488/B1052/9/G.

38 Crawford to Brenchley, 16 May 1967, TNA: FCO 8/17.

39 National Intelligence Estimate 34-66, 'Iran', 24 March 1966: CIA: FOIA.

40 CIA intelligence memorandum, 'The Arab threat to Iran', 21 May 1966, LBJL: National Security File, Country File, Middle East, Box 104.

41 Rouhollah K. Ramazani, *The Foreign Policy of Iran 1941–1973: A Study of Foreign Policy in Modernizing Nations* (Charlottesville, VA: University Press of Virginia, 1975), pp. 395, 408.

42 Crawford to Brown, 30 December 1966, TNA: PREM 13/2209.

43 Healey, 18 January 1967, *HC Debates*, Vol. 739, cc. 403–4; Healey, 5 June 1967, *HC Deb*, Vol. 747, cc. 139–40; Brown, 12 June 1967, *HC Debates*, Vol. 748, cc. 76–8; Brown, 20 July 1967, *HC Debates*, Vol. 750.

44 Roberts to Crawford, 19 June 1967, TNA: FCO 8/843.

45 Balfour-Paul to Roberts, 7 January 1967, TNA; FCO 8/828; Brown, 20 July 1967 *HC Debates*, Vol. 750, cc. 2494–2495.

46 'Defence expenditure study No. 6: Long-term policy in the Persian Gulf', SC (67) 38, 28 September 1967, TNA: FCO 49/10.

47 Crawford to Brown, 8 December 1967, TNA: FCO 8/828.

48 Minister of State's visit to the Persian Gulf, November 1967, Brief No. 1, TNA: FCO 8/142.

49 *HC Debates*, Vol. 753, cc. 997–8.

50 Balfour-Paul, *End of Empire*, p. 123.

51 'The impact of Britain's devaluation of the pound', CIA intelligence memorandum, November 1967, LBJL: National Security File, Country File, Box 211.

52 Jeffrey Pickering, 'Politics and "Black Tuesday": Shifting power in the Cabinet and the decision to withdraw from East of Suez, November 1967–January 1968', *Twentieth Century British History*, Vol. 13, No. 2 (2002), p. 152.

53 Shohei Sato, 'Britain's decision to withdraw from the Persian Gulf, 1964–1968', *Journal of Imperial and Commonwealth History*, Vol. 37, No. 1 (2009), pp. 107–9, 111.

54 'Long term policy in the Persian Gulf. Note by the Secretaries', 7 June 1967, OPDO (DR) (67) 28 (Final), TNA: CAB 148/57; *HC Debates*, 15 November 1967, Written Answers (Defence), Vol. 754.

55 'Likely developments in the Persian Gulf and their probable effects for British interests', JIC (68) 35 (Final), 7 June 1968, TNA: CAB 158/70.

56 Wm. Roger Louis, 'The British withdrawal from the Gulf, 1967–69', *Ends of British Imperialism: The Scramble for Empire, Suez and Decolonization* (London: I.B. Tauris, 2006), p. 878.

57 *SWB*, Part 4, The Middle East and Africa, 6 April 1965.

58 Memo by Berthoud, 'The Iranians, the Arabs and the Persian Gulf', 15 July 1964, TNA: FO 371/174492/B1073/7.

59 Walker to Posnett, 2 December 1964, enclosing report of the Arab League mission to the Gulf, TNA: FO 371/174493/B1073/57.

60 Persian Gulf annual review for 1964, 21 January 1965, TNA: FO 371/179738/B1011/1.

61 Boustead to FO, 24 October 1964, TNA: FO 371/174493/B1073/37.

62 Brown to Snellgrove, 4 November 1964, ibid., B1073/46.

63 Luce to Stewart, Persian Gulf annual review for 1965, 7 January 1966, TNA: FO 371/185162/B1011/1.

64 Luce to FO, 21 June 1965, No. 528, TNA: PREM 13/3326.

65 Crawford to Milner-Barry, 26 April 1965, TNA: FO 371/179916/BT1103/62.

66 Philips to Brenchley, 19 July 1965, No. 16930G, TNA: CAB 163/116.

67 Luce to Crawford, 25 January 1965, TNA: FO 371/179754/B1072/16.

68 Minister of State's talks in Washington, Persian Gulf: The Arab League and the Trucial States, 22 June 1965, TNA: FO 371/179919/BT1103/233.

69 Crawford to Luce, 12 February 1965, TNA: FO 371/179743/B103116/4/G.

70 Luce to Crawford, 8 February 1965, ibid., B103116/4/G.

71 Foreign Office guidance telegram, 4 June 1965, TNA: FO 371/179918/BT1103/141.

72 Luce to FO, 16 May 1965, No. 354, TNA: FO 371/179916/BT1103/84.

73 Luce to Crawford, 24 May 1965, TNA: FO 371/179750/BT1051/43.

74 Tripp to FO, 13 June 1965, No. 501, TNA: FO 371/179918/BT1103/170/G.

75 Luce to FO, 21 June 1965, No. 528, ibid., BT1103/195.

76 Current Intelligence Bulletin, 16 June 1965, CIA: FOIA.

77 Luce to FO, 21 May 1965, TNA: FO 371/179917/BT1103/93.

78 TOS intelligence report No. 45, 19 June 1965, TNA: WO 337/15.

79 Vallett to Elwyn Jones, 8 June 1965, TNA: FO 371/179919/BT/1103/201; von Bismarck, *British Policy in the Persian Gulf*, pp. 143–5.

80 For a personal account of the deposition of Saqr, see, Sultan bin Muhammad Al-Qasimi, *My Early Life* (London: Bloomsbury, 2011), pp. 220–8.

81 See, in particular, TNA: FO 371/179903, in which numerous papers have been withheld until 2026.

82 Record of a meeting at the Political Residency, Bahrain on Sunday, 9 May 1965, TNA: FO 371/179740/B1016/18; FO to Bahrain, 16 June 1965, TNA: FO 371/179918/BT1103/179.

83 Balfour-Paul to FO, No. 161, 24 June 1965, TNA: FO 371/179903/BT1015/42.

84 Foreign Office guidance telegram to certain missions, 24 June 1965, ibid., BT1015/44. A more detailed account can be found in Tait to Luce, 14 July 1965, TNA: FO 371/179920/BT1103/251.

85 Von Bismarck, *British Policy in the Persian Gulf*, p. 149.

86 'Defence Expenditure Study No. 6: Long-term policy in the Persian Gulf: Report by the Defence Review Working Party', 7 June 1967, OPD (67) 8, TNA: CAB 148/80.

87 TOS intelligence summary No. 46, 26 June 1965, TNA: WO 337/15.

88 Central Intelligence Bulletin, 26 June 1965, CIA: FOIA.

89 President's Daily Brief, 25 June 1965, ibid.

90   Said Zahlan, *Making of the Modern Gulf States*, p. 117.

91   *SWB*, Part 4, The Middle East and Africa, 30 June 1965.

92   Balfour-Paul to Luce, 1 January 1966, annual review of events in the Northern Trucial States, TNA: FO 371/185523/BT1011/2.

93   Parsons to Crawford, 10 February 1969, TNA: FCO 8/1001.

94   NIE 36.1-65, 'Problems and prospects for the United Arab Republic', 31 March 1965, LBJL: National Security File, National Intelligence Estimates, Box 6.

95   Luce to Stewart, 7 January 1966, Persian Gulf annual review for 1965, TNA: FO 371/185162/B1011/1.

96   Luce to Stewart, 21 July 1965, TNA: FO 371/179740/B1016/25.

97   This is because the relevant papers have been withheld from public view until 2026 and 2027. See, for example, TNA: FO 371/179906/BT1016/1-15, 24, FO 371/185526/BT1016/4, 9-19 and FO 1016/738.

98   Lamb to Luce, 12 October 1965, TNA: FO 371/179906/BT1016/25.

99   Lamb to Brenchley, 8 November 1965, ibid., BT1016/28.

100 Lamb to Brenchley, 26 February 1966 and 16 April 1966, TNA: FO 371/185526/BT1016/2 and 5.

101 Anthony Parsons, *They Say the Lion: Britain's Legacy to the Arabs: A Personal Memoir* (London: Jonathan Cape, 1986), pp. 126–7.

102 Luce to Stewart, 19 July 1966, TNA: FO 371/185167/B1016/51.

103 Man to FO, 20 February 1968, TNA: FCO 8/751.

104 Lamb to Crawford, 5 November 1966, TNA: FO 371/185529/BT1016/79; Lamb to Crawford, 2 January 1967, Abu Dhabi annual review for 1966, TNA: FCO 8/827.

105 Nuttall to FO, 6 August 1966, TNA: FO 371/185527/BT1016/21.

106 Balfour-Paul, *Bagpipes in Babylon*, pp. 203–5.

107 Antony Cawston and Michael Curtis, *Arabian Days: The Memoirs of Two Trucial Oman Scouts*, Foreword by Major General Ken Perkins, CB, MBE, DFC (Michael Curtis, 2011), pp. 122–6. Personal information provided to the author.

108 Summarised in Gent to Nuttall, 2 September 1966, TNA: FO 371/185529/BT1016/62/G. See *The Daily Telegraph*, 8 August 1966, p. 16, and *The Times*, 8 August 1966, pp. 6 and 9.

109 Defence Expenditure Study No. 6: Long-term policy in the Persian Gulf: Report by the Defence Review Working Party, 7 June 1967, OPD (67) 8, TNA: CAB 148/80. Reference to the British role in the overthrow of Sheikhs Saqr and Shakhbut have been redacted in the Foreign Office version of this document. See SC (67) 38, 28 September 1967, TNA: FCO 49/10.

110 FO minute, 9 August 1966, TNA: FO 371/185527/BT1016/30.

111 Persian Gulf annual review for 1966, 20 January 1967, TNA: FCO 8/2.

112 Minute by Brenchley, 28 September 1966, TNA: FO 371/185529/BT1016/68.

113 Roberts to Crawford, 30 December 1966, northern Trucial States annual review for 1966, TNA: FCO 8/829.

114 Lamb to Crawford, 5 November 1966, TNA: FO 371/185529/BT1016/79.

115 Lamb to Crawford, 6 November 1966, ibid., BT1016/82.

116 Lamb to Crawford, 24 October 1967, TNA: FCO 8/834.

117 Luce to Walmsley, 5 August 1961, TNA: FO 371/157038/BT1201/51.

118 Hawley, *The Emirates*, p. 291.

119 Report of the working party on the future of the Trucial Oman Scouts, Annex A, 18 June 1968, TNA: T 317/1431.

120 Luce to Walmsley, 12 December 1961, TNA: FO 371/157038/BT1201/62.

121 Rossiter, 'Britain and the development of professional security forces', pp. 205–6.

122 Ford to Cranefield, 29 April 1961, TNA: FO 371/156692/B1192/4/G.

123 Horner to DOS, 1 April 1964, NARA: RG 59, CFPF 1964–1966 Pol 23-3 Trucial St, Box, 2745.

124 Luce to Brenchley, 16 July 1966, TNA: FO 1016/736.

125 Man to Walmsley, 28 April 1961, TNA: FO 371/157062/BT1641/16.

126 Luce to Walmsley, 5 August 1961, ibid., BT1641/26.

127 Brown to McCarthy, 12 February 1964, enclosing 'directive to the commander Trucial Oman Scouts on operation of the police wing', TNA: FO 371/174718/BT1201/2.

128 Tripp to Given, 9 January 1963, TNA: FO 371/168951/BT1641/1.

129 TOS intelligences summaries Nos. 69 and 70, 29 February and 7 March 1966, TNA: WO 337/15.

130 'The threat to the Lower Persian Gulf until the end of 1966', 15 October 1965, JIC(65) 42 (Final), Appendix C, TNA: CAB 158/58.

131 Mann, *Trucial Oman Scouts*, p. 139.

132 Boustead to Luce, 20 January 1964, Abu Dhabi annual review for 1963, TNA: FO 371/174697/BT1011/1.

133 Minute by Edwards, 22 May 1964, TNA: T 317/801.

134 Minute by Brenchley, 10 August 1965, TNA: FO 371/179929/BT1202/9.

135 Slater to Brenchley, 3 August 1964, TNA: FO 371/174719/BT1203/2.

136 Luce to Brenchley, 17 April 1965, TNA: FO 371/179929/BT1202/2.

137 Slater to Weir, 16 May 1965, ibid., BT1202/6.

138 Howard to Arabian Department, 14 October 1964, TNA: FO 371/174719/BT1203/11.

139 Rossiter, 'Britain and the development of professional security forces', pp. 208–10.

140 Lamb to Brenchley, 23 April 1966, TNA: FO 371/185551/BT1202/3.

141 De Butts to Crawford, 25 January 1967, TNA: FCO 8/883.

142 Lamb to Gent, 7 June 1966, TNA: FO 371/185551/BT1202/6.

143 Craig to Luce, 29 September 1964, TNA: FO 371/174700/BT1015/28.

144 Bartholomew to Brigadier Holme, 7 March 1964, TNA: FO 371/174718/BT1201/4.

145 War Office to the Foreign Office, 20 July 1961, TNA: FO 371/157038/BT1201/48.

146 'The threat to the Lower Persian Gulf until the end of 1966', 15 October 1965, JIC (65) 42 (Final), TNA: CAB 158/58.

147 Bahrain Residency to Brenchley, 22 March 1965, TNA: CAB 163/116.

148 War Office to FO, 20 July 1961, TNA: FO 371/157038/BT1201/48.

149 Bahrain Residency memo, 'The case for an improved intelligence organisation in the Persian Gulf', 21 March 1965, TNA: CAB 163/116.

150 Summary record of discussions at the Political Agents conference, 7 to 9 December 1965, TNA: FO 371/185177/B1051/2.

151 Minutes of a meeting of the Counter-Subversion Committee, 19 May 1966, TNA: FO 371/185167/B1016/47/G.

152 MOD memorandum, 'Counter-subversion in the Persian Gulf', 8 July 1966, TNA: DEFE 28/149.

153 Lamb to Luce, 22 June 1966, TNA: FO 371/185575/BT1691/4.

154 Luce to Brenchley, 10 May 1966, enclosing a memorandum titled, 'The internal security situation in the Trucial States (less Abu Dhabi)', TNA: FO 1016/851.

155 'The outlook for the Persian Gulf and South Arabia up to the end of 1968', JIC (66) 37 (Final), 25 May 1966, TNA: CAB 158/63.

156 De Butts to Holme, 10 May 1966, TNA: FO 1016/735.

157 Admiral Le Fanu to Field Marshal Hull, 12 May 1966, TNA: DEFE 11/478.

158 De Butts to Crawford, 25 January 1967, TNA: FCO 8/883.

159 Luce to Brenchley, 16 July 1966, TNA: FO 1016/736.

160 Minute by Brenchley, 24 January 1967, TNA: FCO 8/881.

161 Balfour Paul to Weir, 11 November 1967, TNA: FCO 8/884.

162 Fogarty to Allen, 13 December 1966, TNA: T 317/1431.

163 Crawford to Weir, 20 October 1967, TNA: FCO 8/884.

164 Crawford to Weir, 20 June 1967, TNA: FCO 8/883.

165 Crawford to Brenchley, 20 June 1967, ibid.

166 Freddie de Butts, *Now the Dust has Settled: Memories of War and Peace, 1939–1994* (Padstow: Tab House, 1995), pp. 193–4.

167 Weir to Crawford, 5 October 1967, TNA: FCO 8/884.

168 Crawford to Weir, 20 October 1967, ibid.

169 'Special Branches – Trucial States', August 1967, TNA: FCO 8/100.

170 Counter-subversion Committee, Working Group on the Persian Gulf (including Kuwait), record of a meeting on 12 December 1967, TNA: CAB 163/73.

171 NIE 30-1-67, 'The Persian Gulf States', 18 May 1967, LBJL: National Security File, National Intelligence Estimates, Box 6.

172 'The threat of sabotage in the Persian Gulf until the end of 1966', 14 January 1966, JIC (65) 41 (Final), TNA: CAB 158/58.

173 COS 63rd Meeting, 29 November 1966, TNA: DEFE 4/209.

174 JIC (67) 1st Meeting, 5 January 1967, TNA: CAB 163/117.

175 Roberts to Crawford, 10 and 19 June 1967, TNA: FCO 8/843.

176 Crawford to Brown, 28 July 1967, TNA: FCO 8/44.

177 Counter subversion committee, Working group on the Persian Gulf (including Kuwait), 9 August 1967, TNA: FCO 8/100.

178 SNIE 36.1-67, 'The situation and prospects in Egypt', 17 August 1967, CIA: FOIA.

179 'Nasser's limited options', Board of National Estimates Special Memorandum, 15 April 1968, ibid. The CIA produced several insightful intelligence estimates that commented on Nasser and his standing in the Arab world between the Suez Crisis and the aftermath of the Six Day War. See, for example, NIE 36.1-57, 'The outlook for Egypt and the Nasser regime', 12 November 1957, CIA: FOIA.

180 'Britain and the Persian Gulf: The next six months', 27 October 1967, JIC (67) 53 (Final), TNA: CAB 158/67.

181 Crawford to Brown, 6 March 1967, TNA: OD 34/176.

182 Minute Goulding, 6 April 1965, TNA: FO 371/179916/BT1103/47.

183 Weir to Raw, 14 April 1965, TNA: OD 34/68.

184 Thomson to FO, 16 May 1965, No. 355, TNA: FO 371/179916/BT1103/83; *HC Debates*, 20 July 1965, Vol. 716, c. 1366.

185 Sharp to Rae, 8 April 1965, TNA: OD 34/68.

186 There are numerous Treasury minutes that challenge the Foreign Office's thinking in TNA: T 317/666.

187 Minute by Trend, 25 May 1965, TNA: PREM 13/3326.

188 Summarised in 'Trucial States', OPD (65) 85, 24 May 1965, TNA: CAB 148/21.

189 OPD (65) 27th meeting, 26 May 1965, TNA: CAB 148/18.

190 McKenzie Johnston to Derrick, 20 November 1968, TNA: FCO 8/1226.

191 Trucial States annual review for 1966, TNA: FCO 8/829.

192 Abu Dhabi Petroleum Company Ltd annual review for 1967, BP Archive: 52087.

193 Abu Dhabi Petroleum Company Ltd annual review for 1971, ibid., 242128.

194 Lamb to Howell, 'Economic study of Abu Dhabi', 1 March 1967, TNA: FCO 8/869.

195 Northern Trucial States annual review for 1967, 10 January 1968, TNA: FCO 8/839.

196 Bullock to Balfour-Paul, 26 January 1967, TNA: OD 34/285.

197 Crawford to Brown, 5 January 1968, TNA: FO 1016/882.

5. All politics and no strategy

1   Record of a meeting with Shaikh Zaid, 9 January 1968, TNA: FO 1016/753; Roberts to Crawford, 11 January 1968, TNA: FCO 8/754.

2   *HC Debates*, 16 January 1968, Vol. 756, c. 1580.

3   Saul Kelly, 'Vanishing act: Britain's abandonment of Aden and retreat from the Gulf',
    in Robert Johnson and Timothy Clask (eds), *At the End of Military Intervention:*
    Historical, Theoretical and Applied Approaches to Transition, Handover and
    Withdrawal (Oxford: Oxford University Press, 2014), p. 184.

4   'Persian Gulf commitments', 27 March 1968, OPD (68) 25, TNA: CAB 148/36.

5   Louis, 'British withdrawal', p. 879.

6   D.C. Watt, 'The decision to withdraw from the Gulf', *Political Quarterly*, Vol. 39,
    No. 3 (1969), p. 310.

7   Crawford to Brown, 29 January 1968, TNA: FCO 8/31.

8   Crawford to Weir, 19 January 1968, TNA: FCO 8/828.

9   Crawford to Brown, 31 January 1968, TNA: FCO 8/33.

10 Parsons, *They Say the Lion*, pp. 134–5; BDOHP, interview with Sir Anthony Parsons,
    22 March 1996, p. 12.

11 Lamb to Crawford, 11 January 1968, TNA: FCO 8/48; Foreign Office guidance
    telegram, 2 February 1968, TNA: FCO 8/49.

12 Healey comments on BBC *Panorama*, January 1968, TNA: PREM 13/2218.

13 Roberts to the rulers, 24 January 1968, TNA: FCO 8/49.

14 Kelly, 'Vanishing act', p. 185.

15 Arabian Department minute, 10 January 1968, TNA: FCO 8/48.

16 Tehran to FCO, 7 January 1968, No. 50, TNA: PREM 13/2209.

17 For a detailed account of the King's views, see, Allen to DOS, 14 January 1968,
    No. 462, NARA: RG 59, CFPF 1967–1969, POL 33 Persian Gulf, Box 2418; Man to
    Brown, 22 February 1968, TNA: FCO 8/751.

18 Petersen, *The Decline of the Anglo-American Middle East*, pp. 117–19.

19 Dean to Brown, 4 March 1968, TNA: DEFE 25/265.

20 Battle to Rusk, 12 February 1968, NARA: RG 59, CFPF 1967–1969, POL 33 Persian
    Gulf, Box 2418. See also, background paper on the Gulf for Wilson meeting,
    2 February 1968, LJBL: NSF Country File UK, Box 215.

21 C. (68) 22, 12 January 1968, TNA: CAB 129/35.

22 Johnson to Wilson, 11 and 14 January 1968, TNA: PREM 13/1999.

23 Record of a conversation between Wilson and Johnson, 8 February 1968, TNA:
    PREM 13/2455.

24 Jeffrey R. Macris, 'Why didn't America replace the British in the Persian Gulf?', in
    Jeffrey R. Macris and Saul Kelly (eds), *Imperial Crossroads: The Great Powers and the*
    Persian Gulf (Annapolis, MD: Naval Institute Press, 2012), pp. 65–8.

25 Battle to Rusk, 9 February 1968, POL 33 Persian Gulf, NARA: RG 59, CFPF
    1967–1969, Box 2418.

26 Brewer to Battle, 24 April 1968, NARA: RG 59, Records Relating to the Persian Gulf
    and Arabian Peninsula, 1952–1975, Box 3.

27 'Future Soviet policy in the Persian Gulf', 16 March 1971, JIC (A) (71) 7, TNA: CAB 186/8.

28 'Moscow moves in the Persian Gulf', 28 February 1972, Def 1 Near E, NARA: RG 59, SNF 1970–73, Box 1774.

29 'The outlook for Kuwait', 13 January 1971, JIC (A) (71) 41, TNA: CAB 186/6.

30 Private information provided to the author.

31 Memo by Budd, 23 May 1971, NAM: 2016-03-40.

32 Stephen to McCarthy, 24 April 1968, TNA: FCO 8/885.

33 Derrick to Stirling, 19 June 1968, TNA: T 225/3144.

34 Trucial Oman Scouts: Measures needed to maintain the force in being, 9 October 1969, OPDO (DR) (69) 8, TNA: CAB 148/97.

35 Ministry of Defence, *Supplementary Statement on Defence Policy*, Cmnd. 3701 (London: HMSO, July 1968).

36 Dhahran to DOS, 7 August 1968, DEF 6 Trucial St, NARA: RG 59, CFPF 1967–1969, Box 1613.

37 Dhahran to DOS, 'Abu Dhabi Defence Force and Trucial Oman Scouts: Recent developments', 7 August 1968, DEF 6 Trucial St, NARA: CFPF 1967–1969, Box 1635.

38 Report of the CGS on his visit to the Gulf, 28 August 1968, TNA: FCO 8/81.

39 Dubai and the Northern Trucial States annual review for 1968, 5 January 1969, TNA: FCO 8/1210.

40 Abu Dhabi annual review for 1968, 4 January 1969, ibid.

41 Clark to Weir, 9 July 1968, TNA: FCO 8/888.

42 Minute by Eyers of a meeting with Sheikh Rashid, 1 August 1968, ibid.

43 'The police and security forces of Bahrain, Qatar and the Trucial States', 29 February 1969, TNA: FCO 8/96.

44 Report on the Advisory Mission on Defence of the Union of Arab Emirates, 20 April 1969, TNA: FCO 8/982.

45 Crawford to McCarthy, 9 April 1969, TNA: FO 1016/756.

46 Abu Dhabi annual review for 1969, 19 December 1969, TNA: FCO 8/1509.

47 Minutes of a meeting at the Foreign Office, 11 June 1969, TNA: FCO 8/997.

48 Brief No. 8 'Operation Oboe', June 1969, TNA: FCO 8/998.

49 Weir to Bullard, 13 January 1969, TNA: FCO 8/1245.

50 Rossiter, 'Britain and the development of professional security forces', pp. 227–32.

51 David Nield, *A Soldier in Arabia*, Foreword by HH Sheikh Saud bin Saqr Al Qasimi, ruler of Ras Al Khaimah (Surbiton: Medina Publisher, 2015), pp. 100–6, 110.

52 Luard to Douglas-Home, 3 November 1969, TNA: FCO 8/1245.

53 Bullard to Weir, 18 November 1969, ibid.

54 'The rundown and total withdrawal of British forces from the Gulf by 31st December 1971', Annex B, TNA: CAB 163/115.

55 Coles to Weir, 20 July 1970, TNA: FCO 8/1511.

56 Al-Qasimi, *My Early Life*, p. 270.

57 Coles to Weir, 23 July 1970, TNA: FCO 8/1511.

58 Dubai and the Northern Trucial States annual review for 1970, 10 December 1970, TNA: FCO 8/1510.

59 Crawford to Douglas-Home, 25 July 1970, TNA: FCO 8/1318.

60 Douglas-Home to Heath, 26 November 1970, PM/70/138, TNA: PREM 13/538.

61 Minute Acland, 7 December 1970, TNA: FCO 8/1311.

62 'Assistance to police forces and special branches in the Gulf', March 1971, TNA: FCO 8/1629.

63 Hodges to Acland, 26 April 1971, ibid.

64 DP Note 208/71 (Final), 21 June 1971, Residual UK military presence in the Gulf after 1971, Note by the Defence Policy Staff, TNA: DEFE 13/1388.

65 Minute by Luce, 27 September 1971, TNA: FCO 8/1623; FCO minute, 11 November 1971, TNA: FCO 8/1637; de Butts, *Now the Dust has Settled*, p. 229.

66 Luce–Arthur meetings with Sheikh Zayed and Sheikh Rashid, 15 September 1971, TNA: FCO 8/1623.

67 INR Research Study RNAS-15 revised, 'Persian Gulf; implications of British withdrawal', 3 September 1971, POL 33 Persian Gulf, NARA: RG 59, SNF 1970–73, Box 1996.

68 JIC (A) (71) 46, 21 September 1971, TNA: CAB 186/9.

69 Arthur to Douglas-Home, 23 December 1971, TNA: FCO 8/1628.

70 Arthur to Douglas-Home, 21 January 1972, TNA: FCO 8/1939.

71 De Butts, *Now the Dust has Settled*, p. 230.

72 Memo on frontiers, 29 April 1965, MECA: Paxton Collection, Box 5/5; Crawford to Douglas-Home, 25 July 1970, TNA: FCO 8/1318.

73 Crawford to Weir, 19 January 1968, TNA: FCO 8/828.

74 OPDO (DR) (69) 4, 1 October 1969, TNA CAB 148/97.

75 Balfour-Paul, *End of Empire*, p. 126.

76 Smith, *Britain's Revival*, p. 73.

77 Crawford to Brown, 8 December 1967, TNA: FCO 8/828.

78 Battle to Rostow, 8 April 1968, NARA: RG 59, CFPF 1967–1969, POL 33 Persian Gulf, Box 2418.

79 Government of Qatar memorandum for the formation of the UAE, 25 February 1968, MECA: Sir Geoffrey Arthur Collection, file 1.

80 H. G. Balfour-Paul, 'Recent developments in the Persian Gulf', *Journal of the Royal Central Asian Society*, Vol. 56, No. 1 (1969), p. 17

81 INR memorandum, 'Bahrain and Qatar: The two Gulf States in search of a new identity', 29 May 1968, NARA: RG 59, CFPF 1967–1969 POL 19 FAA, Box 2083. State Department documents call the Union the Federation of Arab Amirates (FAA).

82 INR research memorandum, 'Federation of Arab Amirates to be born on March 30', 22 March 1968, NARA: RG 59, CFPF 1967–1969 POL 3 Trucial St, Box 2543.

83 INR research memorandum, 'Persian Gulf rulers still searching for unity', 12 July 1968, NARA: RG 59, CFPF 1967–1969 POL 19 FAA, Box 2083.

84 Crawford meeting with Sheikh Rashid, 16 March 1968, TNA: FO 1016/859.

85 Abu Dhabi annual review for 1968, TNA: FCO 8/1210.

86 Parsons to Crawford, 4 January 1969, TNA: FCO 8/1004.

87 Dubai and Northern Trucial States annual review for 1968, 5 January 1969, TNA FCO 8/1210.

88 For an assessment of the different rulers, see, annex in Crawford to Stewart, 10 June 1968, TNA: FO 1016/863.

89 Minister of State meeting with Sheikh Rashid, 27 June 1968, TNA: FO 1016/865.

90 Crawford to Stewart, 14 June 1968, TNA: FO 1016/747.

91 Anglo-US talks on the Middle East at the State Department, 13 September 1968, TNA: FO 1016/867.

92 'Note on a visit to the Trucial States on 28 December, 1968 to 3 January 1969', DUL: Hawley Papers, HAW 63/14/1-6.

93 Parsons to Crawford, 17 June 1968, TNA: FO 1016/865.

94 Persian Gulf annual review for 1968, 14 January 1969, TNA: FCO 8/927.

95 Morris to Stewart, 27 November 1968, TNA: FO 1016/870.

96 Kelly, *Arabia*, p. 55.

97 Henderson to Balfour-Paul, 20 April 1968, TNA: FO 1016/860.

98 ADDF booklet for perspective officers, undated, DUL: Hawley Papers, HAW 9/7/10.

99 Nuttall to Crawford, 5 October 1969, TNA: FCO 8/848.

100 Crawford to Stewart, 17 February 1969, TNA: FCO 8/917.

101 Minute by McCarthy, 18 March 1969, ibid.

102 Anglo-American talks on the Middle East held at Washington, 10–11 March 1969, TNA: FCO 8/934.

103 US–UK Persian Gulf talks, 11 March 1969, NARA: RG 59, Records Relating to the Persian Gulf and Arabian Peninsula, 1952–1975, Box 3.

104 Smith, *Britain's Revival*, pp. 137–8.

105 Bahrain annual review for 1969, 28 December 1969, TNA: FCO 8/1360.

106 Qatar annual review for 1969, 29 December 1969, TNA: FCO 8/1472.

107 Crawford to Stewart, 10 July 1969, TNA: FO 1016/876.

108 Crawford to Stewart, 15 July 1969, TNA: FCO 8/920.

109 Minute by Coles, 21 May 1969, TNA: FO 1016/874.

110 Weir to McCarthy, 4 June 1969, TNA: FO 1016/875.

111 Stewart to Crawford, 13 August 1969, TNA: FCO 8/920.

112 DP Note 3/68 (revised), 19 February 1968 TNA: DEFE 6/106; DP note 207/68, 8 April 1968, ibid.

113 'The Persian Gulf and Kuwait: British forces Gulf', 8 December 1967, TNA: DEFE
     25/265.

114 Bond to Acland and Tesh, 22 April 1971, TNA: FCO 46/723.

115 INR Research Study RNAS-15 revised, 'Persian Gulf: Implications of British
     withdrawal', 3 September 1971, POL 33 Persian Gulf, NARA: RG 59, SNF 1970–73,
     Box 1996.

116 Bullard to Crawford, 8 July 1969, TNA: FO 1016/876.

117 Crawford to Stewart, 11 November 1969, TNA: FCO 8/925.

118 Dubai and the Northern Trucial States annual review for 1969, 30 December 1969,
     TNA: FCO 8/1509.

119 Dubai and Northern Trucial States annual review for 1970, 10 December 1970,
     TNA: FCO 8/1510.

120 Minute by Acland, 14 February 1970, TNA: FCO 8/1357.

121 Dubai and the Northern Trucial States annual review for 1969, 30 December 1969,
     TNA: FCO 8/1509.

122 See, for example, correspondence in TNA: FCO 8/1314, and especially Falle to
     Acland, 10 June 1970, and Crawford to Acland, 23 June 1970.

123 Details of Luard's talks with the rulers can be found in TNA: FCO 8/1516. See
     also, minute by Luard, 11 May 1970, TNA: FCO 8/1292.

124 Wright to Douglas-Home, 26 July 1971, TNA: FCO 8/1562.

125 'Developments in the external relations with Iran', 2 July 1971, JIC (A) (71) 19,
     TNA: CAB 186/9.

126 Persian Gulf annual review for 1970, 1 January 1971, TNA: FCO 8/1570.

127 Minute by Acland, 15 May 1970, TNA: FCO 8/1333.

128 Saudi Arabia annual review for 1970, 31 December 1970, TNA: FCO 8/1734.

129 Richard Schofield, 'The crystallisation of a complex territorial dispute: Britain and
     the Saudi Arabian borderland, 1966–71', *Journal of Arabian Studies*, Vol. 1, No. 1
     (2011), pp. 44–5.

130 Bahrain to FCO, 14 May 1970, No. 188, TNA: FCO 8/1332. Many of the
     documents in this file have been redacted under Section 27 of the Freedom of
     Information Act.

131 Crawford to McCarthy, 16 March 1970, TNA: FCO 8/1331.

132 Saudi Arabia annual review for 1970, 31 December 1970, TNA: FCO 8/1734.

133 Murphy to Sisco, 27 September 1971, NARA: RG 59, Records Relating to the
     Persian Gulf and Arabian Peninsula, 1952–1975, Box 3.

134 Smith, *Britain's Revival*, p. 34.

135 Records of Heath's talks in the Middle East, March 29–11 April 1969, TNA: PREM
     15/122. For discussion of the implications of Heath's visit, see TNA: FCO 8/979.

136 Crawford to McCarthy, 9 April 1969, TNA: FO 1016/756.

137 Balfour-Paul, *End of Empire*, p. 225 n. 79.

138   Daly, *Last of the Great Proconsuls*, p. 274.

139   Henderson to Crawford, 26 April 1969, TNA: FO 1016/756.

140   Crawford to Douglas-Home, 25 July 1970, TNA: FCO 8/1318.

141   Minute by Acland, 20 July 1970, ibid.

142   Gause III, 'British and American policies', pp. 254–5.

143   Minutes of a meeting at 10 Downing Street, TNA: PREM 15/538.

144   Tore T. Petersen, 'Richard Nixon, Great Britain, and the Anglo-American strategy of turning the Persian Gulf into an Allied lake', in Macris and Kelly (eds), *Imperial Crossroads*, p. 81.

145   Defence Expenditure Study No. 5, The Kuwait commitment in the period to 1970/71, 10 April 1967, TNA: FCO 49/27.

146   Balfour-Paul to Brown, 11 April 1970, TNA: FCO 8/1539.

147   Crawford to Douglas-Home, 22 July 1970, ibid.

148   *HC Debates*, 20 July 1970, Vol. 804, cc. 14–15.

149   Louis, 'The British withdrawal', p. 898.

150   Alec Douglas-Home, *The Way the Wind Blows* (London: William Collins & Sons, 1976), p. 261. Summarised in a minute to Heath, 29 June 1970, TNA: PREM 15/538, PM/70/73.

151   Minutes of a meeting held at 10 Downing Street, 22 July 1970, ibid.

152   William Luce, 'Britain and the Persian Gulf: Mistaken timing over Aden', *The Round Table*, Vol. 57, No. 227 (1967), pp. 280–2.

153   Sir William Luce, GBE, KCMG, 'Britain's withdrawal from the Middle East and the Persian Gulf', lecture given at RUSI on 26 November 1968, *Royal United Services Institution Journal*, Vol. 114, No. 653, p. 7.

154   William Luce, 'A naval force for the Gulf: Balancing inevitable Russian penetration', *The Round Table*, Vol. 59, No. 236 (1969), pp. 349–50, 355–6.

155   Daly, *Last of the Great Proconsuls*, pp. 268–72.

156   Luce meeting with the Chiefs of Staff, 4 August 1970, TNA: DEFE 4/249.

157   For a detailed discussion of Luce's role, see, Daly, *Last of the Great Proconsuls*, pp. 280–304.

158   Memo by McCarthy, 'Lessons from South Arabia', 20 November 1967, TNA: FCO 8/41.

159   Crawford to Douglas-Home, 25 July 1970, TNA: FCO 8/1318.

160   Bullard to Crawford, 10 December 1970, TNA: FCO 8/1510.

161   Douglas-Home to Heath, 26 November 1970, PM/70/138 TNA: PREM 13/538.

162   Dinsmore to DOS, 28 October 1970, No. A-89, POL 2 Trucial St, NARA: RG 59, SNF 1970–73, Box, 2631.

163   Douglas-Home to Heath, 26 November 1970, PM/70/138, TNA: PREM 13/538.

164 Both reports were enclosed in Douglas-Home to Heath, 26 November 1970, TNA: PREM 13/538. An unredacted copy can found in DOP (70) 44, 8 December 1970, TNA: CAB 148/102.
165 Trend to Heath, 10 December 1970, TNA: PREM 15/538.
166 DOP (70) 12th meeting, 11 December 1970, TNA: CAB 148/101.
167 DOP (70) 47, 28 December 1970, TNA: CAB 148/102.
168 Bullard to Arthur, 10 December 1970, TNA: FCO 8/1510.
169 Arthur to Douglas-Home, 21 October 1971, TNA: FCO 8/1724.
170 *HC Debates*, 1 March 1971, Vol. 812, cc. 1227–32. For an analysis of Douglas-Home's statement, see the State Department INR memo REUN-13, 'UK: Heath Government defines Persian Gulf policy', 5 March 1971, DEF 1 Near E, NARA: RG 59, SNF 1970–73, Box 1774.
171 D. C. Watt, 'Can the Union of Arab Emirates survive?', *The World Today*, Vol. 27, No. 4 (April 1971), p. 144.
172 'Britain and the Gulf: The arithmetic of withdrawal', *Financial Times*, 12 March 1971, p. 12.
173 Arthur to Douglas-Home, 19 April 1971, TNA: FCO 8/1572.
174 Wright to Douglas-Home, 26 July 1971, TNA: FCO 8/1562.
175 Sato, *Britain and the Formation of the Gulf States*, pp. 104–5.
176 A copy of the agreement can be found in Coles to Everard, 19 July 1971, TNA: FCO 8/1562.
177 Minute by McCarthy, 1 February 1970, TNA: FCO 8/1301.
178 Arthur to Douglas-Home, 19 January 1972, TNA: FCO 8/1922.
179 Persian Gulf annual review for 1971, 24 January 1972, TNA: FCO 8/1804.
180 Heard-Bey, *Trucial States*, p. 363.
181 Grattan to Moon, 3 January 1972, TNA: PREM 15/1763.
182 'The outlook for Saudi Arabia', 8 September 1971, JIC (A) (71) 29, TNA: CAB 186/9.
183 Morris to Douglas-Home, 28 April 1971, TNA: FCO 8/1733.
184 'Persian Gulf: Factors inhibiting Saudi-Iranian cooperation in the Gulf', INR memo RNAN-7, 12 February 1970, POL 33 Persian Gulf, NARA: RG 59, SNF 1970–73, Box 1994.
185 'Policy in the Gulf: The Union of Arab Emirates (UAE)', 30 June 1971, DOP (71) 37, TNA: CAB 148/116.
186 Wright to Douglas-Home, 26 July 1971, TNA: FCO 8/1562.
187 BDOHP, interview with Sir Antony Acland, 23 April 2001, pp. 20–2.
188 Minute by Acland, 6 August 1971, TNA: FCO 8/1572.
198 Morris to Douglas-Home, 28 April 1971, TNA: FCO 8/1733.
190 Dinsmore to DOS, 6 December 1970, No. A-103, POL 2 Trucial St, NARA: RG 59, SNF 1970–73, Box 2631.

191   'Developments in the external relations of Iran', 2 July 1971, JIC (A) (71) 19, TNA: CAB 186/9.

192   Douglas-Home meeting with the Shah at Brussels, 10 July 1970, TNA: FCO 8/1316; minute by Douglas-Home, 13 July 1970, TNA: PREM 13/538.

193   Lord Carrington to Heath, 29 September 1971, TNA: PREM 15/1763.

194   Persian Gulf annual review for 1971, 24 January 1972, TNA: FCO 8/1804.

195   In 1969, the Chiefs of Staff developed a plan to deter the Iranians from invading the islands. See 'Deterrence of Iranian action against Abu Musa and Tunb – Joint Theatre Plan (Gulf) No. 1 (Operation Pensum)', 21 March 1969, COS 19/69, TNA: DEFE 5/181.

196   Lord Carrington to Heath, 16 November 1971, TNA: PREM 15/1763.

197   President's Daily Brief, 19 November 1971, CIA: FOIA; 'Iran: the Persian Gulf Islands Dispute', CIA research paper, 4 May 1980, ibid.

198   DOP (71) 22nd meetings, 30 November 1971, TNA: CAB 148/115.

199   Smith, *Britain's Revival and Fall*, p. 107; Louis, 'The British withdrawal', p. 902; DOP (71) 21st meeting, 9 November 1971, TNA: CAB 148/115.

200   Grattan to Moon, 28 August 1971, TNA: PREM 15/1763.

201   Memo by Admiral Hill-Norton, 30 April 1971, TNA DEFE 13/1388.

202   Arthur to Douglas-Home, 2 February 1972, TNA: FCO 8/1814.

203   Arthur to Home, 21 February 1972, TNA: FCO 8/1922.

204   Dinsmore to DOS, 20 November 1971, No. A-136, POL 18 Trucial St, NARA: RG 59, SNF 1970–73, Box, 2631.

205   Undated memorandum, 'The Trucial States (Trucial Oman)', TNA: OD 34/246.

206   CIA intelligence memorandum, 'The Persian Gulf Amirates: Economic assets and prospects', April 1970, CIA: FOIA.

207   Balfour-Paul to Urwick, 30 March 1968, TNA: OD 34/246.

208   The Persian Gulf, Representative's Annual Report, 1967–1968, TNA: BW 114/10.

209   Heard-Bey, *Trucial States*, pp. 332–4.

210   See, for example, the Abu Dhabi Petroleum Company Ltd annual report for 1971, BP Archive: 242128.

211   CIA intelligence memorandum, 'The Persian Gulf Amirates: economic assets and prospects', April 1970, CIA: FOIA.

212   Abu Dhabi annual review for 1968, 4 January 1969, TNA: FCO 8/1210.

213   K. G. Fenelon, *United Arab Emirates: An Economic and Social Survey*, 2nd edn (London: Longman, 1976), pp. 80–1. 1 BD = $2.10.

214   Kendall to Roberts, 6 May 1968, TNA: FCO 8/862.

215   ECSSR, *With United Strength*, pp. 149–51.

216 'Abu Dhabi – The sour smell of success', *Financial Times*, 30 October 1969, p. 20. Jayanti Maitra, *Zayed: From Challenges to Union* (Abu Dhabi: National Archives, 2015), pp. 226–37.

217 Treadwell to Crawford, 5 October 1969, TNA: FCO 8/1229.

218 Abu Dhabi annual review for 1969, 19 December 1969, TNA: FCO 8/1509.

219 Persian Gulf annual review for 1970, 1 January 1971, TNA: FCO 8/1570.

220 Minute by Luce, 8 September 1970, TNA: FCO 8/1319.

221 McKenzie Johnston to Derrick, 30 November 1968, TNA: FCO 8/1226.

222 Howell to Crawford, 14 March 1969, ibid.

223 Ibid.

224 Fenelon, *United Arab Emirates*, p. 26.

225 Dubai and the Northern Trucial States annual review for 1968, 5 January 1969, TNA: FCO 8/1210.

226 Dubai and the Northern Trucial States annual review for 1969, 30 December 1969, TNA: FCO 8/1509.

227 *Financial Times*, 5 November 1968, p. 24.

228 *Financial Times*, 22 April 1970, p. 9.

6. Epilogue

1 Robin W. Winks, 'On decolonization and Informal Empire', *American Historical Review*, Vol. 81, No. 3 (1976), pp. 541–2.

2 Lucas to Roberts, 30 June 1974, TNA: FCO 8/3152.

3 Personal information provided to the author.

4 Foreign and Commonwealth Office, *Diplomatic Service List*, 1971 and 1980 (London: HMSO, 1971 and 1980).

5 Treadwell to Home, 10 June 1973, TNA: FCO 8/2126.

6 Minute by McCarthy, 5 March 1974, TNA: FCO 8/2359.

7 Hollis, 'From force to finance', p. 214.

8 Kelly, 'Vanishing act', p. 191.

9 Personal information provided to the author.

10 Minute by Parsons, 9 May 1972, TNA: FCO 8/1806.

11 Alan Munro, *Keep the Flag Flying: A Diplomatic Memoir* (London: Gilgamesh Publishing, 2012), pp. 125–6.

12 Anthony Parsons, *The Pride and the Fall: Iran 1974–1979* (London: Jonathan Cape, 1984), pp. 37–8.

13 Roberts to Owen, 29 March 1978, TNA: FCO 8/3140.

14 Minister of State's visit to the Gulf: 4–19 February 1975, TNA: FCO 8/2396.

15 Ennals to Callaghan, 19 February 1975, TNA: FCO 8/2395.

16 McCarthy to Lucas, 11 March 1975, ibid.

17 McCarthy to Douglas-Home, 31 December 1973, TNA: FCO 8/2354.

18 McCarthy to Wright, 24 June 1974, TNA: FCO 8/2359.

19 Henderson to Douglas-Home, 24 September 1974, TNA: FCO 8/2291.

20 Brant to Owen, 1 May 1978, TNA: FCO 8/3222.

21 CIA Staff Notes: Middle East, Africa South Asia, 18 February 1975, No. 0431/75, CIA: FOIA.

22 Passmore to Muir, UAE steering brief for the Secretary of State of Energy tour of the UAE, 17 September 1980, TNA: FCO 8/3457.

23 Roberts to Owen, 13 November 1977, TNA: FCO 8/2910.

24 Stirling to Douglas-Home, 23 May 1972, TNA: FCO 8/1824.

25 McCarthy to Hunt, 16 March 1973, TNA: FCO 8/1950.

26 Walker to Treadwell, 25 and 31 January 1972, TNA: FCO 8/1925.

27 Personal information provided to the author. See a report by Colonel Watson, Commanding Officer of the UDF, 26 January 1972, TNA: FCO 8/1925.

28 Fromherz, *Qatar*, pp. 77, 79–80. See also Henderson to Douglas-Home, 7 March 1972, TNA: FCO 8/1892.

29 Personal information provided to the author.

30 Ibid.

31 Roberts to Owen, 20 July 1978, TNA: FCO 8/3141.

32 Treadwell to Wright, 8 May 1973, TNA: FCO 8/2128.

33 Treadwell to Wright, 8 May 1973, TNA: FCO 8/2126.

34 McCarthy to Home, 31 December 1973, TNA: FCO 8/1539.

35 UAE annual review for 1975, TNA: FCO 8/2659.

36 McCarthy to Lucas, 17 January 1976, TNA: FCO 8/2660.

37 UAE annual review for 1975, TNA: FCO 8/2659.

38 McCarthy to Callaghan, 19 October 1975, TNA: FCO 8/2424.

39 Roberts to Owen, 29 March 1978, TNA: FCO 8/3140.

40 Henderson to Acland, 28 March 1972, TNA: FCO 8/1894.

41 Walker to Treadwell, 27 February 1972, TNA: FCO 8/1923.

42 Treadwell to Home, 11 February 1972, ibid.

43 UAE annual review for 1976, 5 January 1977, TNA: FCO 8/2888.

44 Gregory F. Gause III, *The International Relations of the Persian Gulf* (Cambridge: Cambridge University Press, 2010), pp. 29–33.

45 Roberts to Lord Carrington, 25 April 1981, TNA: FCO 8/3910.

46 Personal information provided to the author.

47 Kelly, *Arabia*, p. 205.

48 Memorandum on Anglo-US talks on the Middle East, 28 September 1973, TNA: FCO 8/1950.

49 Agar to Treadwell, 'Annual report by the Defence Attaché United Arab Emirates', 21 January 1973, TNA: FCO 8/2138.

50 Ibid.

51 Treadwell to Wright, 3 July 1972, TNA: FCO 8/1926; personal information provided to the author.

52 Helms to Kissinger, 31 March 1973, CIA: FOIA.

53 National Intelligence Estimate 30–1–73, 'Problems in the Persian Gulf', 7 June 1974, Richard Nixon Library: NSC Subject Files: National Intelligence Estimates, Box 362.

54 DP Note 206/73 (Revised Final), July 1973, DEFE 11/741.

55 'Command and administrative instructions for the Military Advisory Team Gulf', 8 December 1971, TNA: FCO 8/1939.

56 McCarthy to Douglas-Home, 31 December 1973, TNA: FCO 8/2354.

57 Clark to McCarthy, 7 February 1974, TNA: FCO 8/2366.

58 Treadwell to Douglas-Home, 29 January 1973, TNA: FCO 8/2138.

59 McCarthy to Wright, 5 March 1974, TNA: FCO 8/2359.

60 'Defence sales to the Middle East', 3 May 1973, OPD (74) 11, TNA: CAB 148/145.

61 'Arms Transfers to the Persian Gulf: Trends and Implications', Intelligence Assessment, August 1982, CIA: FOIA.

62 Roberts to Lucas, 25 July 1978, TNA: FCO 8/2123.

63 Annual report for 1976 by the Defence Attaché UAE, 30 January 1977, TNA: FCO 8/2897.

64 Kelly, *Arabia*, p. 206.

65 United Arab Emirates: Annual review for 1978, 1 January 1979, TNA: FCO 8/3319.

66 Roberts to Owen, 20 July 1978, TNA: FCO 8/3141.

67 Minute by Lucas, 17 May 1978, TNA: FCO 8/3140.

68 Roberts to Lucas, 25 July 1978, and Lucas to Smith, 15 August 1978, TNA: FCO 8/2123.

69 Valedictory report by the Defence Attaché UAE, June 1978, TNA: FCO 8/3105.

70 Roberts to Owen, 18 June 1978, ibid.

71 Julian Walker, 'Practical problems of boundary delimitation in Arabia: The case of the United Arab Emirates', in Richard Schofield (ed.), *Territorial Foundations of the Gulf States* (New York: St. Martin's Press, 1994), pp. 109–16.

72 Julian Walker, 'The United Arab Emirates and Oman frontiers', in Clive H. Schofield and Richard N. Schofield (eds), *The Middle East and North Africa: World Boundaries*, Vol. 2 (London: Routledge, 1994), pp. 176–83.

73 For a survey of the diplomacy surrounding the Buraimi dispute, see Treadwell to Callaghan, 'The character of the "Buraimi" dispute and the sequence to its settlement', 7 August 1974, TNA: FCO 8/2357.

74 MD to TRM, 'Border discussions', 7 June 1977, MECA: Julian Paxton Collection, Box 5/1.

75 Schofield, 'The crystallisation of a complex territorial dispute', p. 49.

76 Meeting at the State Department, 26 June 1972, TNA: FCO 8/1806.

77 Minute by Parsons, 23 February 1973, TNA: FCO 8/1959.

78 Minute by Wright, 23 May 1973, TNA: FCO 8/2129.

79   Michael Quentin Morton, *Buraimi: The Struggle for Power, Influence and Oil in Arabia* (London: I.B. Tauris, 2013), pp. 223–5.

80   Kuwait Embassy to Abu Dhabi Embassy, 2 March 1974, available at: https://wikileaks.org/plusd/cables/1974KUWAIT00809_b.html (accessed 4 July 2018); McCarthy to Callaghan, 7 August 1974, TNA: FCO 8/2357.

81   Akins to DOS, 31 July 1974, No. 4458, available at: https://wikileaks.org/plusd/cables/1974KUWAIT00809_b.html (accessed 4 July 2018).

82   Horn to DOS, 31 July 1974, No. 4458, NARA: CFPF 1973–1979.

83   Sterner to DOS, 30 July 1974, No. 1009, NARA: CFPF 1973–1979.

84   Kelly, *Arabia*, p. 210.

85   *Middle East Economic Survey*, 19 June 1995, pp. D1–D3.

86   Richard Schofield, with Elizabeth Evans, *Arabian Boundaries: New Documents*, Vol. 15: *1974* (Cambridge: Cambridge University Press, 2009), p. xii. Schofield provides a detailed commentary about the Saudi–UAE Boundary Agreement of 1974 on pp. xii–xv.

87   Oberwetter and Sison to DOS, 10 September 2005, available at: https://wikileaks.org/plusd/cables/05ABUDHABI3851_a.html; see also, Sison to DOS, 6 July 2005, available at: https://wikileaks.org/plusd/cables/05ABUDHABI3008_a.html (both accessed 4 July 2018).

88   Personal information provided to the author.

89   FCO Planning Staff memo, 'Consequences of the fall of the Shah', 6 February 1979, TNA: FCO 8/3280.

90   Personal information provided to the author.

91   'Royal Tour of Eastern Arabia: Her Majesty's Ambassadors at Kuwait, Bahrain, Jedda, Doha, Abu Dhabi and Muscat', February–March 1979, TNA: DEFE 70/631.

92   Royal tour political steering brief, undated, TNA: FCO 8/3298.

93   Owen to Callaghan, 22 February 1979, TNA: FCO 8/3280.

94   'Royal Tour of Eastern Arabia', TNA: DEFE 70/631.

95   'UK policy towards the Gulf and Saudi Arabia', 27 February 1979, TNA: FCO 8/3280.

96   Personal information provided to the author.

97   Roberts to Parsons, 5 May 1979, TNA: FCO 8/3281.

98   Parsons to Wilton, 2 April 1979, ibid.

99   Report by Parsons, 15 June 1979, TNA: FCO 8/3287.

100   Parsons to FCO, 8 June 1979, TNA: PREM 19/92.

101   Munro, *Keep the Flag Flying*, p. 128.

102   'Defence Options in the Gulf, Red Sea and North West Indian Ocean', 21 August 1980, DP 7/80 (Final), TNA: PREM 16/2169.

Bibliography

Archives

British Library, London: India Office Records

L/P&S/12	Political (External) Department, Annual Files
L/P&S/18	Political and Secret Department Memoranda
L/P&S/20	Political and Secret Department Library
R/15/1	Political Residency, Bushire

Churchill College, Cambridge University

British Diplomatic Oral History Programme (BDOHP)
    Sir Antony Acland
    Sir John Coles
    Sir James Craig
    Sir Donald Hawley
    Sir Archie Lamb
    Sir Ivor Lucas
    Sir John Moberly
    Sir Anthony Parsons
    Sir Clive Rose
    Sir Harold Walker

Georgetown University Library, Washington, DC

William Mulligan Papers

HSBC Group Archives, London

British Bank of the Middle East

Lyndon Baines Johnson Presidential Library (LBJL), Austin, TX

National Security File

John F. Kennedy Presidential Library, Boston, MA

Robert W. Komer Papers

Palace Green Library, Durham University (DUL)

Sir Donald Hawley Papers

The National Archives, Kew, Richmond

BW	British Council
CAB	Cabinet Office
DEFE	Ministry of Defence
FCO	Foreign and Commonwealth Office
FO	Foreign Office
ODA	Ministry of Overseas Development
PREM	Prime Minister's Office
T	Treasury
WO	War Office

The National Army Museum (NAM), Chelsea, London

Miscellaneous Papers on the Trucial Oman Scouts

Richard M. Nixon Presidential Library and Museum, Yorba Linda, CA

National Security Council Files
National Security Council Institutional ('H') Files

Royal Institute of International Affairs (Chatham House), London

Records of Meetings and Memoranda on the Persian Gulf, *c.* 1950–1985

School of Oriental and African Studies (SOAS), London University: Archives and Special Collections

Sir James Norman Dalrymple Anderson Papers

Seeley Mudd Library, Princeton University

John Foster Dulles Papers

St Antony's College, Oxford University: Middle East Centre Archive

Sir Geoffrey Arthur Collection
Sir Richard Beaumont Collection
Norman Corkhill Collection
Julian Paxton Collection
Sir George Rendel Collection
John Slade-Baker Collection

The National Archives and Records Administration (NARA), College Park, MD

RG 59   General Records of the Department of State (DOS)
RG 84   Records of the Foreign Service Posts of the Department of State

Warwick University, Coventry

BP Archive

Published primary sources

Official publications

Aitchison, C. U. *A Collection of Treaties, Engagements and Sanads Relating to India and Neighbouring Countries*, Vol. 11 (Delhi: Manager of Publications, 1933).
Arbitration Concerning Buraimi and the Common Frontier between Abu Dhabi and Saudi Arabia: Memorial Submitted by the Government of the United Kingdom of Great Britain and Northern Ireland (London, 1955).
Arbitration for the Settlement of the Territorial Dispute between Muscat and Abu Dhabi on the One Side and Saudi Arabia on the Other: Memorial of the Government of Saudi Arabia (Cairo, 1955).
Debates, House of Commons (*HC Debates*), and *House of Lords* (*HL Debates*) (London: Hansard, 1903–71).
Foreign and Commonwealth Office, *Diplomatic Service List*, 1971 and 1980 (London: HMSO, 1971 and 1980).
Hughes, R. Thomas, Arabian Gulf Intelligence, *Selections from the Records of the Bombay Government*, New Series, No. 24, 1856: *Concerning Arabia, Bahrain, Kuwait, Muscat*

and Oman, Qatar United Arab Emirates and the Islands of the Gulf, referred to as *Bombay Selections* (Cambridge: Oleander Press, 1985).

Lorimer, J. G., *Gazetteer of the Persian Gulf, Oman and Central Arabia*, Vol. 1: *Historical* (Calcutta: Superintendent Government Printing, 1915).

Lorimer, J. G., *Gazetteer of the Persian Gulf, Oman and Central Arabia*, Vol. 2: *Geographical and Statistical* (Calcutta: Superintendent Government Printing, 1915).

Ministry of Defence, *Statement on the Defence Estimates*, Vols 1 and 2, Cmnd. 2902 (London: HMSO, 1966) and Cmnd. 4290 (London: HMSO, 1970).

Ministry of Defence, *Supplementary Statement on Defence Policy*, Cmnd. 3357 (London: HMSO, 1967), Cmnd. 3701 (London: HMSO, 1968) and Cmnd. 4251 (London: HMSO, 1970).

Saldanha, J. A., *Précis of Nejd Affairs, 1804–1904* (Simla: Office of the Superintendent of Government Printing, 1904).

Saldanha, J. A., *Précis of Correspondence on International Rivalry and British Policy in the Persian Gulf, 1872–1905* (1906).

Saldanha, J. A., *Précis of Correspondence Regarding the Affairs of the Persian Gulf, 1854–1905* (Calcutta: Office of the Superintendent of Government Printing, 1906).

Saldanha, J. A., *Précis of Correspondence Regarding the Trucial Chiefs, 1801–1953* (Calcutta: Office of the Superintendent of Government Printing, 1906).

The Persian Gulf Administrative Reports for 1873–1947 (Gerrards Cross: Archive Editions, 1986).

The Persian Gulf Gazette and Supplements, 1953–1972 (Gerrards Cross: Archive Editions, 1987).

Tuson, Penelope, *The Records of the British Residency and Agencies in the Persian Gulf* (London: India Office Library and Records, 1978).

Foreign Relations of the United States (FRUS)

Foreign Relations of the United States, 1947, Vol. 5: *The Near East and Africa* (Washington, DC: Government Printing Office, 1971).

FRUS, 1949, Vol. 6: *The Near East, South Asia and Africa* (Washington, DC: Government Printing Office, 1977), pp. 88–9, 1624.

FRUS, 1951, Vol. 5: *The Near East and Africa* (Washington, DC: Government Printing Office, 1982).

FRUS, 1955–57, Vol. 13: *The Near East: Jordan–Yemen* (Washington, DC: Government Printing Office, 1988).

Diaries and memoirss

Al-Gurg, Easa Saleh, *The Wells of Memory: An Autobiography*, with an introduction by Sir James Craig GCMG (London: John Murray, 1998).

Al-Qasimi, Sultan bin Muhammad, *My Early Life* (London: Bloomsbury, 2011).

Balfour-Paul, Glencairn, *Bagpipes in Babylon: A Lifetime in the World and Beyond* (London: I.B. Tauris, 2006).

BBC Summary of World Broadcasts, Part 4: *The Arab World, Israel, Greece, Turkey, Persia* (Caversham Park: British Broadcasting Corporation, 1956; *SWB*).

Boustead, Colonel Sir Hugh, *The Wind in the Morning: The Autobiography of Hugh Boustead* (London: Chatto & Windus, 1971).

Burrows, Bernard, *Footnotes in the Sand: The Gulf in Transition, 1953–1958* (Salisbury: Michael Russell, 1990).

Cawston, Antony and Michael Curtis, *Arabian Days: The Memoirs of Two Trucial Oman Scouts*, Foreword by Major General Ken Perkins, CB, MBE, DFC (Michael Curtis, 2011).

de Butts, Freddie, *Now the Dust has Settled: Memories of War and Peace, 1939–1994* (Padstow: Tab House, 1995).

Douglas-Home, Alec, *The Way the Wind Blows* (London: William Collins & Sons, 1976).

Hawley, Donald, *Desert Wind and Tropic Storm: An Autobiography* (Norwich: Michael Russell, 2000).

Hawley, Donald, *The Emirates: Witness to a Metamorphosis* (Norwich: Michael Russell, 2007).

Henderson, Edward, *This Strange Eventful History: Memoirs of Earlier Days in the UAE and Oman* (London: Quartet Books, 1988).

Lamb, Sir Archie, *A Long Way from Swansea* (Pembroke: Starborn Books, 2003).

Luce, Margaret, *From Aden to the Gulf: Personal Diaries, 1956–1966*, Foreword by Lord Home of the Hirsel (Norwich: Michael Russell, 1987).

Memoirs of the Emirates (Abu Dhabi: National Archives, 2012).

Munro, Alan, *Keep the Flag Flying: A Diplomatic Memoir* (London: Gilgamesh Publishing, 2012).

Nield, David, *A Soldier in Arabia*, Foreword by HH Sheikh Saud bin Saqr Al Qasimi, ruler of Ras Al Khaimah (Surbiton: Medina Publisher, 2015).

Parsons, Anthony, *The Pride and the Fall: Iran 1974–1979* (London: Jonathan Cape, 1984).

Parsons, Anthony, *They Say the Lion: Britain's Legacy to the Arabs: A Personal Memoir* (London: Jonathan Cape, 1986).

Rundell, Anthony, *Emirates: All Our Yesterdays: The Trucial States 1960–1962* (Abu Dhabi: National Archives, 2012).

Shuckburgh, Evelyn, *Descent to Suez: Diaries 1951–56* (London: Weidenfeld and Nicolson, 1986).

Walker, Julian, *Tyro on the Trucial Coast* (Durham: Memoir Club, 1999).

Worsnop, Edric, *The Vorsinoporix Chronicle: A Diplomatic Passage* (Oxford: Oxford Book Projects, 2007).

Interviews

Lieutenant Colonel Graham Barnett, telephone interview, 18 March 2018
Christopher Battiscombe, CMG, London, 27 January 2018
Sir Michael Burton, KCVO, CMG, London, 29 February 2018
Sir Terence Clark, KBE, CMG, CVO, London, 12 March 2018
Colonel Tim Courtenay RM, OBE, DL, telephone interview, 29 March 2018
Major Michael Curtis, Winchester, 3 April 2018
Major Cameron Mackie RM, telephone interviews, 23 and 30 March 2018
Sir Alan Munro, KCMG, London, 11 April 2018
Sir Harold Walker, KCMG, London, 21 February 2018

Newspapers and Radio Monitoring Reports

BBC Summary of World Broadcasts (SWB)
The Financial Times
The Guardian
The Times (London)

Books, journal articles and theses

Al-Baharna, Husain M., 'The consequences of Britain's Exclusive Treaties: A Gulf view',
    in B. R. Pridham (ed.), *The Arab Gulf and the West* (Beckenham: Croom Helm, 1985),
    pp. 15–37.
Al-Sayegh, Fatma, 'Merchants' role in a changing society: The case of Dubai, 1900–90',
    Middle Eastern Studies, Vol. 34, No. 1 (1998), pp. 87–102.
Allfree, P. S., *Warlords of Oman* (New York: Barnes & Co, 1967).
Alon, Yoav, *The Making of Jordan: Tribes, Colonialism and the Modern State* (London:
    I.B. Tauris: 2007).
Alon, Yoav, 'British colonialism and orientalism in Arabia: Glubb Pasha in Transjordan,
    1930–1946', *British Scholar*, Vol. 3, No. 1 (2010), pp. 105–26.
Alon, Yoav, 'From Abdullah (I) to Abdullah (II): The monarchy, the tribes and shaykhly
    families in Jordan, 1920–2012', in Uzi Rabi (ed.), *Tribes and States in a Changing
    Middle East* (London: Hurst and Company, 2016), pp. 11–35.
Anscombe, Frederick F., *The Ottoman Gulf: The Creation of Kuwait, Saudi Arabia, and
    Qatar* (New York: Columbia University Press, 1997).
Ashton, Nigel, 'Britain and the Kuwait Crisis, 1961', *Diplomacy and Statecraft*, Vol. 9,
    No. 1 (1998), pp. 163–81.

Balfour Paul, H. G., 'Recent developments in the Persian Gulf', *Journal of the Royal Central Asian Society*, Vol. 56, No. 1 (1969), pp. 12–19.

Balfour-Paul, Glencairn, *The End of Empire in the Middle East: Britain's Relinquishment of Power in Her Last Three Arab Dependencies* (Cambridge: Cambridge University Press, 1991).

Bamberg, James, *The History of the British Petroleum Company*, Vol. 2: *The Anglo-Iranian Years, 1928–1954* (Cambridge: Cambridge University Press, 1994).

Bannerman, J. P., 'The impact of the oil industry on society in the Arabian Peninsula', in R. I. Lawless (ed.), *The Gulf in the Early 20th Century: Foreign Institutions and Local Resources*, Working Paper, Centre for Middle Eastern and Islamic Studies, University of Durham (1986), pp. 76–90.

Bayly, C. A., *Empire and Information: Intelligence Gathering and Social Communication in India, 1780–1870* (Cambridge: Cambridge University Press, 1996).

Bin-Abood, Saif Mohammad Obaid, 'Britain's withdrawal from the Gulf: With particular reference to the Emirates', PhD thesis, Durham University (1992).

Bismarck, Helene von, 'The Kuwait crisis and its consequences for Great Britain's Persian Gulf policy', *British Scholar*, Vol. 2, No. 1 (2009), pp. 75–96.

Bismarck, Helene von, *British Policy in the Persian Gulf, 1961–1968: Conceptions of Informal Empire* (London: Palgrave Macmillan, 2013).

Blyth, Robert J., 'Britain versus India in the Persian Gulf: The struggle for political control, c. 1928–48', *Journal of Imperial and Commonwealth History*, Vol. 28, No. 1 (2000), pp. 90–111.

Blyth, Robert J., *The Empire of the Raj: India, Eastern Africa and the Middle East, 0000–1947* (Basingstoke: Palgrave Macmillan, 2003).

Bradshaw, Tancred, 'The dead hand of the Treasury: The economic and social development of the Trucial States, 1948–60', *Middle Eastern Studies*, Vol. 50, No. 2 (2014), pp. 325–42.

Bradshaw, Tancred, *The Glubb Reports: Glubb Pasha and Britain's Empire Project in the Middle East, 1920–1956* (London: Palgrave Macmillan, 2016).

Bradshaw, Tancred, 'The hand of Glubb: The origins of the Trucial Oman Scouts, 1948–1956', *Middle Eastern Studies*, Vol. 53, No. 4 (2017), pp. 656–72.

Centre for Strategic and International Studies, *The Gulf: Implications of British Withdrawal*, Special Report Series, No. 8 (Washington, DC: February 1967).

Citino, Nathan J., *From Arab Nationalism to OPEC: Eisenhower, King Saud, and the Making of U.S.–Saudi Relations*, 2nd edn (Bloomington, IN: Indiana University Press, 2010).

Clayton, Peter, *Two Alpha Lima: The First Ten Years of the Trucial Oman Levies and Trucial Oman Scouts (1950–1960)* (London: Janus Publishing, 1994).

Craig, Sir James, *Shemlan: A History of the Middle East Centre for Arab Studies*, Foreword by Lord Hurd of Westwell (Basingstoke: Macmillan in association with St Antony's College, Oxford University, 1998).

Cronin, Stephanie, *Armies and State-Building in the Modern Middle East: Politics, Nationalism and Military Reform* (London: I.B. Tauris, 2014).

Crystal, Jill, *Oil and Politics in the Gulf: Rulers and the Merchants in Kuwait and Qatar* (Cambridge: Cambridge University Press, 1990).

Curzon, George Nathaniel, *Persia and the Persian Question*, Vol. 2 (London: Longmans, Green & Co, 1892).

Daily Telegraph, The 8 August 1966, p. 16.

Daly, M. W., *The Last of the Great Proconsuls: The Biography of Sir William Luce* (San Diego, CA: Nathan Berg, 2014).

Darwin, John, *Britain and Decolonisation: The Retreat from Empire in the Post-War World* (Basingstoke: Macmillan, 1988).

Dickson, H. R. P., *The Arab of the Desert: A Glimpse into Badawin Life in Kuwait and Saudi Arabia* (London: George Allen & Unwin, 1951).

Dockrill, Saki, *Britain's Retreat from East of Suez: The Choice between Europe and the World?* (Basingstoke: Palgrave Macmillan, 2002).

Dresch, Paul, *Tribes, Government and History in Yemen* (Oxford: Oxford University Press, 1989).

Eickelman, Dale F., *The Middle East and Central Asia: An Anthropological Approach*, 4th edn (Upper Saddle River, NJ: Prentice Hall, 2002).

Emirates Centre for Strategic Studies and Research (ECSSR), *With United Strength: H.H. Shaikh Zayed bin Sultan Al Nahyan: The Leader and the Nation* (Abu Dhabi: ECSSR, 2005).

Fabian Society, *Arabia: When Britain Goes*, Fabian Research Series, 259 (London: Fabian Society, 1967).

Fain, W. Taylor, *American Ascendance and British Retreat in the Persian Gulf Region* (New York: Palgrave Macmillan, 2008).

Fenelon, K. G., *The Trucial States: A Brief Economic Survey* (Beirut: Khayats, 1967).

Fenelon, K. G., *The United Arab Emirates: An Economic and Social Survey*, 2nd edn (London: Longman, 1976).

Financial Times, 5 November 1968, p. 24.

Fisher, Michael H., *Indirect Rule in India: Residents and the Residency System, 1764–1858* (New Delhi: Oxford University Press, 1991).

Fromherz, Allen J., *Qatar: A Modern History* (London: I.B. Tauris, 2012).

Fuccaro, Nelida, *Histories of City and State in the Persian Gulf: Manama since 1800* (Cambridge: Cambridge University Press, 2009).

Galpern, Steven G., *Money, Oil and Empire in the Middle East: Sterling and Postwar Imperialism, 1944–1971* (Cambridge: Cambridge University Press, 2009).

Gause III, F. Gregory, 'British and American policies in the Persian Gulf, 1968–1973', *Review of International Studies*, Vol. 11, No. 4 (1985), pp. 247–53.

Gause III, F. Gregory, *Oil Monarchies: Domestic and Security Challenges in the Arab Gulf States* (New York: Council on Foreign Relations Press, 1994).

Gause III, F. Gregory, *The International Relations of the Persian Gulf* (Cambridge: Cambridge University Press, 2010).

Gifford, Prosser, 'Indirect rule: Touchstone or tombstone for colonial policy?', in Prosser
    Gifford and William Roger Louis (eds), *Britain and Germany in Africa: Imperial*
    Rivalry and Colonial Rule (New Haven, CT: Yale University Press, 1967), pp. 351–91.

Guardian, The 'Frightened oil sheikh sits on his millions', 11 April 1964

Hawley, Donald, *The Trucial States* (London: Michael Russell, 1970).

Hay, Rupert, *The Persian Gulf States* (Washington, DC: Middle East Institute, 1959).

Hayman, Mark, 'Inducement and coercion on the Trucial Coast: The First Oil
    Agreements', *Journal of Imperial and Commonwealth History*, Vol. 38, No. 2 (2010),
    pp. 261–78.

Hayman, Mark, 'Economic protectorate in Britain's Informal Empire: The Trucial Coast
    during the Second World War', *Journal of Imperial and Commonwealth History*,
    Vol. 46, No. 2 (2018), pp. 323–44.

Heard-Bey, Frauke, *From Trucial States to United Arab Emirates: A Society in Transition*
    (London: Longman, 1997).

Heard-Bey, Frauke, *Abu Dhabi, the United Arab Emirates and the Gulf Region: Fifty Years*
    of Transformation (Berlin: Gerlach Press, 2017).

Herb, Michael, *All in the Family: Absolutism, Revolution, and Democracy in the Middle*
    Eastern Monarchies (Albany, NY: State University of New York Press, 1999).

Holden, David, 'The Persian Gulf: After the British Raj', *Foreign Affairs*, Vol. 49, No. 4
    (1971), pp. 721–35.

Hollis, Rosemary, 'From force to finance: Britain's adaptation to decline: Transforming
    relations with selected Arab Gulf States, 1965–1985', PhD thesis, George Washington
    University, Washington, DC (1988).

Hopwood, Derek (ed.), *The Arabian Peninsula: Society and Politics* (London: George
    Allen & Unwin, 1972).

Hyam, Ronald, *Britain's Declining Empire: The Road to Decolonisation 1918–1968*
    (Cambridge: Cambridge University Press, 2006).

Jones, Geoffrey, *Banking and Oil: The History of the British Bank of the Middle East*,
    Vol. 2 (Cambridge: Cambridge University Press, 1986).

Joyce, Miriam, *Kuwait 1945–1996: An Anglo-American Perspective* (London: Frank Cass,
    1998).

Joyce, Miriam, *Ruling Shaikhs and Her Majesty's Government* (London: Frank Cass, 2003).

Keddie, Nikki R., *Modern Iran: Roots and Results of Revolution* (New Haven, CT, and
    London: Yale University Press, 2003).

Kelly, J. B., 'The legal and historical basis of the British position in the Persian Gulf', *St*
    Antony's Papers, No. 4: *Middle Eastern Affairs*, Vol. 1 (London: Chatto and Windus,
    1958), pp. 110–40.

Kelly, J. B., *Eastern Arabian Frontiers* (New York: Frederick A. Praeger, 1964).

Kelly, J. B, 'The British position in the Persian Gulf', *The World Today*, June 1964,
    pp. 238–49.

Kelly, J. B., *Britain and the Persian Gulf, 1795–1880* (Oxford: Oxford University Press,
    1968).

Kelly, J. B., *Arabia, the Gulf and the West: A Critical View of the Arabs and Their Oil Policy* (New York: Basic Books, 1980).

Kelly, J. B., *Desert Dispute: The Diplomacy of Boundary-Making in South-Eastern Arabia*, ed. by Saul B. Kelly, 2 vols (Berlin: Gerlach Press, 2018).

Kelly, S. B. (ed.), *Fighting the Retreat from Arabia and the Gulf: The Collected Essays and Reviews of* J.B. Kelly, Vol. 1 (Nashville, TN, and London: New English Review Press, 2013).

Kelly, Saul, 'Vanishing act: Britain's abandonment of Aden and retreat from the Gulf', in Robert Johnson and Timothy Clask (eds), *At the End of Military Intervention: Historical, Theoretical and Applied Approaches to Transition, Handover and Withdrawal* (Oxford: Oxford University Press, 2014), pp. 169–95.

Kelly, Saul and Gareth Stansfield, 'Britain, the United Arab Emirates and the defence of the Gulf revisited', *International Affairs*, Vol. 89, No. 5 (2013), pp. 1203–19.

Khadduri, Majid, *Arab Personalities in Politics* (Washington, DC: Middle East Institute, 1981).

Khalidi, Rashid, 'The impact of the Iraqi Revolution on the Arab World', in Robert A. Fernea and Wm. Roger Louis (eds), *The Iraqi Revolution of 1958: The Old Social Classes Revisited* (London: I.B. Tauris, 1991), pp. 106–17.

Khoury, Philip S. and Joseph Kostiner (eds), *Tribes and State Formation in the Middle East* (Berkeley, CA: University of California Press, 1990).

Khuri, Fuad I., *Tribe and State in Bahrain: The Transformation of Social and Political Authority in an Arab State* (Chicago, IL: University of Chicago Press, 1980).

Kirk-Greene, Anthony, *Britain's Imperial Administrators, 1858–1966* (Basingstoke: Macmillan, 2000).

Lienhardt, Peter, 'Shaikhdoms of Eastern Arabia', DPhil thesis, Oxford University (1957).

Lienhardt, Peter, 'The authority of shaykhs in the Gulf: An essay in nineteenth-century history', in R. B. Serjeant and R. L. Bidwell (eds), *Arabian Studies*, Vol. 2 (London: C. Hurst & Company, 1975), pp. 61–75.

Lienhardt, Peter, *Shaikhdoms of Eastern Arabia*, ed. by Ahmed Al-Shahi (Basingstoke: Palgrave, 2001).

Lienhardt, Peter, 'Town politics in Eastern Arabia in the 1950s', *Journal of Arabian Studies*, Vol. 5, No. 1 (2015), pp. 1–14.

Lienhardt, Peter, *Letters from Kuwait (1953–1955)*, ed. by Ahmed Al-Shahi (Kuwait City: Centre for Research and Studies on Kuwait, 2017).

Louis, Wm. Roger, *The British Empire in the Middle East 1945–1951: Arab Nationalism, the United States, and Postwar Imperialism* (Oxford: Clarendon Press, 1984).

Louis, Wm. Roger, 'Musaddiq and the dilemmas of British imperialism', in James A. Bill and Wm. Roger Louis (eds), *Musaddiq, Iranian Nationalism and Oil* (London: I.B. Tauris, 1988), pp. 228–60.

Louis, Wm. Roger, 'The British and the origins of the Iraqi Revolution', in Robert A. Fernea and Wm. Roger Louis (eds), *The Iraqi Revolution of 1958: The Old Social Classes Revisited* (London: I.B. Tauris, 1991), pp. 31–61.

Louis, Wm. Roger, 'The British withdrawal from the Gulf, 1967–69', *Ends of British Imperialism: The Scramble for Empire, Suez and Decolonization* (London: I.B. Tauris, 2006), pp. 877–903.

Low, Charles Rathbone, *History of the Indian Navy*, Vol. 1 (London: Richard Bentley and Son, 1877).

Luce, William, 'Britain and the Persian Gulf: Mistaken timing over Aden', *The Round Table*, Vol. 57, No. 227 (1967), pp. 277–83.

Luce, William, 'Britain's withdrawal from the Persian Gulf', lecture given at RUSI on 26 November 1968, *Royal United Services Institution Journal*, Vol. 114, No. 653 (1969), pp. 4–10.

Luce, William, 'A naval force for the Gulf: Balancing inevitable Russian penetration', *The Round Table*, Vol. 59, No. 236 (1969), pp. 347–56.

Lunt, James, *Imperial Sunset: Frontier Soldiering in the 20th Century* (London: Macdonald, 1981).

Macris, Jeffrey R., *The Politics and Security of the Gulf: Anglo-American Hegemony and the Shaping of the Region* (London: Routledge, 2010).

Macris, Jeffrey R., 'Why didn't America Replace the British in the Persian Gulf?', in Jeffrey R. Macris and Saul Kelly (eds), *Imperial Crossroads: The Great Powers and the Persian Gulf* (Annapolis, MD: Naval Institute Press, 2012), pp. 61–74.

Macris, Jeffrey R. and Saul Kelly (eds) *Imperial Crossroads: The Great Powers and the Persian Gulf* (Annapolis, MD: Naval Institute Press, 2012).

Maitra, Jayanti, *Zayed: From Challenges to Union* (Abu Dhabi: National Archives, 2015).

Maitra, Jayanti and Afra Al-Hajji, *Qasr Al Hosn: The History of the Rulers of Abu Dhabi 1793–1966* (Abu Dhabi: Centre for Documentation and Research, 2001).

Mann, Michael, *The Trucial Oman Scouts: The Story of a Bedouin Force* (Norwich: Michael Russell, 1994).

Mattair, Thomas, R., *The Three Occupied UAE Islands: The Tunbs and Abu Musa* (Abu Dhabi: Emirates Centre for Strategic Studies and Research, 2005).

Mawby, Spencer, *British Policy in Aden and the Protectorates, 1955–67: Last Outpost of a Middle East Empire* (London: Routledge, 2005).

Middle East Economic Survey, 19 June 1995, pp. D1–D3.

Monroe, Elizabeth, 'British bases in the Middle East: Assets or liabilities?', *International Affairs*, Vol. 42, No. 1 (1966), pp. 24–34.

Morton, Michael Quentin, *Buraimi: The Struggle for Power, Influence and Oil in Arabia* (London: I.B. Tauris, 2013).

Onley, James, 'India's native agents in Arabia and Persia in the nineteenth century', *Comparative Studies of South Asia, Africa and the Middle East*, Vol. 24, No. 2 (2004), pp. 129–37.

Onley, James, 'The politics of protection in the Gulf: The Arab rulers and the British Resident in the nineteenth century', *New Arabian Studies*, Vol. 6 (2004), pp. 30–92.

Onley, James, 'Britain's Informal Empire in the Gulf, 1820–1971', *Journal of Social Affairs*, Vol. 22, No. 87 (2005), pp. 29–45.

Onley, James, *The Arabian Frontier of the British Raj: Merchants, Rulers, and the British in the Nineteenth-Century Gulf* (Oxford: Oxford University Press, 2007).

Onley, James, 'The Raj reconsidered: British India's Informal Empire and spheres of influence in Asia and Africa', *Asian Affairs*, Vol. 11, No. 1 (2009), pp. 44–62.

Onley, James, *Britain and the Gulf Shaikhdoms, 1820–1971: The Politics of Protection* (Education City, Doha: Georgetown University School of Foreign Service, 2009).

Onley, James and Sulayman Khalaf, 'Shaikhly authority in the pre-oil Gulf: An historical-anthropological study', *History and Anthropology*, Vol. 17, No. 3 (2006), pp. 189–208.

Owtram, Francis, *A Modern History of Oman: Formation of the State since 1920* (London: I.B. Tauris, 2004).

Parry, Clive, *Nationality and Citizenship Laws of the Commonwealth and of the Republic of Ireland* (London: Stevens & Sons Limited, 1957).

Petersen, Tore T., 'Anglo-American rivalry in the Middle East: The struggle for the Buraimi Oasis, 1952–1957', *International History Review*, Vol. 14, No. 1 (1992), pp. 71–91.

Petersen, Tore T., 'Crossing the Rubicon: Britain's withdrawal from the Middle East, 1964–1968: A bibliographical review', *International History Review*, Vol. 22, No. 2 (2000), pp. 318–40.

Petersen, Tore T., *The Decline of the Anglo-American Middle East 1961–1969: A Willing Retreat* (Brighton: Sussex Academic Press, 2006).

Petersen, Tore T., 'Richard Nixon, Great Britain, and the Anglo-American strategy of turning the Persian Gulf into an Allied lake', in Jeffrey R. Macris and Saul Kelly (eds), *Imperial Crossroads: The Great Powers and the Persian Gulf* (Annapolis, MD: Naval Institute Press, 2012), pp. 75–90.

Peterson, J. E., 'Tribes and politics in Eastern Arabia', *Middle East Journal*, Vol. 21, No. 3 (1977), pp. 297–312.

Peterson, J. E., 'The nature of succession in the Gulf', *Middle East Journal*, Vol. 55, No. 4 (2001), pp. 580–601.

Peterson, J. E., 'Rulers, merchants and shaikhs in Gulf Politics', in Alanoud Alsharekh (ed.), *The Gulf Family: Kinship Policies and Modernity*, SOAS Middle East Issues (London: Saqi in association with London Middle East Institute SOAS, 2007), pp. 21–36.

Peterson, J. E., *Oman's Insurgencies: The Sultanate's Struggle for Supremacy* (London: Saqi, 2007).

Peterson, J. E., 'Britain and the Gulf: At the periphery of Empire', in Lawrence G. Potter (ed.), *The Persian Gulf in History* (New York: Palgrave, 2009), pp. 277–93.

Peterson, J. E. (ed.), *The Emergence of the Gulf States: Studies in Modern History* (London: Bloomsbury Academic, 2016).

Pickering, Jeffrey, 'Politics and "Black Tuesday": Shifting power in the Cabinet and the decision to withdraw from East of Suez, November 1967–January 1968', *Twentieth Century British History*, Vol. 13, No. 2 (2002), pp. 144–70.

Pieragostini, Karl, *Britain, Aden and South Arabia: Abandoning Empire* (Basingstoke: Macmillan, 1991).

Potter, Lawrence G. (ed.), *The Persian Gulf in History* (New York: Palgrave Macmillan, 2009).

Pridham, B. R. (ed.), *The Arab Gulf and the West* (Beckenham: Croom Helm, 1983).

Rabi, Uzi, 'Britain's "special position" in the Gulf: Its origins, dynamics and legacy', *Middle Eastern Studies*, Vol. 42, No. 6 (2006), pp. 351–64.

Rabi, Uzi, 'Oil, politics and tribal rulers in Eastern Arabia: The reign of Shakhbut (1928–1966)', *British Journal of Middle Eastern Studies*, Vol. 33, No. 1 (2006), pp. 37–50.

Rabi, Uzi, *The Emergence of States in a Tribal Society: Oman under Sa'id bin Taymur, 1932–1970* (Eastbourne: Sussex Academic Press, 2006).

Ramazani, Rouhollah K., *The Foreign Policy of Iran 1941–1973: A Study of Foreign Policy in Modernizing Nations* (Charlottesville, VA: University Press of Virginia, 1975).

Rich, Paul, *Creating the Arabian Gulf: The British Raj and the Invasions of the Gulf* (Lanham, MD: Lexington Books, 2009).

Robinson, Ronald, 'Non-European foundations of European imperialism: Sketch for a theory of collaboration', in R. Owen and B. Sutcliffe (eds), *Studies in the Theory of Imperialism* (London: Longman, 1972), pp. 117–42.

Robinson, Ronald, 'The excentric idea of imperialism, with or without empire', in W. J. Mommsen and J. Osterhammel (eds), *Imperialism and After: Continuities and Discontinuities* (London: Allen & Unwin, 1986), pp. 267–89.

Rossiter, Ash, 'Britain and the development of professional security forces in the Gulf Arab States, 1921–1971: Local forces and Informal Empire', PhD thesis, University of Exeter (2014).

Rugh, Andrea B., *The Political Culture of Leadership in the United Arab Emirates* (New York: Palgrave Macmillan, 2007).

Said Zahlan, Rosemarie, *The Origins of the United Arab Emirates: A Political and Social History of the Trucial States* (New York: St. Martin's Press, 1978).

Said Zahlan, Rosemarie, *The Creation of Qatar* (London: Croom Helm, 1979).

Said Zahlan, Rosemarie, *The Making of the Modern Gulf States: Kuwait, Bahrain, Qatar, the United Arab Emirates and Oman*, Foreword by Roger Owen, revised and updated edn (Reading: Garnett Publishing, 1998).

Salil-ibn-Razik, *The History of the Imams and Seyyids of Oman: From AD 661–1856* (Cambridge: Cambridge University Press, 1871).

Sato, Shohei, 'Britain's decision to withdraw from the Persian Gulf, 1964–1968', *Journal of Imperial and Commonwealth History*, Vol. 37, No. 1 (2009), pp. 99–117.

Sato, Shohei, *Britain and the Formation of the Gulf States: Embers of Empire* (Manchester: Manchester University Press, 2016).

Schofield, Richard, 'The crystallisation of a complex territorial dispute: Britain and the Saudi Arabian borderland, 1966–71', *Journal of Arabian Studies*, Vol. 1, No. 1 (2011), pp. 27–51.

Schofield, Richard (ed.), *Territorial Foundations of the Gulf States* (New York: St. Martin's Press, 1994).

Schofield, Richard, with Elizabeth Evans, *Arabian Boundaries: New Documents*, Vol. 15: *1974* (Cambridge: Cambridge University Press, 2009).

Sluglett, Peter, 'Formal and informal empire in the Middle East', in *The Oxford History of the British Empire*, Vol. 5: *Historiography*, ed. by R. Winks (Oxford: Oxford University Press, 1999), pp.416–36.

Smith, Simon, *Britain's Revival and Fall in the Gulf: Kuwait, Bahrain, Qatar and the Trucial States, 1950–71* (London: Routledge, 2004).

Smith, Simon, 'Britain's decision to withdraw from the Gulf: A pattern not a puzzle', *Journal of Imperial and Commonwealth History*, Vol. 44, No. 2 (2016), pp. 328–51.

Standish, John F., 'British maritime policy in the Persian Gulf', *Middle Eastern Studies*, Vol. 3, No. 4 (1967), pp. 324–54.

Sweet, Louise E., 'Camel raiding of North Arabian bedouin: A mechanism of ecological adaption', *American Anthropologist*, Vol. 67, No. 5 (1965), pp. 1132–50.

Taryam, Abdullah Omran, *The Establishment of the United Arab Emirates 1950–85* (Beckenham: Croom Helm, 1987).

Tetreault, Mary Ann, *Stories of Democracy: Politics and Society in Contemporary Kuwait* (New York: Columbia University Press, 2000).

Thesiger, Wilfred, *Arabian Sands* (London: Longman 1959).

Thomas, Martin, *Empires of Intelligence: Security Services and Colonial Disorder after 1914* (Berkeley and Los Angeles, CA: University of California Press, 2008).

Times, The 26 February 1956, p. 11.

Times, The 'The Sheikh with oil millions to spend', 3 February 1964, p. 11

Times, The 8 August 1966, pp. 6 and 9.

Toth, A. B. 'Control and allegiance at the dawn of the Oil Age: Bedouin, *zakat* and struggles for sovereignty in Arabia, 1916–1955', *Middle East Critique*, Vol. 21, No. 1 (2012), pp. 57–79.

Tripp, Charles, *A History of Iraq* (Cambridge: Cambridge University Press, 2007).

Troeller, Gary, *The Birth of Saudi Arabia: Britain and the Rise of the House of Sa'ud* (London: Frank Cass, 1976).

Vassiliev, Alexei, *The History of Saudi Arabia* (London: Saqi Books, 1998).

Vatikiotis, P. J., *Politics and the Military in Jordan: A Study of the Arab Legion, 1921–1957* (London: Frank Cass, 1967).

Walker, Julian, 'Practical problems of boundary delimitation in Arabia: The case of the United Arab Emirates', in Richard Schofield (ed.), *Territorial Foundations of the Gulf States* (New York: St Martin's Press, 1994), pp. 109–16.

Walker, Julian, 'The United Arab Emirates and Oman frontiers', in Clive H. Schofield and Richard N. Schofield (eds), *The Middle East and North Africa: World Boundaries*, Vol. 2 (London: Routledge, 1994), pp. 173–83.

Watt, D. C., 'Britain and the future of the Persian Gulf States', *The World Today*, November 1964, pp. 488–96.

Watt, D. C., 'The decision to withdraw from the Gulf', *Political Quarterly*, Vol. 39, No. 3 (1969), pp. 310–19.

Watt, D. C., 'Can the Union of Arab Emirates survive?', *The World Today* (April 1971), pp. 144–7.

Wilkinson, J. C., 'Traditional concepts of territory in South East Arabia', *Geographical Journal*, Vol. 149, No. 3 (1983), pp. 301–15.

Wilkinson, J. C., *Arabia's Frontiers: The Story of Britain's Boundary Drawing in the Desert* (London: I.B. Tauris, 1991).

Wilson, Graham H., *Zayed: Man Who Built a Nation* (Abu Dhabi: National Archives, 2013).

Winks, Robin W., 'On decolonization and Informal Empire', *American Historical Review*, Vol. 81, No. 3 (1976), pp. 540–56.

Yapp, Malcolm, 'British policy in the Persian Gulf', in Alvin J. Cottrell (ed.), *The Persian Gulf States: A General Survey* (Baltimore, MD, and London: Johns Hopkins University Press, 1980), pp. 70–98.

Index